YALE STUDIES IN ENGLISH

BENJAMIN CHRISTIE NANGLE, EDITOR

VOLUME 157

JOHN SKELTON'S POETRY

by Stanley Eugene Fish

New Haven and London, Yale University Press

Copyright © 1965 by Yale University.
Second printing, December 1967.
Designed by John O. C. McCrillis,
set in Garamond type,
and printed in the United States of America by
The Carl Purington Rollins Printing-Office of
the Yale University Press, New Haven, Connecticut.
Distributed in Canada by McGill University Press.
All rights reserved. This book may not be
reproduced, in whole or in part, in any form
(except by reviewers for the public press),
without written permission from the publishers.

Library of Congress catalog card number: 65–11177

Published with assistance from the Mary Cady
Tew Memorial Fund.

To Adrienne

For I have gravyd her wythin the
  secret wall
Of my trew hart, to love her best
  of all.

—JOHN SKELTON.

Preface

SKELTON'S only extant play, *Magnificence,* will not be considered in this study. The reader is referred to the edition of R. L. Ramsay, Early English Text Society, extra series no. 98 (London, 1908), A. R. Heiserman's *Skelton and Satire* (Chicago, 1961), D. M. Bevington's *From Mankind to Marlowe* (Cambridge, Mass., 1962), and the articles of William O. Harris cited in the text. Mr. Harris is preparing a book-length essay on the play.

A primary debt is to the researches and insights of William Nelson, H. L. R. Edwards, Robert Kinsman, and Arthur Heiserman; Professor Heiserman's study of Skelton's sources in medieval satire has been particularly helpful.

I am pleased to be able to thank formally the teachers and friends who have read and criticized this essay, first in the form of a dissertation in the English Department of Yale University, subsequently in far too many revisions: George Bland, Cleanth Brooks, James Cline, A. Bartlett Giamatti, Davis Harding, Robert Kinsman, Richard Lanham, Josephine Miles, Leonard Nathan, Michael O'Loughlin, Paul Piehler, Frederick Pottle, Peter Sharkey, and Richard Sylvester. I can only marvel at the patience of David Horne and Benjamin Nangle, who guided an inexperienced author through the mysteries of the making of a book.

And finally I offer this volume as an inadequate recompense for the guidance and inspiration of two men: Maurice Johnson, who years ago convinced me, by his example, that the pursuit of literary studies is a worthy one; and Talbot Donaldson, who while pretending merely to direct a dissertation, brought me to know what poetry is.

S. E. F.

Berkeley, California
July 1964

Contents

1 Introduction

HERESY WILL NEVER DIE

IN APRIL 1489 Henry Percy, fourth earl of Northumberland, was slain near Thirsk as he attempted to reconcile an insurgent mob to an unpopular tax. For the Tudor chronicler Edward Hall, the affair was not a complicated one: "The rude rashe and unadvised people . . . violently set upon the erle by the procurement of a symple felowe called John of Chambre, whom the erle intreated with fayre woordes to come to reason."[1] But in 1622 Francis Bacon, servant of another monarch in another age, offered his own interpretation of the same incident: "the earl assembled the principal justices and freeholders of the country; and speaking to them in that imperious language . . . did not only irritate, but made them conceive . . . that himself was the author."[2]

Bacon is willing to entertain the possibility that monarchy (and the hierarchy it supports) may have obligations (common civility) as well as rights; and in his suggestion of complexity we see the beginnings of the modern idea of history as process rather than crisis. In a very real way, the Northumberland affair was a crisis. Four years after Bosworth, Henry was simultaneously attempting to strengthen a shaky claim on a traditionally shaky throne and win the respect of the European monarchs. Preparations for war with

1. Edward Hall, *Chronicle Containing the History of England* (London, printed for J. Johnson et al., 1809), p. 443. This edition was "carefully collated with the editions of 1548 and 1550."
2. *History of the Reign of King Henry VII*, ed. J. R. Lumby (Cambridge University Press, 1892), p. 65.

France were proceeding under the cover of negotiation, and the civil resistance of the northerners to a necessary military tax was a blow on two fronts. Hall's sense of crisis, however, is less political or military than religious; there is only one consideration—disobedience, and only one reaction—horror. Both chroniclers allude to the possibility of northern sympathy for Richard III and the Yorkist cause. In a diagrammatic image Bacon indicates that the memory of Richard was such "that it lay like lees in the bottom of men's hearts, and if the vessel was but stirred, it would come up."[3] Here cause and effect are anatomized in a way peculiarly Baconian and modern; events are the result of the conjunction of visible and (to some extent) measurable forces. To Hall, Richard is the "secret serpent" whose memory inspires rebellion.[4] The allusion is to that old serpent, Satan, and the phrase itself announces a theory of history where all rebellions are one rebellion, all rebels the first rebel, and all authority divine authority. Hall clearly shares Henry's fear "least yt might appere that the decrees, actes and statutes made and confirmed by him . . . shoulde by hys rude and rusticall people be infringed."[5] The question for him is not economic or social or even political, and the analysis Bacon offers is in no way relevant to a judgment that is made not in a historical context, but *sub specie aeternitatis*.

If we are to understand John Skelton, we must be prepared to accept this apocalyptic view of history as a possibility, and to admit that those who do hold to it are not necessarily reactionary or primitive. In his "Upon the Dolourus Dethe and Muche Lamentable Chaunce of the Most Honorable Erle of Northumberlande,"[6] Skelton anticipates Hall with

3. Ibid.
4. Hall, *Chronicle*, p. 443.
5. Ibid.
6. Dyce, *1*, 6–14. Unless otherwise noted, all quotations from Skelton's works are taken from the edition of Alexander Dyce (2 vols.

a vehemence which is, even from the vantage point of historical reconstruction, surprising. To the fledgling poet, the implications of Percy's murder are enormous, the deed itself, incomprehensible:

> In sesons past, who hath herde or sene
> Of formar writyng by any presidente
> That vilane hastarddis in their furious tene,
> Fulfylled with malice of froward entente,
> Confetered togeder of commonn concente
> Falsly to slee theyr moste singuler good lord?
>
> [22–27]

Their action is not only treasonous,

> the ryght of his prince . . . shold not be withstand;
> For whose cause ye slew him with your owne hand,
> [67–68]

but blasphemous:

> Were not these commons . . . karlis of kind
> To slo their owne lord? God was not in theyr mind.
> [34–35]

"God was not in theyr mind." In this identification of political dissent with godlessness (and, ultimately, heresy) lies the keystone of Skelton's radically unified universe. The temporal and eternal hierarchies are intimately connected, and a challenge to one is a challenge to the other. For Skelton, political and ecclesiastical stability are patterns of the Divine. Disorder is to be feared and resisted. As the representative of an anointed monarch, Northumberland not only commands allegiance but assures stability. Ironi-

London, Thomas Rodd, 1843). The printing of u's and v's has been normalized, and the titles of Skelton's poems are given in modern English spellings.

cally, the rebels have only weakened their position and in
theological terms have called into question their salvation
by striking at the structure which stands between them and
chaos. "He was your chefteyne, your shelde, your chef de-
fence" (57), the poet cries, and in the context of the medieval
orthodoxy Percy defends not only against the iniquities of the
human situation but against the forces of darkness which in
every age threaten to render that situation hopeless. In this
role the slain Earl looms as the bulwark of the nation ("Peregall to dukes, with kynges he might compare, / . . . Lyke to
Eneas benigne in worde and dede, / Valiant as Hector in
every marciall nede") (134–38), and throughout the elegy
Skelton stands incredulous before the very fact that is the
basis of his poem:

> I say, ye comoners, why wer ye so stark mad?
> What frantyk frensy fyll in your brayne?
> Where was your wit and reson ye should have had?
> What wilful foly made yow to ryse agayne
> Your naturall lord? alas, I can not fayne.   [50–54]

Conventional though it may be, the final apostrophe to
Christ seems especially appropriate in a poem where the distinction between the secular and the spiritual does not exist:

> In joy triumphaunt the hevenly yerarchy,
> With all the hole sorte of that glorious place,
> His soull mot receyve into theyr company,
> Thorow bounty of Hym that formed all solace;
> Wel of pite, of mercy, and of grace,
> The Father, the Sonn, and the Holy Ghost,
> In Trinitate one God of myghtes moste!   [211–17]

On December 8, 1527, two young clerics, Thomas Bilney
and Thomas Arthur, formally abjured their heretical opinions at St. Paul's. Forty years have passed since the death

of Percy, and the order that Skelton championed in 1489
faces a more direct attack. For the last time Skelton is again
on the scene, and in his *Replycacion Agaynst Certayne Yong
Scolers Abjured of Late* we presumably have the poet's final
statement.[7] He has changed little. If the faithless retainers of 1480
shout "Bluntly as bestis with boste and with crye" (83), the
literally faithless abjurers of 1527 are "braynlesse beestes"
(263) who jangle "lyke pratynge poppyng dawes" (39). If
the poet cannot comprehend the rationale of political dissent in 1489 ("why wer ye so stark mad? . . . alas, I can not
fayne"), he is more amazed in 1527 in the presence of doctrinal dissenters whose abjuration, he suspects, is only
formal:

> I saye, thou madde Marche hare,
> I wondre how ye dare   [35–36]
>
> Wotte ye what ye sayed
> Of Mary, mother and mayed?   [46–47]
>
> And yet some men say,
> Howe ye are this day,
> And be nowe as yll,
> And so ye wyll be styll
> As ye were before.   [176–80]

The easy transformation of the rhetoric of politics into the
rhetoric of theology emphasizes again the unity of the Skeltonic vision. Rebellion against civil authority equals rebellion against ecclesiastical authority equals rebellion against
God. In the early poem this equation is implicit, but here
the relationship between the flight from authority and the
possibility of chaos (damnation) is defined through the
ramifications of heresy. As preachers, Bilney and Arthur have

7. Dyce, *1*, 206–24.

exposed countless others to the possibility of damnation, have

> devyllysshely devysed
> The people to seduce,
> And chase them thorowe the muse
> Of your noughty counsell,
> To hunt them into hell;   [210–14]

and in his final burst of invective, Skelton hypothesizes a chain reaction leading to total anarchy:

> Ye cobble and ye clout
> Holy Scripture so about
> That people are in great dout
> And feare leest they be out
> Of all good Christen order,
> Thus all thyng ye disorder.   [222–27]

"Thus all thyng ye disorder." Four decades of trial and disillusionment seem not to have affected the poet at all.

For all their similarity of statement and attitude, however, the two poems differ significantly. While the Skelton of 1527 still insists on the necessity of a conformity with the divine patterns of order, he seems less certain than he was in 1489 that this is possible. The elegy concludes on the traditional note of affirmation. Disturbing as it may be, the disruption of order is only temporary, for the younger Percy now steps forward as an assurance that the balance will be restored:

> O yonge lyon, but tender yet of age,
> Grow and encrese, remembre thyn estate;
> God the assyst unto thyn herytage,
> And geve the grace to be more fortunate!
> Agayn rebellyones arme the to make debate.
>   [162–66]

In formal terms, the almost rigid conventionality of the
poem provides a parallel reassurance. The transition from
lamentation to apotheosis proceeds within the graceful rigor
of rhyme royal. His orthodoxy is no less literary than religious; Skelton is conspicuously faithful to the elegiac tradition: the muses, the gods, and the spirit of the deceased
are addressed in the familiar manner, and at the elegy's turn
he borrows from Geoffrey de Vinsauf's *Poetria Nova* the
very *exclamatio* Chaucer had parodied a century before:

> O cruell Mars, thou dedly god of war!
> O dolorous tewisday, dedicate to thy name,
> When thou shoke thy sworde so noble a man to mar!
> O ground ungracious, unhappy be thy fame,
> Which wert endyed with rede bloud of the same.[8]
>   [113–17]

In the *Replication,* however, the formal and "public"
rhyme royal has given way to the formless and idiosyncratic
Skeltonic. Patches of alliterative prose alternate haphazardly
with Latin refrains and the unique extended rhyme leashes;
the emotional irresponsibility of the rhetoric of abuse has
replaced the control of tradition:

> Sive per aequivocum,
> Sive per univocum
> Sive sic, sive nat so,
> Ye are brought to, Lo, lo, lo!
> Se where the heretykes go,
> Wytlesse wandring to and fro!
> With, Te he, ta ha, bo ho, bo ho!   [68–74]

Affirmation has disappeared along with formality. While
half the earlier poem emphasizes the restoration of order,

8. See *Nun's Priest's Tale,* lines 3338–54.

the poetic voice of the *Replication* apostrophizes and laments
for three hundred lines:

Helas, ye wreches, ye may be wo!   [77]

And curse both nyght and day,
When ye were bredde and borne.   [79–80]

ye wolde appere wyse,
But ye were folysshe nyse.   [129–30]

With chatyng and rechatyng,
And your busy pratyng.   [217–18]

Come forthe, ye popeholy,
Full of melancoly.   [247–48]

doutlesse ye shalbe blased,
And be brent at a stake.   [294–95]

There is no final and tranquil prayer to Christ, no promise of
a Messiah-like figure who will assure the suppression of
schism, and the final line, the last Skelton is to write, suggests that, in terms of this world, the triumph of order is by
no means a certainty: "Heresy wyll never dye." In the Skeltonic universe, heresy comprehends and implies all aberra-
tions from the divine patterns of order, and by acknowledging its durability, the poet reveals an awareness of the frailty
of mortality which is not his in 1489. It is not his faith in
the eternal (immutable) but his faith in the ability of man
to pattern himself after the eternal which has altered. And
although this alteration can be partially defined in terms of
a formal and tonal comparison, its significance for Skelton's
art is clear only when we examine the idea that finally sustains him, the doctrine of poetic inspiration.

POETS ARE FEW AND RARE

In his tribute to the Earl of Northumberland, Skelton defers to the muses at what he would call "the usuall rate [amount]":

> Of hevenly poems, O Clyo, calde by name
> In the colege of Musis goddes hystoriall,
> Adres the to me, whiche am both halt and lame
> In elect uteraunce to make memoryall.   [8–11]

This is as conventional as the "modesty *topos*" which follows ("My wordes unpullysht be, nakide and playne"), and Skelton refers later in the poem to the "divine *afflatus*" theory of poetry only to deny its applicability in his case:

> If the hole quere of the Musis nyne
> In me onely wer set and comprysed,
> Enbrethed with the blast of influence devyne.
>   [155–57]

If I were divinely inspired. In 1489 the idea of inspiration is little more than a rhetorical throwaway and its relationship to the central tenet of Skelton's philosophy (a rage for order) is not at all clear. Half the *Replication,* on the other hand, is an extended "confutacion responsyve" addressed to anonymous critics who believe

> that poetry
> Maye not flye so hye
> In theology,
> Nor analogy,
> Nor philology,
> Nor philosophy
> To answere or reply
> Agaynst suche heresy.   [306–13]

"Why," Skelton queries, "have ye . . . disdayne / At poetes, and complayne / Howe poetes do but fayne [make fictions]," obviously replying to an anonymous revival of Plato's charge (*Republic* 10.595–606) that since the artist imitates at a third remove from reality, he necessarily lies. The aging poet responds with a fully articulated and confident assertion of his divinity:

> there is a spyrituall,
> And a mysteriall,
> And a mysticall
> Effecte energiall
> As Grekes do it call,
> Of suche an industry,
> And suche a pregnacy,
> Of hevenly inspyracion
> In laureate creacyon,
> Of poetes commendacion,
> That of divyne myseracion
> God maketh his habytacion
> In poetes whiche excelles,
> And sojourns with them and dwells. [365–78]

This is hardly the conventional deference to the inspirational muse we see in *The Earl of Northumberland*. In fact it recalls the attempt of Plotinus and later Neoplatonists to fit the inspired artist into a comprehensive philosophical system. Plotinus maintains that in our material world lying at the outer limits of the Divine influence, the artist is in direct contact with the "One." The arts "give no bare reproduction of the thing seen but go back to the Ideas from which nature derives, and furthermore . . . much of their work is all their own; they are moulders of beauty and add where nature is lacking. Thus Pheidias wrought the Zeus upon no model among things of sense, but by apprehending what form

Zeus must take if he chose to become manifest to sight."[1] Still, the relevance of this passage to the business at hand (an attack on heresy) seems at first no less questionable than the casual statement of 1489. But if we explore the implications of Skelton's position, we see that Bilney and Arthur have fallen through their reliance on ways of knowing that deny the primacy of the visionary or poetic. They are condemned for having gone too far in their "perihermeniall [exegetical] principles," for proceeding on the basis of "A lytell ragge of rhethorike, / A lesse lumpe of logyke, / A pece or patche of philosophy," (1–3) for "tumbling" in theology, in short for believing that their faculties could unaided lead them to truth. It is "your owne foly," Skelton concludes, which has infected you with "the flye / Of horryble heresy" (84–86). For "foly" we may read "trust in the intellect" or merely "rationality," as the relationship between his assault on heresy and this defense of poetry is made explicit in a Latin epigraph: "Sunt infiniti, sunt innumerique sophistae / sunt infiniti, sunt innumerique logistae. / Innumeri sunt philosophi, sunt theologique, . . . / sed sunt pauci rarique poetae" (Dyce, *1*, 223). Poets are few and rare. And—he might have added—saved. For this is a peculiarly Christian afflatus,

> By whose inflammacion
> Of spyrituall instygacion
> And divyne inspyracion,
> We are kyndled in suche facyon
> With hete of the Holy Gost,
> Which is God of myghtes most,
> That he our penne dothe lede,
> And maketh in us suche spede.   [379–86]

1. Plotinus, *Works*, trans. Stephen Mackenna (5 vols. London, 1917–1930), *Ennead* 5.8.1. For a discussion of Plotinus' significance for literary theory see W. K. Wimsatt, Jr., and Cleanth Brooks, *Literary Criticism: A Short History* (New York, 1957), pp. 112–35.

A series of marginal notes simultaneously ascribe this doctrine to Ovid, Jerome, Baptuus Mantuus, and David, and it is clear that through a unique juncture of personal, intellectual, and theological history, the grace of orthodox Christianity, which assures salvation, the poetic intuition of the neo-Plotinian aesthetic, and the muse of classical invocation are one in the mind of this early Tudor poet. An examination of the poetry written between 1489 and 1527 suggests the terms in which this identification is made. For the young Skelton, the stability of the temporal reflects and guarantees the benignity of the eternal; there is no need for a theory of divine inspiration. As he matures, the increasingly obvious fallibility of temporal sources of authority (including the Church) forces him to become aware of a disparity between what he sees and what he believes. In our age such an awareness often leads to a denial of the eternal (disbelief); in the early 1500s the same awareness brought many to Protestantism; but a peculiarly medieval ability to transcend the testimony of fact enabled Skelton to make an adjustment that was in some ways predictable and traditional. As his reliance on physical manifestations of the ideal (institutions, laws, scriptural interpretation) fades, his reliance on faith or intuition increases proportionally. The theory of divine inspiration, once a mere rhetorical convenience, now becomes an important reinforcement of faith, as the intuition of poetry and the illumination of grace are gradually fused. The realization that the world he lives in does not, and perhaps will not, conform to the divine patterns of order is a difficult one for Skelton. It is poetry which allows him to confront this difficulty, and in his last poem the components of that confrontation are on display:

> Heresy wyll never dye.
> Poets are few and rare.

IF I AM TELLING THE TRUTH, WHY DON'T YOU BELIEVE ME?

While the fusion of grace and inspiration allows Skelton to resolve the conflict between appearance and his particular reality on a conceptual level, this very resolution presents him, on a moral level, with a new problem. Simply stated, where does the seer's private awareness of another and better world leave him in relation to this one? In terms of his own aesthetic, the gift of poetry is also an assurance of salvation. The *Replication* is more than a defense of poetry; it is a virtual canonization of the poet, for Skelton identifies the true poet with the psalmist:

> if this noble kyng [David]
> Thus can harpe and syng
> With his harpe of prophecy
> And spyrituall poetry   [343–46]
>
> Why have ye than disdayne
> At poetes?   [351–52]

As the *vates* of God, Skelton again and again speaks to an erring humanity, "All noble men, of this take hede,"[2] but noble men do not, it seems, take heed. Skelton comes to see only too clearly that in terms of his ideal, the world is yielding to the forces of chaos. Heresy indeed will never die, and although he assures his audience that the voice of his poetry is the voice of God ("With trouthe it is ennewde: / Trouth ought to be rescude, / Trouthe should nat be subdude"),[3] his readers will not hearken. In the epigraph to *Against the*

---

2. The opening line of *Why Come Ye Not to Court?* Dyce, 2, 26.
3. From *The Douty Duke of Albany*, Dyce, 2, 80, lines 419–22.

Scots, Skelton asks, "Si veritatem dico, quare non creditis mihi? If I am telling the truth, why don't you believe me?"[4] This cry echoes the repeated laments of the Old Testament prophets, who are, in the poet's mind, his predecessors. Traditionally without honor in their own lands, they trumpet the message of the Lord only to be reviled and ignored as the people give themselves to the gods of Egypt, Babylon, Assyria. Each of them comes at one time to feel that his prophetic gift confers obligations he cannot fulfill. Jeremiah demands of his Lord: "Remember me, Lord. . . . When I found your words, I devoured them; they became my joy and the happiness of my heart, because I bore your name, O Lord, God of hosts. I did not sit celebrating in the circle of merrymakers; under the weight of your hand I sat alone because you filled me with indignation. Why is my pain continuous, my wound incurable, refusing to be healed? You have indeed become for me a treacherous brook, whose waters do not abide!"[5] And when Phassur, son of Emmer, imprisons him in the stocks, he cries out in accusation: "You duped me, O Lord, and I let myself be duped."[6] It is at these moments that the prophet attempts to reject his gift and the mission it enjoins. Jeremiah: "Whenever I speak, I must cry out, violence and outrage is my message; the word of the Lord has brought me derision and reproach all the day. I say to myself, I will not mention him, I will speak in his name no more."[7] But the presence of the divine word does not depend on the acquiescence of the vessel: "But then it becomes like fire burning in my heart, imprisoned in my bones; I grow weary holding it in, I cannot endure it. Yes,

4. Dyce, *1,* p. 189.
5. Jer. 15:15–16, 18. Quotations from the Scriptures are from the *New American Catholic Edition, Confraternity Version* (New York, 1961).
6. 20:7.
7. 20:8–9.

I hear the whisperings of many: 'Terror on every side! Denounce! let us denounce him!' "[8]
For Jeremiah there is no peace; prophecy and alienation are visited upon him simultaneously, and he can only despair and ask the inevitable question: "Why did I come forth from the womb, to see sorrow and pain, to end my days in shame?"[9] Why of all men, he asks, should I be cursed with the obligation of offering a truth which is repeatedly rejected. I will not speak. The temptation to retreat, to yield before the apparent futility of the battle against disorder, to retire into a private and silent peace is always there for the scorned prophet, and Skelton is no exception. Twice he retires from London and the engagement it symbolizes. Again and again his heroes (who are also poet-prophets) find themselves forced to choose between involvement in a world they know by intuition to be hopelessly fallen and therefore hostile, and withdrawal into the personal security afforded them by their poetic gift. In terms of the Skelton credo I have attempted to construct, disillusionment pulls the poet toward inaction even as an intense awareness of the necessity of action urges him on; for although the assurance of salvation seems to free him from a concern with a recalcitrant humanity, the knowledge that his special gift is also a special mandate will not allow him to rest.

In a very real way, then, Skelton's poetry is a verbal dramatization of the problem of moral action. The word verbal is important here for, since Skelton and his heroes are poets, their sphere of action is pre-eminently verbal. In their universe "to act or not to act" becomes "to write or not to write," and correspondingly the ethically methodological question of how to act is translated into the poetically methodological question of how to write. Consequently, a Skelton poem often proceeds on two levels, which we may

8. 20:9–10.
9. 20:18.

designate as narrative and verbal.[1] On the narrative level
the protagonist is faced with a choice that is dramatically
conceived—to act or not to act (*Bouge of Court*), to believe
or not to believe (*Colin Clout*), to speak or not to speak
(*Speak, Parrot!*), to love or not to love (*Philip Sparrow*). In
each case he is suspended (in Eliot's words) between the emotion and the response, and the objective correlative of the
emotion is historical (the Calais Conference, the dissolution
of the monasteries) and autobiographical (the infatuation
for Jane Scrope, the retreat to Diss). In the last analysis,
every choice is the choice between involvement and withdrawal as the same problem is presented again from varying
angles. On the verbal level the dramatic choice is mirrored
by a clash of styles. In some poems Skelton will introduce
the problem of style directly, asking, in effect, "How shall
I write? What forms shall I employ? How shall I choose
my vocabulary?" In others he will merely offer alternative
stylistic patterns, relying on the reader to recognize the question posed by the alternation. Invariably the choice is between
the aureate or veiled style, which becomes identified with
withdrawal, and the "plain" or truthful style, which indicates acceptance of involvement. And since the problem of
expression is obviously one aspect of the problem of moral
action, the two levels of a Skelton poem will merge at the
moment of resolution, and the decision will be made in
terms of both.

What makes this dramatic use of style possible for Skelton and viable for his audience is the quite public debate
in literary circles concerning (1) the adequacy of the English

1. By narrative I mean that part of a poem's action which is visible
on the surface. The narrative level involves an agreement between poet
and reader on the problem of a poem and the subsequent consideration
of the problem. The verbal level involves the reflection in a clash or
alternation of styles of the narrative problem. In some poems, when the
narrative problem is how to write, the two levels may be one; in others
they will gradually merge.

language, (2) the nature of poetic diction, and (3) the relationship between the art of poetry and rhetoric. Veré Rubel writes, "At no previous time in the history of English literature did diction come so near to being a central concern among the generality of writers as it did in the early decades of the Tudor period,"[2] and Elizabeth Sweeting correctly extends the area of concern beyond the single problem of diction: "The atmosphere of change and controversy reflected in the prose, poetry and translation of the late fifteenth and early sixteenth century, the discussion of style and diction, the evidence of fashions in language, the disuse of old forms or their modification for new purposes—all these trends show that it was a time for the considerations of decisions literary and linguistic."[3] The establishment position on these questions is fully articulated in the work of Stephen Hawes, Skelton's literary enemy, who declared again and again that (1) English is completely inadequate as a vehicle for the expression of fine ideas and noble sentiments, that (2) consequently the only proper diction is the heavenly latinate "aureate," which allows the poet to "cloke" a "trouthe" behind a veil of stylized obscurity, and that (3) poetry *is* rhetoric, and by rhetoric he means the third of the five classical divisions, *elocutio* or style, which codifies and illustrates all possible figures of speech.[4]

Miss Rubel is mistaken, I think, when she groups Skelton with Hawes and argues that no serious reaction to the

2. *Poetic Diction in the English Renaissance* (New York, 1941), p. 1.
3. *Early Tudor Criticism* (Oxford, 1940), pp. 21–22.
4. Lines 1160–69 of his *Pastime of Pleasure* are a fair sample of his literary pronouncements: "He shall attaste / the well of fruytfulnesse / Whiche Vyrgyll claryfyed and also Tullyus / With latyn pure swete and delycyous / From whens my master Lydgate derysyde / The depured rethoryke in englysshe language / To make our tongue so clerely puryfyed / That the vyle termes shoulde nothynge arage / As lyke a pye to chattre in a cage / But for to speke with Rethoryke formally / In the good ordre withouten vylany" (ed. W. E. Mead, Early English Text Society, orig. ser. 173 [London, 1928], 49).

aureate aesthetic is discernible "until the second quarter of the sixteenth century."[5] The mistake is not at all an unnatural one. Caxton, the most prominent contemporary commentator on Skelton, praises him in terms which might well apply to Hawes: "I praye mayster John Skelton late created poete laureate in the unyversite of oxenforde to oversee and correcte this sayd booke. And taddresse and expowne where as shalle be founde faulte to theym that shall requyre it. For hym I knowe for suffycyent to expowne and englysshe euery dyffyculte that is therin For he hath late translated the epyst-lys of Tulle and the boke of dyodorus syculus. and diverse other werkes oute of latyn in to englysshe not in rude and olde langage. but in polysshed and ornate termes craftely."[6] And Skelton himself would seem to corroborate the point in *Philip Sparrow* when he complains "Our naturall tong is rude, / And hard to be enneude / With pullysshed termes lusty; / Our language is so rusty, / So cankered, and so full / Of frowardes, and so dull, / That if I wolde apply / To wryte ornatly, / I wot not where to fynd / Termes to serve my mynde."[7] But this linguistic judgment is delivered in the poem not by Skelton but by Jane Scrope, who prefaces these lines with a warning that has unfortunately been ignored, "I am but a yong mayd."[8] I cannot touch here on the many ways in which this statement is true or on the care Skelton takes to establish in the first half of this poem a personality distinct from his own. Suffice it to say that it is dangerous to equate her words with his, and safer to listen to the poet in an obiter dictum which is more clearly didactic: "Go litill quaire, / Demene you faire; / Take no dispare, / Though I you wrate / After this

5. *Poetic Diction,* p. 6.
6. *The Prologues and Epilogues of William Caxton,* ed. W. J. B. Crotch, Early English Text Society, orig. ser. 176 (London, 1928), 109.
7. Dyce, *1,* 74–75, lines 774–83.
8. Line 770.

rate / In Englysshe letter; / So moche the better / Welcome shall ye / To sum men be."[9] Skelton is consistently less interested in stylistic ingenuity than in communication. In fact, on all these matters, he departs from the Hawesian stance: English is his chosen language, the plain style his style, and rhetoric his servant rather than master. It will take the following chapters and a great deal more to document and qualify these assertions, but something of the complexity of Skelton's position can be seen in his relatively early "Knolege, aquayntance, resort,"[1] which reads at first like a typically aureate compliment. The opening stanzas are a perfect example of what Miss Rubel calls the "mellifluous sesquipedality" of the aureate style:[2] "Allectuary arrectyd to redres / These feverous axys, the dedely wo and payne / Of thoughtfull hertys plungyd in dystres; / Refresshyng myndys the Aprell shoure of rayne. / Condute of comforte, and well most soverayne" (8–12). In other and more comprehensible words the woman in question is a medicinal force ("allectuary") who is able to assuage ("arrectyd to redres") the horrible pains of love-melancholy ("These feverous axys"). The second half of line 9 ("the dedely wo and payne") is no more than a translation of the first half ("These feverous axys"), an example of what Puttenham called "synonymia." What the aureate style can do is pile up superlatives which are more exotic than accurate. The impression is of an excellence beyond expression, but expression is the problem of the poem, and at this point the hyperbolic incantation of the aureate stands between the speaker and a communicable statement of his beloved's perfections. In the first three stanzas, only "Of lusty somer the passyng goodly quene" (14) is relatively "natural," and that

---

9. Dyce, *1*, 422, lines 1533–40. The lines are from an envoy to the *Garland of Laurel.*

1. Dyce, *1*, p. 25.

2. *Poetic Diction,* p. 31.

is a patent echo of Chaucer and other "dream vision" poets.
The fourth stanza marks a turning point as the speaker himself becomes aware of his failure. He admits that his language cannot mirror the beauty of his lady's face, which is
"Illumynyd with feturys far passyng my reporte" (23); and
in the last line of this same stanza he hints at the sentiment
"cloked" beneath the elaborateness of "Saphyre of sadnes,
envayned with indy blew," or "Geyne surfetous suspecte the
emeraud comendable" (17, 20):

> Whych to behold makyth hevy hartys glad.   [28]

This line signals a shift in tactics; the speaker turns from his
lady to his reaction to her: "Of your bownte and of youre
womanhod, / Which makyth my hart oft to lepe and
sprynge, / And to remember many a praty thynge" (31–33).
However, this is merely another way to avoid the problem
as the reader is invited to share the response of the poet to
an object which is still not described; he can refer to, but
not recreate, these "praty thynges." And when he attempts
to explain why the lady's absence affects him so markedly
he is forced to say, "if ye lyst to know the cause why so, /
Open myne hart, beholde my mynde expres: / I wold ye
coud" (38–40), surely an anticipation in every way of Sidney's "look in thy heart and write." By this point aureate
diction has almost disappeared, yet the lover is no more
satisfied with his power of expression than he was in the
earlier stanza. The "I wold ye coud" ("open myne hart")
of line 40 is as much an admission of failure as the "far
passyng my reporte" of line 23. Stalemated by language's
inability to mirror reality perfectly, he can only move back
and forth between two ultimately unsatisfactory modes of
diction. In the last stanza he turns momentarily to a modified
form of the aureate: "Nothynge yerthly to me more desyrous
/ Than to beholde youre bewteouse countenaunce" (43–44).
But he finally decides that while only the opening of his

heart will yield a true reading of her excellences and his passion, what would be found there, beyond the reach of language as it is, is still closer in spirit to the natural statement of the plain style than to the artificial statement of the aureate. The final couplet says nothing of the lady or of her effect on him, but merely asserts baldly the single "fact" which makes the effort of writing the poem necessary:

> I have gravyd her wythin the secret wall
> Of my trew harc, to love her best of all.   [48-49]

What Skelton is *not* doing is parodying the courtly compliment. The opening stanzas are not bombastic or cacophonous; the rhythms are regular and the patterning of vocalic and consonantal sounds in a line like "*Tran*s*end*y*ng* ple*s*ure, *s*urmoun*t*y*ng*e all *dys*por*te*" (7) is fluidly effective. There is grace and a dignity in the aureate when it is done well, and Skelton does it very well; the objection to the style is not that it fails to please, but that it does not do the job. Accuracy, in the sense of a faithful transmission of ideas and sentiments, not grace, is the impossible goal here. Again, Skelton does not condemn artificiality or convention; the poem can be read as a succession of fifteenth-century lyric conventions—*descriptio* (1-22), "modesty" topos (23), "pains of absence" (27-46), "sweet thought" (47-49)—and as a collation of innumerable antecedents:

> Fresshe lusty beaute, joyned with gentylesse,
> Demure appert, glad chere with gouvernaunce.[3]

>   thoughe I be nott able,
> To wrytte to your goodly person.[4]

3. *The Minor Poems of John Lydgate*, Part II, ed. H. N. MacCracken, Early English Text Society, orig. ser. 192 (Oxford, 1934), p. 379, lines 1-2.

4. No. 130 in *Secular Lyrics of the XIVth and XVth Centuries*, ed. R. H. Robbins (Oxford, 1952), p. 126, lines 7-8.

The wynttir nycht ane hour I may nocht sleip,
for thocht of yow.[5]

Allas, it make myn hert to breke.[6]

O wofull hert profound in gret duresse.
Which canst not playn nor opyn thy dysese.[7]

I have pryntyd yow yn my harte soo depe.[8]

In these poems, however, the convention is accepted by the
poet because it allows him to remain within the closed world
of a conceit; it is an adequate vehicle for an effort that is
rhetorical rather than reflective. The courtly versifier is not
concerned with an accurate description of a lady who probably does not exist, even as an ideal, and the modesty topos
permits him to turn his unconcern to advantage. Nor does
the problem of verbalizing an emotion he does not feel tug
at him, and with the "closed-in-my heart" ploy he can make
a virtue of silence. Skelton takes the purely rhetorical pose
and asks a deadly question, "What if this be true?" Commonplaces (literary or philosophical) are valued because their
incantational repetition creates a comfortable screen between
us and the problems that stand behind them; we accord
these problems a position in our mental furniture, and their
reality for us becomes completely verbal. Skelton disturbs
his audience by taking their commonplaces seriously: what
if accuracy of description *is* impossible, what if expression
can never be direct, what if the ideal of sincerity is a
chimera? And in later poems, what if the world is upside
down, what if the Church is corrupt? What does this mean
for me, for you, for us? Skelton's answers to these questions

5. No. 133 in *Secular Lyrics*, p. 132, lines 9–10.
6. No. 127 in *Secular Lyrics*, p. 121, line 39.
7. "An English Friend Of Charles of Orleans," H. N. MacCracken,
PMLA, 1911, p. 160, lines 1–2. The English friend is of course Suffolk.
8. No. 200 in *Secular Lyrics*, p. 206, line 37.

are rarely final and never simple. In "Knolege, aquayntance, resort," he does not ask aureate or plain, courtly or homely, traditional or new, but language or silence, and the answer is as it will be in the forty years that follow, a provisional one in which *a* style, *a* technique, or *a* program of action emerges as the more useful rather than the more correct. The obvious progression in "Knolege, aquayntance, resort," from the formality of the early lines to the almost colloquial freedom of that last couplet appears to be an unqualified statement of the superiority of the informal. But, superimposed on the entire poem, on aureate and plain lines alike, is a formal pattern that reveals Skelton, in his own way, cloaking a truth under a veil: the poem is an acrostic, the first letters of each stanza combining to spell the name of his lady, KATERYN. When we realize that the "truth" of this poetic component is available and complete only in the climactic, plain stanza, the relativity of the poem's aesthetic judgment is given another twist that sets our minds reeling. Perhaps the closest approximation of Skelton's position is Caxton's statement of linguistic indecision: "Loo what sholde a man in thyse dayes now wryte. egges or eyren certaynly it is harde to playse every man by cause of dyversite chaunge of langage. For in these dayes every man that is in ony reputacyon in his countre. wyll ut-ter his commynycacyon and maters in suche maners and termes that fewe men shall understonde theym And som honest and grete clerkes have ben wyth me and desired me to wryte the moste curyous termes that I coude fynde And thus bytwene playn rude and curyous I stande abasshed."[9] Caxton's dilemma, however, is the dilemma of a translator; Skelton's, as we shall see, of a poet for whom the choice of style is a moral and epistemological as well as a technical problem.

To summarize: I read Skelton's poetry as the record of an

9. *Prologues and Epilogues*, pp. 108–09.

attempt to reconcile the implications of certain medieval commonplaces (the immanence of order, the divinity of poetry) with a growing awareness of temporal corruption. In brief, he moves from a reliance on the temporal as a reflection of the eternal to a reliance on the eternal only, and assures his own place in this more elective vision by embracing the doctrine of divine inspiration. This in turn creates a tension between the security of communion with the divine and the moral imperatives of a fallen world, and presents Skelton with a peculiarly human problem. It is this problem (the possibility, for the poet, of moral action) which simultaneously provides the subject for, and determines the formal characteristics of, his poetry.

So important for Skelton's art is his awareness of both tension and problem that any attempt to evade either is poetically disastrous. *The Earl of Northumberland* and the *Replication* are cases in point. I have "sacrificed" these poems to the construction of a Skeltonic aesthetic only because as poems, rather than as documents in the poet's intellectual history, they are unsuccessful. Skelton's finest poetry, I shall argue, is the result of a direct and unflinching confrontation of the conflict inherent in his position as poet-priest and fallen man. Any resolution of this conflict is only temporary; as a supremely political man, he is again and again faced with an unforeseen complication (the proliferation of Lutheranism, the possibility of Wolsey as Pope) which forces him to re-evaluate his position and fashion a new accommodation. "Poetry," writes T. S. Eliot, "is . . . an escape from emotion." Whether or not this is acceptable as a general poetic, it is certainly a description of Skelton's poetic. "But, of course," Eliot adds, "only those who have . . . emotions know what it means to want to escape."[1] For Skelton, however, poetry is an escape from emotional conflict in the sense that it is a vehicle for the resolution of emotional conflict.

1. *Selected Essays, 1917–1932* (New York, 1932), pp. 10–11.

In other words, the escape is not so much from emotion as from an emotional treadmill; the problem of the minute is absorbed into the larger (but still personal) problem which stands behind it. When, however, the poetry ignores the problem or slights its complexity, the result is at best rhetoric (*The Earl of Northumberland*) and at worst propaganda (*Replication*).

What I am suggesting is that Skelton's muse needs the control which a conscious effort to define the relationship between his commitment to a fixed reality and his unavoidable involvement with an unstable humanity provides. In *The Earl of Northumberland* the uncritical acceptance of temporal sources of authority precludes any such effort; in the *Replication* the process of definition has hardened into a new kind of acceptance, and the effort is no longer necessary. In both cases the absence of real conflict is, in effect, the absence of an ordering principle. The traditional form of the elegy gives the earlier poem the illusion of control, although it is obvious that the tradition rather than Skelton is the source of the illusion. The tradition which stands behind the *Replication* (clerical satire) is itself characterized by a certain formlessness, and in the absence of conflict Skelton surrenders to it. In short, he proclaims rather than defines, and produces a poetry of abuse.

I am describing the laws that govern Skelton's poetry. For other poets, it is the mode of proclamation which best channels their creative energies. I am not offering a distinction between poetry written in the heat of passion and poetry written after recollecting in tranquility. Either mode involves a conscious fiction, and the difference lies in the kind of impression the respective fictions convey. In poetry which defines, the reader is asked to observe and perhaps join a mind in the *process* of making moral choices; in the poetry of proclamation, the reader is asked to accept the distilled wisdom of a mind that has made its choices long ago. The dis-

tinction is a technical one, and it would hardly be legitimate
to equate different approaches to the literary presentation of
experience with different approaches to life. It does seem to
me, however, that for the consideration of certain problems
the poetry of definition is the superior vehicle, and that one
such problem is the problem of identity. Skelton's heroes
repeatedly ask, "Who am I?" "What am I doing here?" For
the reasons suggested in the preceding pages, Skelton comes
naturally to these questions, and it is through the poetry
of definition that he fashions his answer.

HISTORY AND CRITICISM

In the chapters that follow, then, we shall examine a poetry
in which the accidents of history provide the raw material
for a drama that is essentially interior. However important
the issues of his time are to Skelton the man, they are significant for the poet only as they seem to demand a reconsideration of his relationship with that which is outside time. If,
as Eliot writes, "it is . . . the intensity of the artistic process,
the pressure . . . under which the fusion takes place, that
counts,"[2] the pressures that lead to Skelton's "fusion" are
certainly to be found in history; and insofar as a personal
(and therefore poetic) readjustment usually attends a political or ecclesiastical crisis, a consideration of Skelton's
poetry is a consideration of the early sixteenth century. Yet
the facts an intelligent reader must have at his command
are minimal: he must know that as tutor to Henry VIII
Skelton saw himself as in a real way responsible for the
preservation of the English state ("The honor of Englond
I lernyd to spelle, / In dygnyte roialle that doth excelle"),[3]
that the rise of the parvenu Wolsey seemed to undercut his

2. Ibid., p. 8.
3. Dyce, *1, 129*, lines 95–96. The couplet is from Skelton's third
flyting against Christopher Garnish.

responsibility and threaten that state, that in the cold war between the old nobility and the architects of the Renaissance state, Skelton stands with the great houses and the feudal hierarchy which created them, that the poet's rejection of humanistic values follows inevitably from his religious and political position.

Yet, while a completely satisfactory reading of a poem depends, in part, on the awareness of what we may call the fabric of history, there is always a danger, especially in the case of a minor figure, that the poem will be lost in that fabric; and since the Skelton "renaissance" of the thirties, his poetry *has* been absorbed by several disciplines. For some, the entire canon is a document in the history of that most imposing of English prelates, Cardinal Wolsey. The antihistorical bias of twentieth-century criticism, however, has led to a gradual abandonment of this extreme position; and as William Harris points out in an impressive article, "If every charge . . . in Skelton's poems were taken to be a possible reference to Wolsey . . . the field of allusions would rapidly expand to impossible proportions."[4] A less obviously misleading approach involves the identification of critical questions with the questions of "intellectual" history. Does Skelton herald the English Renaissance, or is he the last medievalist? Is he a humanist, and of the Lutheran party without knowing it, or a traditionalist defender of the faith? Since the critic who asks these questions defines his terms subjectively, very different Skeltons are offered to us. For Ian Gordon, H. L. R. Edwards, and, more recently, Judith Larsen, Skelton triumphs as he rejects a tired medievalism and decides for the spirit of the new age:

> Middle Ages and Renaissance jostle each other uneasily in the poetry of Skelton. . . . His significance . . . is that

4. "Wolsey and Skelton's Magnyfycence: A Re-evaluation," *Studies in Philology*, 57 (1960), 108.

he was the first poet to catch the transitional spirit of his times and express the aspirations of a new society.[5]

In his devotion to the things of this world, in his healthy robustness of perception, in his independence . . . he expresses the English counterpart of the earthy, Catholic paganism of the High Renaissance.[6]

The use of living speaking characters in place of the medieval straw personifications is another aspect of Skelton's ability to develop his medieval basis into something more complex and useful.[7]

In the same framework, another critic condemns him because he does not decide for the spirit of the new age:

In this time, seething with life, in which every . . . value is dyed in a new bath . . . John Skelton stood like a solid rock of conservatism.

Skelton's conservatism . . . was sufficiently strong to prevent him from siding with the pioneers. It had a bad effect on his achievements as an artist.[8]

Each of these assessments can be challenged on its own terms. In the course of this study I shall argue that Skelton (a) disapproves of the "aspirations of a new society," (b) rejects (intellectually, if not personally) the "things of this world," (c) writes a poetry that is "complex" and "useful" precisely because of his "medieval" basis, (d) owes the power of his poetry to his determination to remain in one sense

5. Ian Gordon, *John Skelton, Poet Laureate* (Melbourne, 1934), p. 69.

6. H. L. R. Edwards, *Skelton: The Life and Times of an Early Tudor Poet* (London, 1949), p. 23.

7. Judith Larsen, "What Is the *Bouge of Courte?*" *Journal of English and German Philology*, 61 (1962), 295.

8. T. Tillemans, "John Skelton, a Conservative," *English Studies*, 28 (1946), 142, 145.

"a solid rock of conservatism." But it is the terms of the assessment rather than the assessment itself which seem questionable. As A. R. Heiserman remarks,

> All these studies attempt to precipitate out of Skelton's poetry a consistent set of political, ethical and theological ideas. . . . By searching out the familiar and unfamiliar, the critic who assigns different values to the two can easily decide what is good . . . and bad . . . in Skelton's work . . . one can call his work as a whole either revolutionary or reactionary—depending on one's predilections.[9]

In short, the considerations which guide the critical process here are nonliterary and perhaps extraliterary; a criticism which classifies on the basis of the history of ideas is necessarily superficial. Yet Heiserman's alternative approach is no less superficial and insofar as it *seems* literary, even more misleading. For ideas he substitutes conventions: "For the present study . . . conventions of technique are the essentials of literary tradition and the proper subject of literary history . . . they are the traditional means by which poets achieve their effects."[1] And in his attempt to "comprehend [Skelton's] relations to the traditions of medieval satire,"[2] the poet is reduced to a manipulator of conventions.

What does not emerge from any of these approaches is a recognition of the patterned conflict so central to a Skelton poem. A reading that depends on the reconstruction of political, intellectual, and literary history will hardly exhaust the complexity of any body of poetry and will not approach the mainspring of a poem written in the mode of definition. If I am correct, the locus of a Skelton poem is the narrator's mind; and since the drama is internal, it will reveal itself

9. *Skelton and Satire* (Chicago, 1961), p. 11.
1. Ibid., p. 3.
2. Ibid., p. 13.

to a reading which attends to the psychology of the speaker
and proceeds from there to a consideration of scene, which
moves, in short, from the internal to the external; conversely
a concentration on the scene will yield a reductive interpretation. In the last analysis my quarrel is with the almost
conspiratorial unwillingness to admit that Skelton is in any
way involved in his own poetry.[3] We are offered Skelton,
the political propagandist; Skelton, the voice of his age;
Skelton, the student of convention; but not Skelton, the man,
as he confronts a collision between his ideal and an unwel-
come reality in terms that are historically and personally
unique. Literary criticism is parasitical, and critics sometimes suppress an awareness of their dependence on a poet
by implicitly denying his existence. Something like this lies
behind Heiserman's declaration of critical faith: "Poets have
little new to say; to say once again that love is painful, that
power is ignorant, that God lives, and to say it movingly,
they must constantly freshen and modify the conventions by
which their predecessors moved men."[4]

"Poets have little new to say." In a very real way this
statement is behind the entire range of Skelton criticism;
and of course in one sense it cannot be challenged but in another sense it is irrelevant. In poetry the measure of "new-
ness" is the strength of the poet's *personal* intuition. Philosophically there may be nothing new under the sun; but if
the questions are always the same and the answers often the
same, both are new to the mind challenged for the first time
to make sense of what Wordsworth calls "the weary weight
of all this unintelligible world." Skelton's world is the world
of Lydgate, Hoccleve, Barclay, and Hawes, and his superiority lies neither in a "revolutionary" spirit nor a technical

---

3. Heiserman writes, "We do not consider John Skelton the man
but a few of the works written by him" (*Skelton and Satire*, p. 19). I
confess that I cannot see how this is a virtue.
4. Ibid., p. 3.

facility, but in the uniqueness and intensity of his *personal* response to the complexities of the human situation. One hears a great deal about commonplaces in Skelton criticism. His ideas are so typical that his commitment to them has been assumed to be automatic and unthinking. Yet this assumption ignores the possibility that a commonplace, to which most men pay only lip service, could, in the service of a mind committed to it, be part of a poetic statement that is not commonplace. In Skelton's case the theory of divine inspiration is just that.

The literary historian might possibly explain away his claims of illumination by including him in a number of available traditions: (1) Plato's ironic suggestion in the *Ion* that poetry is written in a trance-like state akin to madness; (2) the Neoplatonic modification of (1) which allows the artist a unique intuition of "the Ideas from which nature derives" and prepares the way for the "golden world" of Sidney's apology;[5] (3) the rabbinical and patristic tradition of exegesis which (a) allows the Church Fathers to interpret "embarrassing" passages of Scripture by assuming that the Bible is a network of types and interchangeable meanings, and (b) makes possible (4) the Christian humanist extension of the Ciceronian defense of poetry as an especially effective vehicle of moral instruction by applying typological criticism to secular and pagan literature.[6] In the *Replication* Skelton would seem to touch on each of these: The gift of poetry is "an effecte energiall / As *Grekes* do it call"; in a reversal of the patristic celebration of the psalmist ("David . . . Simonides noster, Pindarus, et Alcaeus"), every poet becomes a potential David: "Than, if this noble kyng / Thus can harpe and syng / With his harpe of prophecy / And

5. See above, p. 11, n. 1.
6. See D. W. Robertson, Jr., *A Preface to Chaucer: Studies in Medieval Perspectives* (Princeton, 1962), pp. 286–365, for a discussion of Christian allegory and Christian humanism.

spyrituall poetry, / As saynt Jerome saythe, / . . . Why
have ye then disdayne / At poetes";[7] and the epigraph which
begins "Sunt infiniti, sunt innumerique sophistae" and ends
"sed sunt pauci rarique poetae" echoes Boccaccio (*Genealogia Deorum Gentilium*, 14.7)[8] who in turn echoes Cicero
(*De oratore*, 1.3). But any attempt to place Skelton in these
traditions breaks down immediately: more often than not,
it is the enemies of poetry who put forward the "divine
frenzy" argument (Socrates forces Ion to admit that he is
"either dishonest or mad"); in the same way the patristic
attitude toward poetry is to say the least equivocal, and
Aquinas suggests that its similarity to theological discourse
is superficial:

> Poetic knowledge concerns matters which through a
> deficiency in their truth cannot be laid hold of by the
> reason; hence the reason has to be beguiled by means
> of certain similitudes. Theology, on the other hand,
> deals with matters which are above reason. So the
> symbolic mode is common to both types of discourse;
> neither type is suited to reasoning.[9]

Skelton hardly fits here. When the humanists attach themselves to scriptural theory, they take with it the fourfold
interpretation and eventually the Hawesian aesthetic of obscurity (*allegoria*) which Skelton firmly rejects in *Speak,*

---

7. Dyce, *1*, 221, lines 344–49.
8. "This poetry, which ignorant triflers cast aside, is a sort of fervid
and exquisite invention. . . . It proceeds from the bosom of God, and
few, I find, are the souls in whom this gift is born; indeed so wonderful
a gift it is that true poets have always been the rarest of men." From
*Boccaccio on Poetry Being the Preface and the Fourteenth and Fifteenth
Books of Boccaccio's Genealogia Deorum Gentilium*, trans. and ed.
Charles G. Osgood (Princeton, 1930), p. 39.
9. Quoted from Brooks and Wimsatt, *English Literary Criticism*,
p. 131. The passage is to be found in *Commentum in Primum Librum
Sententiarum Magistri Petri Lombardi, Prologus*, q.1, a5, ad 3m.

Parrot. In the sixteenth century the reformers used the same
theory of inspiration to argue that since the Bible is inspired,
it is blasphemy to rearrange Scripture and ignore the literal
level; Skelton condemns the "literalist" heresy in the
Replication.

It becomes increasingly obvious that his adaptation of the
theory is unique. In pre-Skeltonian aesthetics (and in early
Skelton), the deference to divine inspiration is merely formal. For the fathers and schoolmen, Frederick Farrar maintains, it is a ritual that has no relation to practical criticism
or poetics.[1] Surely in the English tradition of the late Middle
Ages it is no more than a rhetorical throwaway. Gower may
say, "God commands me to write with the pen he has
furnished";[2] but this is merely gesture and, as Curtius points
out, a gesture strangely incongruous in view of the poetic
handbooks:

> If we now look back at the Middle Ages, we can see
> that the theory of "poetic madness"—the Platonic
> interpretation of the doctrine of inspiration and en-
> thusiasm—lived on. . . . "Lived on" is perhaps too
> pretentious an expression. As it did with so many other
> coinages of the Greek spirit, the Middle Ages took this

1. *History of Interpretation* (New York, 1886), p. xx.
2. Heiserman quotes this line in *Skelton and Satire* (p. 290), adding
in a note, "Writers of political 'prophecies' would be most prone to
make this claim." The claim itself was made again and again, but it is
the intensity of his statement that sets Skelton apart. One might compare the obviously mechanical deference to the theory in Barclay's prologue to his first eclogue: "The glorious sight of God my saviour, /
Which is chiefe shepheard and head of other all, / To him for succour
in this my worke I call / And not on Clio nor olde Melpomene, / My
hope is fixed of him ayded to be / That he me direct, my mynde for
to expresse: / That he, to good ende my wyt and pen adresse." From
The Eclogues of Alexander Barclay, ed. Beatrice White, Early English
Text Society, orig. ser. 175 (London, 1928), 4, lines 114–20. This is,
as one would expect from Barclay, pious, but what he asks for is the
general protection afforded to every Christian in the performance of

one from late Rome, preserved it, and copied it to the
letter, until the creative Eros of the Italian Renaissance
reawakened the spirit in the letter. That the poetic
μανια found a refuge in the medieval *scriptoria* with
the rest of the authoritative stock of antique learning
is a paradox when one considers that it was precisely
in the Middle Ages that writing poetry was considered
to be sweat-producing labor and was recommended as
such.[3]

For the traditionalists, then, the theory is only a means to
sometimes contradictory ends—the denial of poetic truth,
the scriptural justification of an ecclesiastical establishment,
the defense of belles lettres as an honorable profession. Ideal-
ly, the formulation of an aesthetic involves an attempt to
locate the poet in the hierarchy of moral (in the largest sense
of the word) agents; but the Platonists are philosophers, the
exegetes theologians, the humanists propagandists, before
they are poets, and their aesthetics sometimes become detached from the central problems of existence. For Skelton,
poetry *is* philosophy, theology, propaganda ("Sunt infiniti
. . . sophistae . . . logistae . . . philosophi . . . theologique . . .
doctores") and it is this total commitment that is new, that
is far from commonplace. The late C. S. Lewis implies that
Skelton's successes are accidents: "The result is good only
when he is either playful or violently abusive, when the
shaping power which we ordinarily demand of a poet is

---

his work. There is no sense of the intensely personal communion between the Christian muse and the vessel that we find in Milton's in-
vocations and in Skelton's pronouncements. It is this, I think, which
justifies J. W. H. Atkins' statement that in Skelton's work, "for the
first time the doctrine of poetic inspiration was being expounded in
English" (*English Literary Criticism: The Medieval Phase* [Cambridge
University Press, 1934], p. 176).
   3. *European Literature and the Latin Middle Ages,* trans. Willard
Trask (New York, 1953), p. 475.

either admittedly on holiday or may be supposed to be suspended by rage."[4] The "shaping power" Lewis seeks in vain is surely there. It has, however, been sought in the wrong places, in the issues of an epoch, on the battlefield of ideas, in literary traditions which are partly the creation of the literary historian, rather than in the mind that makes use of these things. Why does Skelton consistently proclaim the divinity of his art and mission? Why does he write a poetry so different and unclassifiable that criticism seems only to distort it? When the answers to these questions are found, the shaping power will be found, found in the accommodation of one man to a universe that is not arranged to please its inhabitants.

4. *English Literature in the Sixteenth Century, Excluding Drama,* Oxford History of English Literature, 3, ed. F. P. Wilson and Bonamy Dobrée (Oxford, 1954), 142.

2   This World Is But a Cherry Fair

THE LYRICS

IN HIS INTRODUCTION TO *Secular Lyrics of the XIVth and XVth Centuries,* Rossell Hope Robbins remarks on the anonymity of most fifteenth-century lyrics:

> Most of the poems in this anthology deal with the realities of the daily life of the period; they had a reason for existing, and were associated with many activities —drinking, begging, seducing, bringing in the boar's head. Their naturalness and simplicity come from the fact that they were meant for daily use. They lack the storm and stress of psychological conflict which come in later poetic . . . art, when the artist becomes a unique person.[1]

The argument of my opening chapter could be reduced to the assertion that in Skelton's poetry interest turns from the "realities of daily life" to the "psychological conflict" of the "unique person" who must face and order them. Skelton characteristically assumes the more anonymous fifteenth-century stance but, through an unexpected complication in the narrative or public situation, he forces the reader to examine the personality which presents it to him. As the questions he considers become more comprehensive, and the psychology of his protagonists more complex, the relationship between his poem and its antecedents is less and less obvious. Fortunately, in his early work, a group of "love lyrics," that relationship can be analyzed with the kind of

1. P. lv.

precision that will be impossible when we come to explicate the poems of his maturity.

The fifteenth-century love lyric presents Skelton with two traditions, identified by Robbins' distinction between "Courtly Love Lyrics" and "Popular Songs." The classification is made in terms of theme and diction: the themes of the courtly lyric are limited—the praise of the beloved ("A Catalogue of Delights"),[2] the inconstancy of the beloved ("A Fickle Mistress"),[3] the unapproachability of the beloved ("A Pitiless Mistress"),[4] the pains of love ("The Wounds of Love"), the pains of separation ("Parting Is Death"),[5] the inevitable farewell:

> Fayre-wele my Ioye, my comfort and solace,
> fayre-wele the floure fayrest of beute,
> fayre-wele the godly feture of youre face,
> fayre-wele my gladnes and felicyte,
> fayre-wele my helth & my prosperyte,
> fayre-wele my herttes lyve & my plesance,
> fayre-wele disport, & fayre-wele dalyance.[6]

As Robbins prints them the poems form a narrative of the typical courtly love affair from first sight to final envoy, and of course each of the themes has its "anti-theme"—the reaction of the unsuccessful lover who decides that his mistress' eyes are nothing like the sun ("her eyen byn holow and grene as any grasse"),[7] that her fickleness is matched only by his indifference ("But sythe that ye / So strange wylbe / As toward me . . . I trust, percase, / to fynde some

2. Ibid., p. 120.
3. Ibid., p. 136.
4. Ibid., p. 141.
5. Ibid., both poems, p. 150.
6. Ibid., p. 207.
7. This line is from "The Dyscryving of a Fayre Lady," number 48 in Henry A. Person's *Cambridge Middle English Lyrics* (Seattle, 1953).

grace / ... & spede as well!"),[8] that her faithlessness is characteristic:

> O Wicket wemen, wilfull, and variable,
> richt fals, feckle, fell, and frivolus,
> Dowgit, dispytfull, dour, and dissavable,
> Unkynd, crewall, curst, and covettus,
> Ovirlicht of laitis, unleill, and licherus,
> Turnit fra trewth, and taiclit With treichery,
> Unferme of faith, fulfillit of fellony![9]

The point is that all the situations and attitudes are so conventional that they are predictable; even the scorn and cynicism is mannered. What one hears is the voice of the tradition—the graceful, but repetitive, aureate vocabulary, the familiar exclamatio's ("O woeful heart") and descriptio's (golden hair, ivory neck, ruby lips), in short, the endless echoes of de Vinsauf and other rhetoricians—rather than the voice of a "unique individual."

In the more native tradition the themes are not dissimilar, although the vocabulary is more English and the "stations" of the love affair are less clearly indicated; there are the same oppositions—the praise of woman ("A woman ys a worthy wight, / she servyth a man both daye and nyght")[1] and the abuse of woman ("women list to smater, / Or Agaynst ther husbondes for to clater")[2]—lovers' pleas ("Myn owne dere ladi fair & fre, / y pray ow in herte ye ruwen on me")[3] and rejected lover's indifference ("I am sory for her sake, / yc may wel ete & drynke; / wanne yc sclepe yc may not wake, / so muche on here yc thenke").[4] In addition there are

8. Robbins, *Secular Lyrics*, p. 139.
9. Ibid., p. 225.
1. Ibid., p. 31.
2. Ibid., p. 36.
3. Ibid., p. 13.
4. Ibid., p. 34.

themes that would not apply to the courtly love relationship
as we know it: the trials of marriage ("A man that wedyth a
wyfe whan he wynkyth, / But he star afterward, wonder me
thynkyth"),[5] the henpecked husband ("If I aske our dame
fleych, / che brekit myn hed with a dych")[6] the serving
maid's seduction by beau or clerk or master ("wan ic to his
chambur com / . . . thout y on no gyle")[7] and the seduced
serving maid's lament ("I go with childe, wel I wot; / I
schrew the fadur that hit gate").[8] Again while the diction is
less "pullyshed," the genre itself is as stylized as its courtly
opposite. The situations, themes, and attitudes are common
property, and the differences between the two traditions have
less to do with such critical terms as artificiality and realism
than with tone, the detachment and grace (even in anger)
of the one, and the boisterousness and good humor (even
in cynicism) of the other; and in both the tone is public
rather than personal. In his lyrics Skelton joins the voice and
often the diction of the unsuccessful courtly lover to the low
humor of the betrayed-serving-maid-ballad. Two things follow: (1) The politesse of the courtly tradition is undercut
and revealed as perfumed coarseness (far worse than un-
adorned coarseness), while the redeeming boisterousness of
the native tradition is negated by the ridicule of a courtly
burlesque; (2) the narrative voice or the voice behind the
narrative becomes the center of attention. Skelton invites the
reader familiar with the fifteenth-century lyric to assume
he is reading a certain kind of poem only to frustrate his
responses by inserting the diction and *topoi* of another, forcing him to turn from the narrative which is no longer a
reliable focal point to the mind which may be. What one
remembers from a reading of Skelton's lyrics is that mind:

5. Ibid., p. 37.
6. Ibid., p. 39.
7. Ibid., p. 23.
8. Ibid., p. 20.

its sophistication, its bitterness, its negativity, its uniqueness.

In these poems the principals in the affair are joined by an observer who either comments directly on them or allows his attitude to emerge in the sum of theirs. The latter is the case in "Womanhod, wanton, ye want," where, if there is a third voice, it is heard only in the last two lines.[9] This lyric is usually read as a monologue, and since the music which possibly accompanied it has not survived, it is difficult to establish with any certainty the division of lines, or indeed that any division is necessary; but as a dialogue the poem is closer in spirit to the Skeltonic lyric tone as it emerges from other poems. The internal evidence is strong: at several points an apparently weak transition could indicate a change in speaker, and lines that are unaccountably vehement are understandable if we read the poem as a sexual flyting; the most telling argument is the unmistakably phallic imagery of the fourth stanza.

In what I read as an exchange of insults, neither antagonist is attractive. The man begins with a charge of shrewishness: "Womanhod, wanton, ye want; / Youre medelyng, mastres, is manerles; / Plente of yll, of goodnes skant, / Ye rayll at ryot, recheles" (1–4). His mistress' censoriousness, he goes on, is belied by her actions; she is, in fact, putting on undeserved airs: "To prayse youre porte it is nedeles; / For all your draffe yet and youre dreggys, / As well borne as ye full oft tyme beggys," (5–7) and a probable pun on port (either carriage or gate) anticipates the later charges of promiscuity. The response is in kind: "Why so koy and full of skorne," she retorts, and mockingly attributes his bluster to a fear that the price of her favors will rise:

> "Myne horse is sold," I wene, you say;
> My new furryd gowne, when it is worne,
> Put up youre purs, ye shall non pay.   [9–11]

9. Dyce, *1,* 20.

This neat turnabout only further infuriates her paramour,
who replies with the traditional warning:

> By crede, I trust to se the day,
> As proud a pohen as ye sprede,
> Of me and other ye may have nede.   [12–14]

What she spreads is, he implies, her tail (pudendum), and
again she appropriates his vocabulary for her own reply:

> Though angelyk be youre smylyng,
> Yet is youre tong an adders tayle,
> Full lyke a scorpyon styngyng
> All those by whom ye have avayle.   [15–18]

This last line can be read in two ways. If the scorpion's sting
is merely metaphorical for a vitriolic tongue and "avayle"
is taken to mean advantage, the import of the passage is
something like this: "You direct your accusations at every-
one within range, especially at those who have at some time
helped you." If, on the other hand, the sting in question is
phallic, and "All those by whom ye have avayle" means all
those whom you have at an advantage, the charge is more
specific and personal. Whichever reading he accepts, the
man decides that this has gone far enough: "Good mastres
Anne, there ye do shayle: / What prate ye, praty pyggysny?
/ I truste to quyte you or I dy" (19–21). The ironically
familiar and affectionate "pyggysny" is an attempt to rewin
the advantage, and the double pun on "quyte" (abandon
or requite or do one's part) and "dy" is simultaneously a
threat and an invitation. In the fourth stanza the resources
of the language and the ambiguity of sexual imagery join
in a tour de force, a duet in which the two voices sing the
same words, but produce contrasting statements:

> Youre key is mete for every lok,
> Youre key is commen and hangyth owte;

Youre key is redy, we nede not knok,
Nor stand long wrestyng there aboute;
Of youre doregate ye have no doute.   [22–26]

This can be read as her characterization of him as a male
whore. The "key" that is hanging out and common, the key
that is "mete" (meat) is the phallus, and the lock(s) the
pudendum; but from his point of view the key that is common and hangs out is the sign of her availability, and the
doorgate again the pudendum. Line 27 ("But one thyng is,
that ye be lewde") is common property and the 28th ("Holde
youre tong now, all beshrewde!") seems to be an editorial
comment on the entire performance. (Skelton will do the
same thing in *Eleanor Rumming,* breaking off that interminable poem in disgust, "God gyve it yll hayle! / ... I have
wrytten to mytche / Of this mad mummynge / Of Elynour
Rummynge.") The final lines stand apart from the lyric
proper:

To mastres Anne, that farly swete,
That wonnes at the Key in Temmys strete.

[29–30]

The tone is softer and the note of polite salutation indicates
that the voice who offers them offers the entire poem. His
is the third voice, and the sign of the key in all its meanings
is the sign of the poem as well as Mistress Anne's business
card. If there was music for this love song, the melody of
the envoy-like couplet was no doubt lilting and romantic.

"Manerly Margery Mylk and Ale" is Skelton's version of
the clerk-and-the-serving-maid-ballad.[1] Although William
Cornish's music survives, there is some controversy as to
how accurately it allows us to assign individual lines to the
two and possibly three voices. J. M. Berdan is confident that
the music helps "us to a more correct distribution of the

1. Ibid., p. 28.

parts in the dialogue,"[2] but unfortunately he does not document his confidence. John Stevens, who identifies the piece as a "refrain song, through set . . . with musical as well as literary refrain" decides that the "text is unusually difficult to interpret with any certainty."[3] The music is written for three voices, a soprano (female), tenor (male), and bass (supporting voice) which we may tentatively identify with Margery, her clerk, and the narrator. In any one line two voices are singing, the third silent; all join in the refrains with the exception of the last, which presents a special problem. I agree with Stevens that a completely satisfactory distribution of lines is impossible; but if the voice which seems to carry the melody of a line is given responsibility for it, a text can be proposed that does not contradict the philological evidence and is thoroughly Skeltonic (the clerk's lines are within quotation marks):

> Ay, besherewe yow! Be my fay
> This wanton clarkis be nyse allway,
> Avent, avent, my popagay!
> "What, will ye do nothing but play?"
> Tully, valy, strawe, let be I say!
> Gup, Cristian Clowte, gup, Jak of the Vale,
> With manerly Margery, milk and ale.

> "Be Gad, ye be a prety pode,
> And I love you an hole cart-lode."
> Strawe, Jamys foder, ye play the fode;
> I am no hakney for your rode;
> Go watch a bole, your bak is brode.
> Gup, Cristian Clowte, gup, Jak of the Vale,
> With manerly [Margery, milk and ale].

2. *Early Tudor Poetry* (New York, 1920), p. 165.
3. *Music and Poetry in the Early Tudor Court* (London, 1961), p. 379.

I-wiss, ye dele uncurtesly;
What, wolde ye frompill me now? fy, fy!
"What, and ye shal be my piggesnye?"
Be Crist, ye shal not! No, no, hardely!
I will not be japed bodely.
Gup, Cristian Clowte, gup, Jak of the Vale,
With manerly Margery, [milke and ale].

"Walke forthe your way, ye cost me nought;
Now have I fownd that I have sought,
The best chepe flessh that evyr I bought."
Yet for his love that all hath wrought
Wed me or els I dye for thought!
Gup, Cristian Clowte, your breth is stale,
With manerly Margery, milke and ale;
Gup, Cristian Clowte, gup, Jak of the Vale,
With manerly Margery, [milke and ale].[4]

Here the love situation is complicated by the introduction
of class distinctions. The clerk is "nyse" in both senses of
the word. He is courteous and perhaps even courtly in a
"courting" situation, but his niceness is also the reserve (or
fastidiousness) of a social superior, and as *mannerly* Margery
the serving girl is quite conscious of the condescension involved in his dalliance; he is not only foppish ("popagay")
and lecherous (wanton) but in terms of any postseduction
relationship, irresponsible (wanton). Of course her protests
("let be I say") are made "under the forme," and his question "What will ye do nothing but play," is a circumlocution
for "when are we to get down to business?" The result of
the negotiation is never really in doubt.

4. This is Stevens' text. In an appendix to his study of music and
poetry in the early Tudor period, he reprints the poems from British
Museum Additional MS 5465, known as The Fayrfax MS. "Manerly
Margery" is number 41 in the manuscript.

In the second stanza the social antagonism is translated into a stylistic clash. The opening couplet is possibly split between Margery and the clerk, respectively. The second line, which draws the I'm-sure-you-say-that-to-all-the-other-girls response ("Strawe Jamys foder, ye play the fode") is certainly his and illustrates the distinctions Skelton can convey through small stylistic variations. "And I love you an hole cart-lode" is a filler, a line that is obviously contrived. Whether he writes in Skeltonics or the more traditional meters, there is a crispness and rapidity about Skelton's verse that is quite distinctive and not at all like the awkward doggerel which results from a monosyllabic line with an open vowel pattern ("you an hole") and the forced rhyming of "cart-lode" and "fode." When Skelton does this kind of thing (he uses it to great advantage in *Philip Sparrow*), the contrivance is to be attributed to the voice in the poem rather than to the poet. In this line the "nyse" clerk attempts to minimize the liability (from the point of view of his immediate objective) involved in his station by adopting Margery's idiom. He fails, both for the reader and for Margery, who replies almost as if she were saying to him, "If you would frame your conversation in barnyard dialogue allow me to show you how it is done." "I'll not be the mare to your rod," she exclaims, "go watch a bull." The refrain "Gup, Cristian Clowte, gup, Jak of the Vale, / With manerly Margery, milk and ale" seems to mock his effort to step down to the level of her other beaus.

This fencing through style continues in the third stanza with the semi-formality of "I-wiss, ye dele uncurtesly." Although this line could be assigned to either "lover," I read it as Margery's counterattempt to ape the clerk's diction. We are to imagine, I think, physical advances and retreats between the lines and stanzas, and when her courtly "I-fear-you-are-not-acting-toward-me-as-you-should" elicits only a physical response, Margery returns instinctively to her more direct manner. "What wolde ye frompill me now?" In the same way his now defensive declaration of affection ("ye shal be my piggesnye") is emphatically rejected: "I will not be japed bodely."

In the last stanza the hard lines of the "contest" become blurred in a way we shall recognize as typically Skelton. Margery does indeed protest too much and predictably she is "japed bodely" in the interval between the third and fourth stanzas. Unexpectedly, the triumphant clerk does not leave her with hypocritical promises of undying devotion; instead he taunts his victim immediately, admitting to her face that she is nothing to him but "chepe flessh." Margery's reply is the traditional one of the betrayed maiden, "Marry me or I am ruined," but the pathos hardly rings true when one recalls her unmaidenlike vocabulary and her questionable innocence. What Skelton consistently denies us in these poems is a sympathetic figure; this couplet is, in context, her answering taunt, and could be paraphrased "as if I cared." The issue here is not virtue or virginity, but supremacy in a battle of wits where sex is a weapon. The extra lines in the fourth refrain are an extension of Margery's counterattack. The clerk is simultaneously associated with the country louts she prefers and mocked for a physical inadequacy ("your breth is stale"). It is possible to hear the voice of the observer, who always steps in at this point in a Skelton lyric, in this penultimate thrust. If the clerk is going to adopt the physical standard implied in cheap flesh, he leaves himself open to the observation that physically *he* is no bargain. The reader is literally left with a bad taste in his mouth as he listens to the pleasant but mockingly incongruous melody of the refrain.

The cast of characters is larger and the cynicism more intensive in "The auncient acquaintance, madam," a seemingly inoffensive courtly compliment:

The auncient, acquaintance madam, betwen us twayn,
The famylyarte, the formar dalyaunce,
Causyth me that I can no myself refrayne
But that I must wryte for my plesaunt pastaunce:
Remembryng your passyng goodly countenaunce,
Your goodly port, your bewteous visage,
Ye may be countyd comfort of all corage.[5]

We learn from this first stanza that the speaker and the
lady he addresses are old friends. The nature of their relationship is not clear, though the "famylyarte" and "dalyaunce" of line 2 suggest the possibility of sexual intimacy.
At this point, however, this is only a possibility, and one
which would seem to fade before the conventionality of "all
your feturs favorable to make tru discripcion, / I am in-
suffycent to make such enterpryse" (8–9). When the shift
comes, it is almost unnoticed. Almost apologetically he intimates that her good name is being slandered:

Yet so it is that a rumer begynnyth for to ryse,
How in good horsmen ye set your hole delyght,
And have forgoten your old trew lovyng knyght.
[12–14]

On a second reading the sexual innuendo of "ryse" is unmistakable, and the lewdness of "hole delyght" unpleasant.

5. Dyce, *1, 23*. This lyric has affinities with Robbins, *Secular Lyrics,*
number 208, "A Mocking Letter to Her Lover." That piece begins as
does Skelton's, with a typical address: "Unto you, most froward, this
lettre I write, / Whych hath causyd me so longe in dyspayre; / The
Goodlynesse of your persone is esye to endyte, / for he levyth nat that
can youre persone appayre." But the descriptio which follows reveals
the true sentiments of the letter-writer: "Youre manly visage, shortly
to declare, / your forehed, mouth, and nose so flatte, / In short conclusyon, best lykened to an hare / Of alle lyvyng thynges, save only a
catte" (p. 219). The irony of the performance depends on maintaining
the *form* of the compliment while inserting the *substance* of an insult.
Skelton's departure from the model is more pronounced, and his irony
more vicious.

What any reader will notice is the gradual abandonment of aureate diction and the colloquial lilt of "your old trew lovyng knyght." Suddenly the speaker seizes on the word "horsmen" and bursts into a galloping meter. At the same time the lady, who was above praise a few lines ago, becomes a mare, "ridden" (in the act of sexual intercourse) by the "horsmen" she is said to favor:

> Wyth bound and rebound, bounsyngly take up
> Hys jentyll curtoyl, and set nowght by small naggys!
> Spur up at the hynder gyrth, with, Gup, morell, gup!
> With, Jayst ye, jenet of Spayne, for your tayll waggys!
> Ye cast all your corage uppon such courtly haggys.
> Have in sergeaunt ferrour myne horse behynde is bare;
> He rydeth well the horse, but he rydeth better the mare.
>
> [15–21]

The image is continued with a precision that is pornographic: "She kykyth with her kalkyns and keylyth with a clench; / She goyth wyde behynde, and hewyth never a dele. / It is perlous for a horseman to dyg in the trenche" (23–24, 26). The perils of digging in the trench are many—a reference to the "clappys they cach" suggests venereal disease—but the speaker emphasizes the familiar and probably autobiographical danger which allows him to return to the aureate: "Thys grevyth your husband, that ryght jentyll knyght, / And so with your servauntys he fersly doth fyght" (27–28). The phrase "ryght jentyll knyght" (echoing perhaps Chaucer's "parfit gentil knyght") and the word "servauntys" recall the world of the first two stanzas. Now, of course, the politesse of "servauntys" rings false, and the entire first section of the poem becomes ironic in retrospect. When the speaker falls again into the formal style, there is a subtle change. The syntactical framework remains (the inversions, the full phrases), but the now pseudo-respectability of the

form is undercut by the prominence of noneuphemistic non-
aureate words like "clene," "game," and "shame":

> For your jentyll husband sorowfull am I,
> How be it, he is not furst hath had a los:
> Advertysyng you madame, to warke more secretly,
> Let not all the world make an owtcry;
> Play fayre play, madame, and loke ye play clene,
> Or ells with gret shame your game wylbe sene.
>
> [37-42]

There are four actors in this little drama, and no one of them
engages: the lady, seemingly above reproach, is shown to
be no better than she should be; the "good horsman" for
whom she deceives her husband is nothing but a farrier
("ferrour") or common blacksmith; the husband, at first a
gentle knight, is in the end the traditional cuckold. The
speaker is more complicated; pretending to be a courteous
(in the sense of courtly) admirer of the lady, he is, we discover, her former lover, now so disillusioned that he can
ironically feign a regard for her honor and express concern
for a man he has cuckolded. The sophisticated irony of the
poem is less amusing than disturbing when we realize that
it is only a cover for his bitterness.

In "Lullay, Lullay" Skelton combines courtly diction, a
less than courtly situation, and the echo of a religious lyric
form—the dialogue between the Blessed Virgin and child
—to present a particularly intense statement of his characteristic cynicism:

> With, Lullay, lullay, lyke a chylde,
> Thou slepyst to long, thou art begylde.
> My darlyng dere, my daysy floure,
> Let me, quod he, ly in your lap.
> Ly styll, quod she, my paramoure,
> Ly styll hardely, and take a nap.

Hys hed was hevy, such was his hap,
All drowsy dremyng, dround in slepe,
That of hys love he toke no kepe,
    With, Hey, lullay, &c.
With ba, ba, ba, and bas, bas, bas,
She cheryshed hym both cheke and chyn,
That he wyst never where he was;
He had forgoten all dedely syn.
He wantyd wyt her love to wyn:
He trusted her payment, and lost all hys pay:
She left hym slepyng, and stale away,
    Wyth, Hey, lullay, &c.
The ryvers rowth, the waters wan;
She sparyd not to wete her fete;
She wadyd over, she found a man
That halsyd her hartely and kyst her swete:
Thus after her cold she cought a hete.
My lefe, she sayd, rowtyth in hys bed;
I wys he hath an hevy hed,
    Wyth, Hey, lullay, &c.
What dremyst thou, drunchard, drousy pate!
Thy lust and lykyng is from the gone;
Thou blynkerd blowboll, thou wakyst to late,
Behold, thou lyeste, luggard, alone!
Well may thou sygh, well may thou grone,
To dele wyth her so cowardly:
I wys, powle hachet, she bleryd thyne I.[6]

In the religious analogues[7] the Virgin rocks the Christ child
in her lap, lamenting as she does the pain and trial which
must terminate his ministry; it is the child himself who must

6. Dyce, *1*, 22–23.
7. Carleton Brown, *Religious Lyrics of the XVth Century* (Oxford,
1938), numbers 1–5. The two following quotations are from numbers
3 and 4.

comfort her in a nice reversal of the more usual mother-
infant relationship:

> bot well I wat as well I may—slepe & be now styll—
> Suffre the paynes that I may; it is my fader wyll.

And in this context the refrain with its suggestion of baby
talk is a gently ironic contrast to the young saviour's wisdom:

> He sayd Ba-Bay;
> sco sayd lullay,
> the virgine fresch as ros in may.

In Skelton's refrain, the innocence and simplicity of the
lullaby, whether it be religious or secular, is complicated at
once by the second line:

> With, Lullay, lullay, lyke a chylde,
> Thou slepyst to long, thou art *begylde* [emphasis mine].

Thus warned, the reader is prepared to find ambiguity in
what follows, and he is not disappointed. In the first stanza
of the narrative proper, the unwary lover's *adnominatio*—
"my daysy floure"—with its aura of purity is deliberately
opposed to the obvious sexuality of "Hys hed [phallus] was
hevy" and "ly in your lap"; and in the second stanza, the "ba,
ba, ba," of the lullaby becomes the "bas, bas, bas" (kiss) of
an assignation, as the "daysy floure" prepares to abandon
a "paramoure" who has failed her physically. There is no
consolation in this relationship. Indeed, the echo of the religious analogue mocks him as she leaves:

> He had forgoten all dedely syn.
> He wanted wyt her love to wyn.   [11–12]

These lines present the paradox which anticipates the poem's
final statement; by falling asleep, the man, if only passively,
defeats the temptation of "dedely syn" (fornication); but
in saving his soul, he loses the world, for his lover deserts

him. The poem becomes a bitter variation on the biblical "For what does it profit a man if he gain the whole world, but suffer the loss of his own soul?"

As in Skelton's other lyrics, the problem for the reader is one of focus, specifically moral focus. Neither lover deserves our sympathy; the choice between a lecher and a whore is a small one. Still, the ballader, the voice of the third person, is making some kind of judgment in his refrain; although at this point it is difficult to interpret its tone. Is the dreamer to be pitied or at least patronized as the more put upon of two scoundrels? This would seem to be the case when our attention is directed, in the third stanza, to the woman whose actions are described in terms frankly animal. At this point the poem is a beast fable in reverse, with human actions figuring forth a subhuman morality. In her haste to find a partner she ignores the discomfort of the stream. "She sparyd not to wete her fete." The iciness of the water is more than balanced, the ballader insists, by the heat of physical contact and of her own body; "She found a man / That halsyd her hartely / . . . Thus after her cold, she cought a hete." The heartiness of their embrace is a verbal echo of "hardely" (l.4) contrasting one man's lethargy with another's force. She herself sets the seal on her metamorphosis by describing her former paramour's inactivity in terms usually associated with a bull: "My lefe she sayd, *rowtyth* in hys bed; / I wys he hath an hevy hed, / Wyth, Hey, lullay" (20–21). The pun on "hed" is obvious and in character.

The final stanza is the narrator's, and in place of irony or ambiguity he offers an authorial *moralitas* which reveals his attitude all too clearly. The possibility of sympathy for the dreamer fades before the fact of his drunkenness; his betrayal is, if we can make judgments in a poem like this, deserved. And, if he "wakyst to late," he wakes to the world as the first-person voice sees it; indeed his failure is a failure

to be immoral (to "dele" with her). The last line is a
viciously exultant welcome to the ranks of the disillusioned:
"Iwys, powle hachet, she bleryd thyne I [eye]."

It is necessary for any authoritative assessment of Skelton's
career to account for the incredible intensity of these poems.
They cannot, however, be dated with complete accuracy,
although the available evidence indicates a period between
1485 and 1504, when Skelton is at the court of Henry VII.
Laureated by that monarch in 1488, he had written for the
Crown, socialized with minor officials and, with his friend
and collaborator William Cornish, prepared royal enter-
tainments. In 1497 Lady Margaret selected him to tutor her
grandson Henry, then Duke of York and destined (so it was
thought) for the Archbishopric. Probably at her insistence
the new tutor entered the church, rising in 1498 from sub-
deacon to deacon to priest.[8] Except for official documents and
occasional anecdotes, we do not see Skelton in these years, but
I think we do see his reaction to London and civilization in
these lyrics. Whatever his thoughts are as a hanger-on, the
conjunction in 1498 of a semi-official position and member-
ship (however nominal) in the spiritual brotherhood seems
to sharpen his sensibilities. The result is the *Bouge of Court*,[9]
the consolidation in the closing hours of the fifteenth century of Skelton's hitherto isolated intuitions into the nature
of the world around him.

8. For the most recent and satisfactory discussion of these early and
sparsely documented years, see Maurice Pollet's *John Skelton* (Paris,
1962), pp. 19–62. M. Pollet remarks of the poems of this period, "Ils
révèlent une veine caustique et joviale, aimant à s'exercer aux dépens
de quelque travers humain. . . . Ils trahissent a cet egard un malaise
qui n'a pu que s'aggraver avec l'entrée du poete dans les ordres" (p. 52).
The joviality in these poems, however, escapes me, and while M. Pollet
identifies this "malaise" only with the Court, it is my argument that
precisely because of Skelton's entrance into orders, his doubts and dis-
satisfactions are more general.

9. Dyce, *1*, 30–50.

THE *BOUGE OF COURT*

Skelton's major poems are usually read as satires; but if, as I believe, their locus is essentially interior, that classification must be either abandoned or qualified. In the kind of satire which has in large measure given us our critical vocabulary, the major emphasis is on a collision between the actions of society and a well-defined system of values, and the speaker is less an individual than a personification or symbol of that system. He remains in the background, evaluating experience by the values which simultaneously sustain and create him, and the singleminded fervor he brings to his task necessarily renders him psychologically uninteresting: "The satirist . . . sees the world as a battlefield between a definite, clearly understood good, which he represents, and an equally clear-cut evil. No ambiguities, no doubts about himself, no sense of mystery trouble him, and he retains always his . . . certainty."[1] In Skelton's poems, however, the speaker, more often than not, is certain of nothing. The battlefield exists in his mind, where the conflict is not so much between good and evil as between a succession of half-goods or greater and lesser evils. He moves not from criticism to affirmation but from criti-

---

1. Alvin Kernan, *The Cankered Muse* (New Haven, 1959), pp. 21–22. Although I do not wish to elaborate the thesis here, the *Bouge of Court* is one of a number of poems in the English literary tradition which bear the characteristics of satire and a tone approaching tragedy. For want of a better term, we may designate these poems "open satires," and I include in this classification Chaucer's *House of Fame*, Sterne's *Tristram Shandy,* and Byron's *Don Juan.* In each case the first person voice would like to adopt the authoritative stance of the closed or traditional satirist, but finds he cannot. My awareness of this "genre" grows out of separate studies of Byron, Chaucer, and Skelton made in the last five years. I have since discovered that other critics have discussed as characteristically associated the attitude and techniques I find in these poems. See especially Irving Babbitt's *Rousseau and Romanticism* (Meridian Edition, 1955), pp. 189–209, Northrop Frye's *Anatomy of Criticism* (Princeton, 1957), pp. 223–39, and Robert Adams' *Strains of Discord: Studies in Literary Openness* (Ithaca, 1958), pp. 11 ff.

cism to criticism and at times toward despair. What we miss in a Skelton "satire" is the moment of resolution, when the speaker rests triumphantly in the security of his own clearly understood principles; instead we are offered a conclusion that is less a resolution than a convenient way out of the poem, and the sense of uneasiness which characteristically initiates the poem's "action" is never really dispelled.

In the earliest of these poems, the *Bouge of Court,* this sense of uneasiness is established in a manner that becomes increasingly familiar to a student of the Skelton canon: the audience is lulled by the early introduction of familiar topoi into accepting his poem as one more in a well-defined tradition, only to find its expectations disappointed and the comfort of the reading experience destroyed along with its familiarity. In this case the tradition reaches back to Boethius' *Consolation,* the *Psychomachia,* and the *Romance of the Rose;* and it includes in the fifteenth century a series of poems that share a common problem—the nature of true authority; a common mode—allegory; and, most important, a common pattern of action—the gradual rejection by a first-person narrator of false authorities and the recognition of the true. For Skelton, and for other poets in this tradition (the authors of the *Kingis Quair,* the *Court of Love,* and the *Court of Sapience*) the model is Chaucer's *House of Fame.* Here the befuddled dreamer moves through the realms of two false authorities, Venus and Fame (who together suggest a third and larger figure, Fortune) toward that moment in the third book when he can assert his independence of them:

> I wot myself best how y stonde;
> For what I drye, or what I thynke,
> I wil myselven al hyt drynke,
> Certeyn, for the more part,
> As fer forth as I kan myn art.   [1878–82]

What this is, essentially, is an acceptance of responsibility for one's actions in a world which seems to assign that responsibility to an arbitrary power. It is, in the context of the poem, a rejection of Venus, Fame, and Fortune, who preach a common doctrine: "I control you; you are helpless before me; I determine and/or judge your actions." The dreamer opts for a higher deity (unnamed in this poem), whose servants these lesser goddesses are, in a plan too large for human comprehension. In this plan, however, man's actions and intentions are his own, and he must answer for them. In short, the dreamer rejects as ultimately unreal the apparent arbitrariness of things of which Fortune is but the man-made name. To deify her is to deify the limited perspective that creates her, to deify oneself. The truth about you, says Mars to Fortune, in a late version of this kind of poem, is that

> poetes hath made a fygure
> Of the for the grete sygnyfycacyon
> The chaunge of man so for to dyscure
> Accordynge to a moralyzacyon.[2]

Juvenal is blunter: "If men had any sense, Fortune would not be a goddess / We are the one who make her so, and give her a place in the heavens."[3]

The excerpt from Hawes illustrates an important development: the poems that follow the *House of Fame* adopt its machinery and make its point with an explicitness that tends toward the mechanical. Chaucer does not offer a didactic indictment of Venus or Fame or Fortune; his poem has the impact of immediate communication because both reader and protagonist discover only gradually that the goddesses who rule its allegorical world are unreliable. In the fifteenth

2. Hawes, *Pastime of Pleasure*, lines 3207–10.
3. *The Satires of Juvenal*, trans. Rolfe Humphries (Bloomington, 1958), p. 134.

century this pattern becomes conventional as the form so hardens that the standard solution to the problem it was created to solve—the nature of authority—is built into it. The same poem is written again and again and its plot is predictable: the speaker muses on the dilemma posed by Fortune, falls asleep, and is guided in a dream to an awareness of Fortune's ultimate unreality. The moral of the poem is always the *House of Fame's* moral, "faith not void of deeds," or as Paul Ruggiers puts it, "Boethius' own lesson well learned";[4] but neither reader nor protagonist participates in its discovery; instead the true authority, often Minerva, appears to "rede" the lesson didactically. In the *Kingis Quair,* the dreamer makes the usual petition to Venus only to be told by that deity that her power to dispose is not as great as it has been said to be:

> This is to say, though it to me pertene,
> In lufis lawe the septre to governe,
> That the effectis of my bemes schene
> Has thaire aspectis by ordynance eterne,
> With otheris bynd and mynes to discerne,
> Quhilum in thingis bothe to cum and gone,
> That langis noght to me to writh allone.
>
> [stanza 107]

The petitioner is sent for more authoritative guidance to Minerva, who proclaims the pointedly Christian moral:

> Tak him before in all thy governance,
> That in his hand the stere has of you all,
> And pray unto his hye purveyance,
> Thy lufe to gye, and on him traist and call,
> That corner-stone and ground is of the wall,

4. "The Unity of Chaucer's *House of Fame,*" *Chaucer Criticism, Volume II,* ed. R. J. Schoeck and J. Taylor (Notre Dame, 1961), 2, 269.

> That failis noght, and trust, withoutin *drede,*
> Unto thy purpos sone he sall the lede.
>
> [stanza 130]

In the *Pastime of Pleasure,* La Graunde Amoure listens attentively as Mars and Fortune debate their respective claims to responsibility for man's actions; but before he can acknowledge the sway of either deity he is led away by a third:

> To here of Mars the mervaylous argument
> And of fortune I was sore amased
> Tyll that I sawe a lady excellent . . .   [3221–23]
>
> To me she came with lowely countenaunce
> And bad me welcome unto that mancyon
> Ledynge me forthe.   [3228–30]

It is three stanzas before the "lady excellent" is identified for us as Minerva; clearly Hawes thinks the name unnecessary, for he can assume that his readers will anticipate her appearance.[5]

5. In no poem is the pattern more stylized or abbreviated than in the *Court of Sapience* (ed. Robert Spindler, Leipzig, 1927), where the entire action of the *House of Fame* is presented in the hundred lines that follow the invocation. The inevitable meditation on worldly arbitrariness evokes a rebuke from reason: "Wyth moble Fortune and false Worldlynesse, / O foole of folles, hast thow thy wyt assayed" (114–15). This leads the protagonist to pray for guidance, and his prayer is answered by sleep: "Thus brought on slepe my spyryte forth gan passe, / And brought I was me thought in place desert, / In wildernes, but I ne wyst, where I was" (127–29). In the *House of Fame,* it is the dreamer's sudden emergence into a similar desert that breaks the artificiality of the dream vision and wrings from him another prayer: " 'O Crist!' thoughte I, 'that art in blysse, / Fro fantome and illusion / Me save!' " (492–94). And the reactions of the respective wanderers to their surroundings are identical: "But now wol I goo out and see, / Ryght at the wiket, yf y kan / See owhere any stiryng man, / That may me telle where I am" (476–79); "I ne wyst, where I was: / In moche derknesse, in caves, in covert, / Wyth wylde bestes in devouryng

By 1498, then, when Skelton comes to write the *Bouge of Court,* the response of his audience to a series of well-defined stimuli is assured. And as the reaction of the reader to this kind of poem becomes self-conscious in a ritualistic way, the poet becomes equally self-conscious in his manner of presentation. In the *House of Fame* Chaucer emphasizes the naïveté of his dreamer, so that we accept his experience as real—that is, as a literary representation of a genuine (but not autobiographical) mental drama. In the fifteenth century the same kind of poem is a literary representation of a literary experience. The sense of disorientation that characterizes the *House of Fame* is controlled, and the poet takes care to distinguish between himself as poet and as temporarily confused hero; he assures us that the former is his true guise, the latter a fiction entertained for the duration of an exercise; it is the performance of a conscious, indeed self-conscious, artist rather than the confrontation of cosmic and personal instability which demands our attention. In short, the fifteenth-century dream vision is a static form in which the reader listens to the comfortably predictable pronouncements of an authority figure. This is a literary situation which finds its parallel in the patterns of traditional satire. There a first-person voice hurls the familiar charges of worldly folly at an audience so inured to them that the presentation is accepted as entertainment rather than criti-

---

expert, / Now woode, now watyr, now hyll, now valey, / Now wynde, now reygne; iwis I knewe no wey" (129–33). In Chaucer's poem 1500 lines pass before the significance of the desert is apparent and the dreamer's prayer answered; in the *Court of Sapience,* Sapience appears at once both to interpret and to assure: " 'Thys desert place of feere, thurgh whyche thow come, / Ys dredefull worldly occupacioun; / Sone! Leve that place' " (162–64); and the immediacy of the hero's reply indicates how far we have moved from the dynamism of the *House of Fame:* "Glad was I tho and on kne fyll a downe, / Helde up myn handes and seyde I wolde fayne / Her servaunt be wyth all subiecciowne" (169–71).

cism; even the satirist is fond of an enemy (evil) which provides him automatically with an occasion and a public. In both genres, then, the reading and writing experiences are insulated ones, and it is this insulation from the imperative of an immediate challenge that Skelton destroys in a particularly effective amalgam of the two forms.

The astrological time signature of the *Bouge of Court* operates, as it does in Chaucer's dream visions, to fix tone as well as season:

> In autumpne, whan the sonne *in Virgine*
> By radyante hete enryped hath our corne;
> Whan Luna, full of mutabylyte,
> As emperes the dyademe hath worne
> Of our pole artyke, smylynge halfe in scorne
> At our foly and our unstedfastnesse;
> The tyme whan Mars to werre hym dyde dres.   [1–7]

It is autumn rather than the more conventional spring; the moon whose baleful influence is traditionally associated with mental instability is joined by the equally ominous red planet in a conjunction that is decidedly threatening. "Smylynge halfe in scorne," the heavens look down at and perhaps cause the "foly" and "unstedfastnesse" which move the speaker to attempt a verbal response:

> I, callynge to mynde the greate auctoryte
> Of poetes olde, whyche full craftely,
> Under as coverte termes as coude be,
> Can touche a trouth and cloke it subtylly
> Wyth fresshe utteraunce full sentencyously;
> Dyverse in style, some spared not vyce to wryte,
> Some of moralyte nobly dyde endyte   [8–14]

> I was sore moved to aforce the same.   [17]

These opening stanzas establish at once the connection between the common problem of a world without stability and the more specific problem of the place for poets in such a world. The speaker in this poem reacts to his astrology by attempting to write satire in the fifteenth-century manner, in covert terms, but discovers that he cannot:

> But Ignoraunce full soone dyde me dyscure,
> And shewed that in this arte I was not *sure;*
> For to illumyne, she sayde, I was to dulle,
> Avysynge me my penne awaye to pulle,
> And not to wryte; for he so wyll attayne
> Excedynge ferther than his connynge is,
> His hede maye be harde, but feble is his brayne,
> Yet have I knowen suche er this;
> But of reproche surely he maye not mys,
> That clymmeth hyer than he may fotynge have;
> What and he slyde downe, *who shall hym save?*
>
> [18–28, emphasis mine]

His fears are at once physical and verbal, symptomatic of a lack of confidence so enervating that it paralyzes. The "not sure" of line 19 qualifies "arte" and is an admission that the pose of the traditional satirist, who is always sure, is one he cannot strike; a more physical danger is suggested by the "climbing" image of 27 and 28, which is in turn tied syntactically to an allusion to the Bellerophon-Pegasus fable ("Excedynge ferther than his connynge is"), traditionally allegorized to point the folly of poetic overextension. The poem's frames of reference spill over into one another. By line 28 the climactic question, "who shall hym save," is asked in a context that will not be limited; an uncertainty that begins with the horror of court intrigue, and is reflected in an inability to satirize that horror, is finally all-encompassing. The words and phrases that give this prologue its

Boethian tone ("sure," "unstedfastnesse," "mutabylyte") will echo throughout until they become as much the subject of the poem as the sinister courtiers who usurp its foreground. Predictably, the inconclusiveness of his meditations proves too much for our hero who falls asleep:[6]

> Thus up and down my mynde was drawen and cast,
> That I *ne wyste what to do was beste;*
> So sore enwered, that I was at the laste
> Enforsed to slepe and for to take some reste.
>
> [29–32, emphasis mine]

In a similar scene, the first-person voice of the *Court of Sapience* admits to parallel difficulties:

> All besy swymming in the stormy flood
> Of frutles worldly meditacioun   [71–72]
>
> And thus to bed I went wyth thought my gest   [77]
>
> So yche astate and worldly governaunce
> In oone eschequer in my mynde I sawe,
> But *I ne wyst what draught was best* to drawe.
>
> [82–84, emphasis mine]

In the earlier poem the dreamer's uneasiness is dispelled immediately by the fortuitous appearance of Sapience, who tells him quite explicitly "what to do was beste"; the dream provides, as we assume it will, an answer to his waking questions. Skelton's dreamer is less successful. He finds him-

---

6. In most dream visions the dreamer falls asleep on a May morning and usually in a meadow. Some have seen in Skelton's localization of the dream at Harwich Port the beginning of a new literary era; but Chaucer also toys with the more conventional forms in the *Book of the Duchess* and the *House of Fame*. See W. O. Sypherd, *Studies in Chaucer's House of Fame*, Chaucer Society, 2nd ser. 39 (London, 1907), pp. 4–5, for a convenient summary of "standard" dream visions and their motifs.

self on a dock where "a shyppe, goodly of sayle, / Come saylynge forth into that haven brood / . . . She kyste an anker, and there she laye at rode. / Marchauntes her borded to see what she had lode" (36–37, 39–40). Moving forward with the crowd, he discovers the ship's name, "the shyp that ye here see, / The Bowge of Courte it hyghte for certeynte" (48–49), and its cargo, "This royall chaffre that is shypped here / Is called Favore" (54–55). Vaguely uncomfortable, he scans the crowd and can "none aquentaunce fynde," but drawn by its brilliance he boards the ship where he comes upon this inscription:

> Garder le fortune, que est mavelz et gode!   [67]
> (Look out for fortune who is both good and evil.)

In the context of the dream vision tradition, this is an unmistakable warning, one which the reader would expect the dreamer to heed; but he does not, and it is at this moment that Skelton formally names his hero, providing us, in a single word, with a genealogy and a psychological history:

> And, as I stode redynge this verse allone,
> Her cheyf gentylwoman, Daunger by her name . . .
> [69–70]

> asked she me, Syr, so God the spede,
> What is thy name? and I sayde, it was Drede.   [76–77]

The revelation is significant; it identifies our protagonist with an abstraction from the world of love allegory and with a word which has a particular significance for fifteenth-century poetry. In the *Romance of the Rose,* Drede, one of the warders who protect the rose, is described as "abasshed, and in gret fere / . . . Of every thing that she may see / Drede is aferd, wherso she be" (3959, 4225–26). In the *Temple of Glass* Lydgate partially anticipates Skelton's use of the name by playing on its possible theological meaning, wanhope or despair:[7]

> Thus ofte tyme with hope I am I mevid
> To tel hir al of that I am so greved,
> And to ben hardi on me forto take
> To axe merci; but drede than doth awake,
> And thurgh wanhope answerith me again,
> That bettir were, then she have disdeyne,
> To deie at onys, unknow of eny wight.
> And there-withal bitt hope anon ryght
> Me to be bold, to prayen hir of grace;
> For sith al vertues be portreid in hir face,
> It were not sitting that merci were bihind.
> And right anone within my self I finde
> A nwe ple brought on me with drede,
> That me so maseth that I se no spede,
> Bicause he seith, that stoneith al my bloode,
> I am so symple & she is so goode.
> Thus hope and drede in me wil not ceasse
> To plete and stryve myn harmes to encrese;
> But at the hardest yit, or I be dede,
> Of my distresse sith i can no rede,
> But stonde doumb stil as eni stone,
> Tofore the goddes I wil me hast anone,
> And complein withoute more sermon;
> Though deth be fin & ful conclusioun
> Of my request, yit I will assai.   [669–93]

Here the lover's fear and indecisiveness are given a color distinctly religious. He stands before one goddess (Venus), doubting the mercy and grace of another (his lady); he runs through the familiar arguments that lead to despair: why should she (or God) be interested in me? I am unworthy.

7. Ed. J. Schick, Early English Text Society, extra ser. 60 (London, 1891), 28–29.

"I am so symple & she is so goode." For a moment the lover is close to paralysis ("stil as eni stone"), but in an act of faith he steps forward to petition. Of course Lydgate is neither platonizing love nor parodying a religious experience; for him the parallel between his hero and the faith-seeking Christian is merely a literary convenience, a witty and elegant way of framing a lover's plaint. In this poem and in the *Romance*, "drede" is that psychological state which prevents the lover from gaining a salvation that is sexual, and his liberation from that state is a necessary (and in the love allegory inevitable) prelude to success. In this context it is disturbing to note that while "drede" plagues the conventional allegorical hero for a time, it is the name—forever —of Skelton's hero; like his predecessor in the *Romance of the Rose,* he fears *everything.* Again the *Court of Sapience* proclaims the moral that will be unavailable in the *Bouge of Court:*

> Who dredeth God, com yn and ryght well come;
> For drede of *God* ys wey of all wysdome.
>
> [944–45, emphasis mine]

As the reader begins to fear for him, Dread ignores even the most explicit of warnings. When "an other gentylwoman / Desyre her name" advises him to "be bolde . . . to speke, for [despite] ony *drede:* / Who spareth to speke, in fayth he spareth to spede," we know that he will not "spede"; and when she describes to him the ship's pilot, he fails to recognize the very Mutability he so wants to escape:

> But of one thynge I werne you er I goo,
> She that styreth the shyp, make her your frende
>
> [106–07]

> Fortune gydeth and ruleth all oure shyppe:
> Whome she hateth shall over the see boorde skyp;
> Whome she loveth, of all plesyre is ryche,

Whyles she laugheth and hath luste for to playe;
Whome she hateth, she casteth in the dyche.   [111–15]

Indeed he accepts Fortune as his saviour and asks, ironically,
the same question he had posed at line 20, "how myghte I
have her *sure?*" "By Bone Aventure," replies Desire, and,
placing his faith in good luck, he commits himself to the
ship and its way of life. The couplet that concludes the
prologue is naively optimistic:

Of Bowge of Court she asketh what we wold have:
And we asked Favoure, and Favour she us gave.

[125–26]

Dread mistakes the capriciousness of Favour for security,
"Favoure we have tougher than ony elme, / That wyll abyde
and never from us fall" (129–30), and in what follows he
reaps the consequences of his error.

Almost at once his new-found confidence leaves him at
the sight of his fellow travelers, "full subtyll persones, in
nombre foure and thre"—Favell, full of flattery, Suspecte
"with face dedely and pale," Harvey Hafter "that well coude
picke a male" (purse), and "other foure of theyr affynyte, /
Disdayne, Ryotte, Dyssymuler, Subtylte" (who later becomes
Deceit).[8] As little pleased by his company as he is by theirs,

8. Lines 133–40. Much of the criticism of the *Bouge of Court* centers
around the question whether it is a renaissance or medieval poem, and
the emphasis in such arguments is on the conspirators rather than
their victim. Ian Gordon (*John Skelton, Poet Laureate*, p. 55) says "His
method . . . shows a curious blend of the abstract sketches of the Middle
Ages with the rotund characterizations of the new age. Disdayne and
Dyssymulacyon both in name and character are hastily conceived. . . .
Ryotte, on the other hand, is an excellent piece of realism." I shall
argue that these figures and their actions are conceived only in their
relationship to Dread. From a historical point of view, Riot's "realism"
is hardly new. One need only turn to the fifth *passus* of *Piers Plowman*
to find his literary ancestor. In general, Skelton's use of detail is not so
much realistic in the nineteenth-century use of the word as it is iconographic. William Nelson (*John Skelton, Laureate*, p. 78) says "The

they recognize in his reticence and timidity something alien:

> They coude not faile, thei thought, they were so *sure*.
>
> [142, emphasis mine]
>
> my dysporte they coude not well endure;
> they hated for to dele with Drede. [145–46]

Already the phrases of his prologue return to mock him. In the anticourt satires Dread would imitate, the satiric voice castigates vice and folly with the sureness that attends a comfortable distance and a firm moral base. Here the positions are reversed: Dread's real doubts leave him defenseless before the artificial and baseless sureness of the enemy. His companions realize immediately that their strength (the appearance of confidence) is his weakness, and the journey becomes a literal nightmare as they conspire to destroy him.

The assault begins immediately. Favell approaches to welcome him:

> Ye be an apte man, as ony can be founde,
> To dwell with us, and serve my ladyes grace;
> Ye be to her yea worth a thousande pounde;
> I herde her speke of you within shorte space.
>
> [155–58]

---

topic of the poem, the treachery and ill manners of courtiers competing for place, is typical Renaissance; the dream form is typical Middle Age." See Heiserman's study of the poem's sources (*Skelton and Satire*, pp. 14–65) for a convincing refutation of this position. Judith Larsen, "What Is the *Bouge of Courte?*" (*Journal of English and German Philology* [1962], p. 295) says "Skelton turns the medieval apologetic attitude into a serious query. . . . The use of living, speaking characters in place of the medieval straw personalities is another aspect of Skelton's ability to develop his medieval basis into something more complex and useful." The implication that medievalism is to be distinguished from seriousness, complexity, and usefulness is indefensible. These are the kinds of schematizations that violate both intellectual history and literature. Skelton would not have understood them.

However, he goes on, all are not equally pleased:

For here be dyverse to you that be unkynde. [161]

Favell does not elaborate, but says barely enough to suggest
a conspiracy: "Thyse lewde cok wattes shall nevermore
prevayle / Ageynste you hardely, therfore be not afrayde"
(173–74). He leaves the largely silent Dread with this assurance, "but this one thynge, ye maye be sure of me," and
moves on. Again the word "sure" seems ominous and ironic.

Dread watches as Favell meets and confers with Suspect.
Drawing near, he hears his "ally" whisper:

He [Drede] sayth, he can not well accorde with the . . .
                                                         [185]

By Cryste . . . Drede is soleyne freke:
What lete us holde him up, man, for a whyle? [187–88]

And the reply, "ye soo, quod Suspecte, he maye us both
begyle." They part, and Suspect addresses Dread: "Ye re-
membre the gentylman ryghte nowe / That commaunde
with you, me thought, a party space? / Beware of him, for,
I make God avowe, / He wyll *begyle* you and speke fayre
to your face" (197–200). By line 200 Favell and Suspect
have betrayed each other to Dread and Dread to each other.
This accounts for all possibilities,[9] and it is obvious that,
in purely physical terms, the dream world is forcing Dread
to the wall. Once again he knows not "what to do."

Their attack is more than physical. Dread is, we know, a
poet; it is his inability to launch a verbal barrage on the
chaos of the human situation that teases him into sleep, and
Favell and company turn his own problem on him. They
defer ostentatiously to the "connynge" he fears to exceed:

9. Cf. lines 1520–1867 of the *House of Fame,* where Fame's replies
to her suitors mathematically define whimsicality.

Noo thynge erthely that I wonder so sore
As of your connynge, that is so excellent,
[Favell, 148–49]

Loo what is to you a pleasure grete,
To have that connynge and wayes that ye have;
[Harvey Hafter, 260–61]

Alas, a connynge man ne dwell maye
In no place well, but foles with hym fraye;
[Dissimulation, 445–46]

but this flattery is only a ploy in their attempt to recreate
the chaos he seeks to escape, as they put forward, as real,
incidents and intrigues that have only a verbal existence.
Dread overhears Suspect ask Favell, "In faythe, quod Suspecte, spake Drede no worde of me?" And Favell answers,
"He sayth, he can not well accorde with the" (183, 185).
We know, and Dread knows, that he has said no such thing,
and that Disdain's later accusation, "Rememberest thou
what thou sayd yester nyght? / Wylt thou abyde by the
wordes agayne?" (323–24) is equally baseless. The conspirators create their own version of reality and involve
Dread in its processes.[1] As part of this they appropriate the
norms and vocabulary of the plain-speaking tradition
which rejects the veiled truth of the aureatians. I am, claims
each of them, the only one of those aboard who will tell you
the truth, who will speak "playnely" rather than artfully
(covertly):

I can not flater, I muste be playne to the;
[Favell, 164]

---

1. Heiserman (p. 22) makes essentially the same point: "the intrigues, the follies, the miseries, the fragile and unaccountable successes
and failures of courtiers are based on and work through nothing more
substantial than words."

> For but I trusted you, so God me save
> I wolde noo thynge so playne be;
>
> [Suspect, 213–14]

> Syr, pardone me, I am an homely knave;
>
> [Harvey Hafter, 264]

> I wolde eche man were as playne as I;
>
> [Dissimulation, 463]

But their pattern of assertion and counterassertion is itself a veil which mocks plainness; in the same way the profusion of the oaths they swear by (from the conventional "God me spede" to the bizarre "the armes of Calyce") destroys the individual force of any one and advances the gradual negation of meaning. Paradoxically their vocabulary is common, but supports seven conflicting and arbitrary "universes." What does beguile mean when a world full of beguilers removes the possibility of a reality that appearance can obscure? What is "connynge" (knowledge) in a world whose flux precludes the attempt to isolate "facts"? The seven create a language in which sounds refer to the phenomena of a world manufactured in their minds rather than to a common experience. Significantly the components of that language are echoes of Dread's own fears: At line 466, Dissimulation, feigning disgust at the hypocrisy of the world, complains, "A man can not wote where to be come." One more strand in the network of lies and illusion surrounding Dread, this is also an ironic echo of his original lament, "I ne wyste what to do was beste." It is Skelton's special triumph that in a poem which makes its point through a studied perversion of language, words and phrases can assume a symbolic significance.

At line 229 Suspect leaves Dread to the successive mercies of Harvey Hafter, Disdain, Riot, Dissimulation, and Deceit, and the dominant pattern of the poem (flattery—intimidation—threat) is reinforced by a series of encounters.

But, as I stode musynge in my mynde,
Harvey Hafter came lepynge, lyghte as lynde [230–31]

To kepe him frome pykinge it was a grete payne:
He gased on me with his gotyshe berde;
Whan I loked on hym, my purse was halfe aferde.
[236–38]

Wyth that came Ryotte, russhynge all at ones,
A rusty gallande, to-ragged and to-rente;
And on the borde he whyrled a payre of bones,
Quater treye dews he clatered as he wente;
Now have at all, by saynte Thomas of Kente!
And ever he threwe and kyst I wote nere what:
His here was growen thorowe oute his hat. [344–50]

Anone Dyscymular came where I stode.
Than in his hode I sawe there faces tweyne;
That one was lene and lyke a pyned goost,
That other loked as he wolde me have slayne;
And to me warde as he gan for to coost,
Whan that he was even at me almoost,
I sawe a knyfe hyd in his one sleve,
Wheron was wryten this worde, *Myscheue.* [427–34]

This mélange of realism and allegory represents the fragmentation of Dread's waking disquiet. Heiserman correctly identifies Dread's dream as an *insomnium* or nightmare[2] "caused," Macrobius explains, "by mental or physical distress or anxiety about the future"; in the resulting dream, he goes on, "the man who fears the plots or might of an enemy . . . is confronted with him in his dream or seems to be flee-

2. *Skelton and Satire*, pp. 34 ff.

ing him."[3] Dread's enemy is Mutability whose manifestation
is sometimes physical (a fall from a high place), sometimes
spiritual (the failure of poetic power), and ultimately all-
encompassing ("full of mutabylyte"). In the same way the
mutability and unsteadfastness of the world of his dream
is perceived on several levels: the danger of a purse-picking
Harvey Hafter is obvious and immediate; the iconographic
threat of Dissimulation is more intellectual and more suggestive, for he is a link with Langland's fifth passus, the
seven deadly sins and a worldly unsteadfastness that goes far
beyond the court. The alternation of these assaults evokes
an emphatic but confused response from Dread and the
reader, and reinforces the poem's major patterns—the progressive annihilation of meaning and the isolation of the
bewildered alien; we might use the plural here, since the
reader is by this point also an alien; the poem literally confronts *him* as well as Dread.

When Deceit appears to press the attack, what follows is
inevitable. He comes from behind, "Er I was ware, behynde
me he sayde, Bo!" (500), and moves automatically for the
pocket, "For, yf I had not quyckely fledde the touche, / He
had plucte oute the nobles of my pouche" (503–04). When
this fails, he turns to the other prong of their strategy and
carries the perversion of language to its logical conclusion
by warning Dread of a nonexistent plot in a code that means
nothing at all:

> by that Lorde that is one, two, and thre,
> I have an errande to rounde in your ere:
> He told me so, by God, ye maye truste me,
> Parte remembre whan ye were there,

3. Macrobius, *Commentary on the Dream of Scipio,* trans. W. H.
Stahl (New York, 1952), p. 88. Stahl writes in his introduction (p. 13),
"The third chapter . . . was sufficient to establish the *Commentary* as
one of the leading dream books of the Middle Ages."

There I wynked on you,—wote ye not where?
In A *Loco,* I mene *juxta* B!
Woo is hym that is blynde and maye not see!

[512–18]

"In A *Loco,* I mene *juxta* B!"—these are Deceit's covert terms; in another reverse of the tradition he uses them to cloak *all* truth and attack the would-be satirist. The last line is especially diabolic. Dread's blindness is forced upon him; his companions have arranged his visibilia in such a way that his own sight and rational processes are drawn into the conspiracy to unbalance him. At this very moment he senses the approach of the remaining conspirators: "And as he rounded thus in myne ere . . . / Me thoughte, I see lewde felawes here and there / Came for to slee me of mortall entente" (526, 528–29). The dramatic and verbal levels of the poem have merged to destroy him, and, unable to act, he desperately flings himself overboard:

And, as they came, the shypborde faste I hente,
And thoughte to lepe; and even with that woke.

[530–31]

The poem concludes with what appears to be a conventional refusal to moralize: "Syth all in substaunce of slumbrynge doth procede: / I wyll not saye it is mater in dede, / But yet oftyme suche dremes be founde trewe: / Now constrewe ye what is the resydewe" (536–39). As traditional as this disclaimer is, Dread is not merely being coy, nor is Skelton, as Heiserman suggests, merely reinforcing his attack "with a pretense of ambiguity."[4] Macrobius maintains that the insomnium is "not worth interpreting," because it has "no prophetic significance."[5] This does not mean that the dream is untrue, but only that its truth is in the accuracy

4. *Skelton and Satire,* p. 34.
5. *Commentary,* p. 88.

with which it reflects the turmoil of the dreamer. Macrobius is far more impressed with the *oraculum* "in which a parent or a pious or reverend man, or a priest or even a god clearly reveals what will or will not transpire, and *what action to take or avoid.*"[6] Its truth stands outside the individual and is therefore truly valuable. The oraculum offers what traditional satire and the fifteenth-century dream vision offer, an authoritative voice, man, priest or god, and a program, however limited, for action. In the end the interpretation and the value of this dream remain problematical because it offers neither the reader nor Dread anything authoritative. As an analysis of his mind, it convinces; as a castigation of vice and folly, it does not. One might say that the satire is written in spite of the narrator's doubts, but the final impression is not of vice condemned or ridiculed, but of vice triumphant. Dread's uncertainty about his dream is ours; there is no moral, no "action to take." In the prologue, Desire warns that those who are not favored by Fortune, "shall over the see boorde skyp" (112). If a moral can be drawn from this, it is strangely nonmoral: "When luck (Bone Aventure) fails, commit suicide."

Whether or not we learn anything from his poem, Dread does not. He recalls his dream and the emotional state that preceded it from the vantage point of time. He writes, he tells us, after the fact: "And, as they came, the shypborde faste I hente, / And thoughte to lepe; and even with that woke, / Caughte penne and ynke, and wrote this lytyll boke" (530–32). There are two Dreads in the poem, the completely ignorant and lost soul who undergoes a very disquieting experience, and the narrator who recalls his experience from the relative security of the present. (The third member of this trinity is, of course, the poet Skelton, who is heard only in the poem's total statement.) Hindsight, however, has not

6. Ibid., p. 90, emphasis mine.

given him insight. He is more aware than he was during the dream of the danger his companions posed (he could not have known before the fact that Favell, for instance, was "full of flatery / Wyth fables false that well coude fayne a tale"), but a familiarity with the face of the enemy is all that he has gained. He awakes in time to escape the dangers of a hostile world where there is nothing to cling to, only to find himself back in the equally hostile world of the opening stanzas, of "mutabylyte" and "unstedfastnesse."[7] A sadder but not a wiser man, he has found no answers, no basis for action; he still complains, "I ne wyste what to do was beste"; he is still unable to write the satire which must await the identification of the true authority, and might well ask with Keats, "do I wake or sleep?" In the prologue, Dread had mused on the problem of one who "clymmeth hyer than he may fotinge have; / What and he slyde downe, who shall hym save?" "Who shall hym save?" The question remains unanswered. To quote Macrobius again, this dream is of no "assistance in foretelling the future."[8]

The advantage of considering a Skelton poem against the tradition of formal satire and the disadvantage of refusing to go beyond the tradition are equally obvious in Arthur Heiserman's chapter on the *Bouge of Court.* Heiserman argues correctly that the poem is demonstrably different from other satirical critiques of court folly, from which Skelton borrows topoi and themes, and he finds the explanation for this difference in Skelton's decision to dramatize the criticism of earlier satirists and thus avoid explicitness.

7. Cf. the dreamer in the *House of Fame* who finds himself lost in a desert from which he is rescued by an eagle. The eagle takes him to the court of Fame where the splendor and opulence are a marked contrast to the wasteland he has fled; but the irony of the situation is that the dazzling detail of the court is unsubstantial and affords him no more of a point of reference than the desert.

8. *Commentary,* pp. 89–90.

"Skelton did *not* make his attack in this explicit way." Rather than harangue court types in an authoritative first-person voice, "he launches a fresh attack on these conventional villainies by converting them into actions performed by allegorical personae." "In *Bowge of Court,* then, Skelton employs a conventional action to attack a conventional complex of objects, but the mixture of action and object is a fresh one."[9] There are many assumptions here and at least one must be challenged. Skelton does avoid explicitness; indeed, were it not for its title, it would be difficult to link the poem explicitly to a court at all. As Lewis remarks, "the particular 'world' or 'racket' described is the court; but almost any man in any profession can recognize most of the encounters."[1] It is also undeniable that the telling distinction between the epistolary satires and anticourt complaint Heiserman examines and the *Bouge of Court* is the latter's dramatic setting. What Heiserman does not consider is that the shift in setting produces (I use the verb provisionally since it is an open question as to what produces what in this poem) a compensatory shift in focus. The abandonment of the authoritative and somewhat detached first-person voice lashing folly from the comfort of a study in favor of the dramatization of an attack on the anticourt "hero" who is threatened *in* the poem, makes the attacked the center of reader attention. Of course, in what Heiserman would call the most direct kind of satire, the attacked are also the center of attention; but in that kind of poem, whether it be Juvenal's, Walter Map's, or Alexander Pope's, our interest is negative: that is, the poet invites us to consider his characters or caricatures as objects of "indignation and scorn"[2]

9. *Skelton and Satire,* pp. 55, 57, 26.
1. Lewis, *English Literature in the Sixteenth Century,* p. 135.
2. Heiserman, *Skelton and Satire,* p. 55. "The indignation and scorn aroused by the poems in that tradition *Bowge of Court* could arise afresh only by indirection."

and he carefully neutralizes his own personality, becomes the *vir bonus*, righteous, moral, and uninteresting, lest we become distracted from his (and he hopes our) castigation of vice by our interest in him. In the *Bouge of Court*, this is exactly what happens, for as Heiserman admits, "It would not be too much to say that the reader *fears* for"[3] Dread, and once the reader becomes concerned in an immediate rather than an academic context for the hero's safety, the dangers or evils of the scene are considered only as the hero reacts to them or is affected by them. In short, we watch him rather than them; his situation (mental and physical), not their exposure, is our point of focus, and insofar as that situation includes conflict within, the drama becomes psychological. Skelton himself seems to say as much when he describes the *Bouge of Court* not in terms of what Heiserman would call the "object of the manifest fiction's attack"[4] (the court), but in terms of its hero, "Item Bowche of Courte, where Drede was *begyled.*"[5]

Heiserman's admirable survey of anticourt satire is the best documentation of my contention. Walter Map's contemptuous and mocking indictment of the court touches on the abuses of the *Bouge of Court*, "but it is constructed as an epistle, involving a correspondent who is eager for news of the court, and a style which at times imitates the method of philosophical treatises . . . we should note that Skelton abandons the epistolary conventions."[6] Exactly. The conven-

3. Ibid., p. 24. Italics are mine.
4. Ibid., p. 298. This is my paraphrase of Edward Rosenheim's definition of satire which Heiserman seems to accept. "Satire consists of an attack, by means of a manifest fiction, upon discernible historic particulars." Heiserman takes the definition from Rosenheim's dissertation, "Swift's Satire in A Tale of a Tub" (University of Chicago, 1953), p. 29. Of course, this may not be the way Skelton would describe his poems at all.
5. Dyce, 2, 409, line 1183, emphasis mine. This is a line from Skelton's versified bibliography in the *Garland of Laurel.*
6. *Skelton and Satire*, p. 37.

tions of epistolary satire carry with them a built-in buffer between the horror of court life or any kind of life as it is experienced, and the letter writer, as he writes, or his correspondent(s), as they read. Heiserman notes that Map, Alain Chartier, and Aeneas Silvius write as literary men and make a point of the court's uncongeniality to the Muse's servants. They have left the court, or are deciding to leave, or are warning others not to come. Again the actual collision between their values and the court's is in the past and is now academic or stalemated. "Those early satires, usually cast as epistles, represent the author as a literary man, employed in but alienated from the court, who persuades his correspondent to eschew the court."[7] Skelton takes the literary man out of an isolation that is a bit unreal and brings him back to the moment of contact when the press of his antagonists is physical. The convention is turned on its head and no longer exists as convention. It is something like what happens to the pastoral when Wordsworth decides to walk through his landscape rather than imagine it; the genre ceases to be a way of thinking and becomes a way of experiencing.

When Heiserman comes to discuss the influence of less restrictive medieval poems (*Piers Plowman, House of Fame*) on the *Bouge of Court,* he marks the absence in Skelton's poem of two commonplace attitudes: (1) a provisional reliance on oneself in the face of doubleness; and (2) a final reliance on God in the face of the same. Commenting on Dunbar's "Hald God thy friend, evir stafill be him stand," Heiserman decides that "Skelton could leave such advice unspoken."[8] But Skelton's hero whose name is Dread, or doubt,

7. Ibid., p. 27.
8. Ibid., p. 56. The line is from Dunbar's *Rewl of Anis Self.* One stanza of the poem reads like a list of the rules Dread fails to follow. "Bewar quhome to thy counsale thow discure, / For trewth dwellis nocht ay for that trewth appeirs: / Put not thyne honour into aventure;

leaves this advice unspoken because it is not available to him in his troubled (doubting) state. This is a poem about the absence of advice and ultimately of faith. Again Heiserman supplies the link when he quotes from the *Book of Vices and Virtues,* "the seventhe braunche of pride is foly drede, that is whan a man . . . doubteth more the world than God."[9] Dread's failure to turn from Fortune to Christ is, to the reader who knows the tradition, a measure of his spiritual aridity; it is the central problem of the poem.

/ Ane freind may be thy fo as fortoun steiris: / In cumpany cheis honorable feiris, / And fra vyle folkis draw the far on syd" (*The Poems of William Dunbar,* ed. W. M. Mackenzie [Edinburgh, 1932], p. 75).

9. *Skelton and Satire,* p. 59. Heiserman's insistence on restricting the *Bouge of Court* to a court satire forces him to misread at several points. "The poem," he says, "traces the fortunes of an ambitious courtier" (p. 21). But in the poem (which is the only place we see him) Dread is anything but ambitious; rather he is progressively more confused and afraid. In the proem, Dread alludes to the danger of "Exceydynge ferther than his connynge is," and Heiserman takes this as an indication of his ambition. But in context that particular fear is a literary one and follows Dread's admission of an inability to find a firm basis for writing satire. In his effort to keep Dread manageable, Heiserman claims that his "murder turns the reader against the objects of the satire" (p. 27). If Dread is murdered, how does he catch pen and ink and write the poem? Or are we to make a distinction between the figure in the poem and the voice in the proem and conclusion? If so, where is that distinction indicated? Of course, if there were such a distinction, and if Dread were murdered, and if his hallmark were ambition, we could separate the figure in the proem from the doubt of his dream surrogate and have our authoritative voice; we could point to a crime that would arouse the reader's anger; we could have a satiric attack on a conventional object. Finally, Heiserman identifies Skelton's purpose as the arousing of "indignation and scorn" (p. 55). This is not I think, the response the poem provokes. The experience of reading the *Bouge of Court* is exactly as C. S. Lewis describes it: "Things overheard, things misunderstood, a general and growing sense of being out of one's depth, fill the poem with a Kafka-like uneasiness" (*English Literature in the Sixteenth Century,* p. 135). And the purpose of the poem is to consider what becomes the persistent Skeltonic problem—the possibility, for the poet, of moral action.

Skelton does here what he will do in other poems; he invokes traditions by borrowing their topoi only to reveal by significant omissions (*Bouge of Court*), structural inconsistencies (*Colin Clout*) or mockery (*Speak, Parrot*) that their utility is either questionable or partial. And in each case, the reader who finds suddenly that he is not reading the kind of poem he has been led to expect, turns from the tradition to the mind it cannot contain.

As the first of these poems, the *Bouge of Court* illustrates formal characteristics we shall see again. Its dominant patterns are established by an alternation rather than a graduated succession of words and images. It is impossible to assess, as the initial stanzas are read for the first time, the significance of a word (sure) or a phrase ("I ne wyste"); but when that word or phrase appears in several (often contradictory) contexts, we begin to discern in these appearances an emerging pattern. In short, Skelton presents his readers with choices (as opposed to commands), forces them to share the burden of decision; while the more traditional satirist, who writes in the hortative mood, draws his lines of demarcation at once and proceeds more or less directly to a logical resolution. In the same way, the relationships between the images of the poem exist only in the poem, not in an external frame of reference where they are also associated. Dissimulation's hood and Harvey Hafter's dicing box do not necessarily suggest each other, but, in combination with other similarly dissimilar images, do suggest a third and larger image, the handy dandy world of deception. The reader, in effect, must put the poem together and thus involve himself in the creation of its structure and imagery. Finally, the ambiguity of its conclusion is typical of Skelton. The conclusion of a traditional satire effects or follows a resolution of conflict; it is, in the context of the particular context, satisfactory. When Pope decides, in the final lines of his *Epistle to Dr. Arbuthnot,* to rise above the petty quarrels of a petty age by following the example of his father, who "walk'd innoxious thro' his Age / No courts he saw, no suits would ever try, / Nor dar'd an Oath, nor hazarded a Lye," he is confident that this course of action will assure him a certain serenity: "Oh grant me thus to live, and thus to die! / Who sprung from Kings shall know less joy than I" (395–97, 404–05). On the other hand, there is nothing satisfactory or confident in Dread's attempt to leap overboard; the Skeltonic problem is characteristically insoluble, at least within the framework of the poem. In later poems there will be an alternative solution—a "leap of faith." In 1498 this possibility is ironically parodied in Dread's leap downward. Throughout his career, Skelton is a Hebraïc or Pauline Christian who looks for inspiration to the Old Testament prophecies and to the epistles. In his poems we often hear the prophets' lamentations of alienation and futility answered by the Apostle's promulgation of the new dispensation. Dread, however, is unable to accept the good news, and he can only repeat Paul's anguished cry: "Non enim quod volo bonum, hoc facio; sed quod nolo malum, hoc ago . . . Infelix ego homo! Quis me liberavit?" (Romans 7:19, 24).[1] Paul's reaction to his own lament is immediate and true: "Gratia Dei per Jesum Christum Dominum nostrum" (Romans 7:25); but it will be more than twenty years before Skelton, as Colin Clout, articulates his mature response to the question this poem poses: "Who shall save me?"

1. "I can not do the good that I would, but the evil I would not do, I perform. . . . O unhappy man! Who shall free (save?) me?"

3   Some Graver Subject

SKELTON AND RHETORIC

FIVE YEARS LATER, no longer at court, Skelton is the rector of Diss, which his latest biographer describes as a "grosse bourgade agricole au débouché de la riante vallée de la Waveney."[1] Whatever its explanation, Skelton's "exile" effectively isolates him from the pressures of a scene that threatened to overwhelm him. He seems to have taken his new responsibilities quite seriously; and except for an occasional visit with old friends is caught up in the affairs of his parish for the next eight years. We need not, however, imagine a bitter exile; this is the Skelton of the *Merrie Tales* (which surely have some foundation in fact), idiosyncratic, quarrelsome, and, in his own way, endearing. And there is reason to suppose that he welcomed an opportunity, as he would again in 1523, to reassess his mission in an interlude he surely believed temporary. The accession of Henry VIII will see him petition for permission to return; but in the years at Diss he will come to terms with the disparity between the complexity of the human situation and the resources of art, and he will return not as a courtier but as a warrior. It is not that Skelton needs to learn his craft; the lyrics and the *Bouge of Court* prove him the most competent versifier in English since Chaucer. But at Diss he will realize that his "mastery" is in some ways only a trick, that the building of structures is easy, and may mask and even contribute to a moral irresponsibility. Skelton's "retirement," like Milton's, will end in a rededication in which his gifts and powers will

1. Maurice Pollet, *John Skelton*, p. 63.

be brought to bear on "some graver subject." As he stands
and waits, he will continue to write, and although his pro-
ductions may seem insubstantial, a closer examination reveals that beneath their surface playfulness is an exploration
of the limits of poetry.

Skelton inherits a tradition in which the whole of poetry
is ornament. Schirmer says of Lydgate that his "conception of
the art of poetry . . . consists solely in mastery of linguistic
technique," and for technique we may read rhetoric.[2] In the
Middle Ages what was once an art with a philosophical
rationale had become a series of formulae for the amplification of commonplace topics. The elements of classical
rhetoric had been subordinated to something larger than the
sum of their parts, i.e. the determination of policy (Delibera-
tive), the presentation of a course of law (Judicial), the
maintenance of public ceremony (Epideictic). Ornament,
verbal or visual (*actio*), was seen merely as a means. But as
political conditions lead to the decay of Judicial and Delib-
erative oratory, rhetoric is more and more identified with the
hyperbolic flourishes of the Epideictic. A good man speaking
well is easily shortened to speaking well. Rhetorical virtuosity is valued for its own sake, and the entire system is fragmented into a collection of unconnected but authoritative
rules. At the same time, other pressures (largely religious)
operate to produce a parallel transformation in the art of
poetry. In a Christian or Platonic society, poetry is always
on the defensive, and the readiest defense is one that sacrifices it to something else. In the Middle Ages that something
is Christianity and poetry becomes a sugared vehicle for the
communication of a truth independent of the artistic effort.

2. Walter Schirmer, *John Lydgate: A Study of the Culture of the
XVth Century,* trans. Ann E. Keep (Berkeley and Los Angeles, 1961),
p. 47; ibid.: "the homage repeatedly paid to Chaucer is rendered him
only as an artist in words, and in his asseverations of modesty he de-
plores his own lack of rhetoric."

What remains to the poet and to the rhetorician are the small tricks with which they decorate and amplify the "sentence" presented to them by others. Inevitably, poetry and rhetoric merge in their common concern with technique. The result is a literature of momentary and theatrical effects produced by men who leave considerations of morality and truth to others, and who have no conception of the artifact as a sustained act of communication. In much of fifteenth-century poetry one looks in vain for a sense of purpose, of moral responsibility, for an awareness of an end beyond the impact of the single word or phrase. As C. S. Baldwin writes, "The Sophistic style can not be escaped. It is always saying, 'here is style.'"

Only in pulpit oratory is the rhetorical unit the whole rather than the *ecphrasis*. Here, of course, we have a purpose which transcends and even denies purely stylistic considerations. "In preaching, the safeguard against sophistic is the distinctive use of the occasion to move men to action. . . . Relying less than political oratory on argument, reasoning less and pleading more, it is even more urgent toward a goal."[3] Taking their cue from Augustine's *De doctrina,* the authors of the *artes praedicandi* warn continually against an emphasis on style. Alan de Lille intones, "Praedicatio enim in se, non debet habere verba scurrilia, vel puerilia, vel ryth-

---

3. C. S. Baldwin, *Medieval Poetic and Rhetoric* (New York, 1928), pp. 50, 230. Baldwin's analysis of the relationship between Augustine and Cicero is helpful: "Augustine has passed . . . from Cicero's three tasks of oratory to his three typical styles by applying to the preacher Cicero's definition of the orator: 'He, then shall be called eloquent who can speak small things quietly, larger things proportionally, great things greatly.' Thus the three styles are *genus submissum* (or *tenue*), *genus temperatum* (or *medium*), and *genus grande*" (p. 68). "Augustine shows . . . the need of variety. . . . No one of the three styles, least of all the third, can be effectively prolonged; the change from style to style gives relief; and subordination of what might be heightened may enhance the emotion of what must be. . . . So . . . the end of all eloquence, in whatever style, is persuasion" (p. 71).

morum melodias et consonantias metrorum, quae potius fiunt
ad aures demulcendas, quam ad animum instruendum: quae
praedicatio theatralis est et mimica, et ideo omnifarie con-
temnenda."[4] The "Aquinas" and "Hesse" tracts censure
imprecision, excessive gestures, irrelevant digressions.[5] Perhaps the most austere of these divine rhetors is Humbert of
Romans:

> A sermon should be simple, and devoid of all the
> empty ornaments of rhetoric, after the example of those
> Asiatic nations who went to battle armed only with a
> plowshare. "Guard against multiplying the solemn Di-
> vine words lest you thereby overburden your speech,"
> is the advice of St. Augustine. . . . Leave the ingenious
> style to art; here it is a question of souls. A sick man
> does not look for eloquence in his doctor; and a doctor
> who gives his prescriptions in flowery language is like
> a ruler who cares more for elegance than *practicality*.

In a later passage Humbert links rhetorical absurdities with
ignorance and even an absence of divine grace as he attempts
to account for the sterility of some sermons. He concludes by
approving a comment of Seneca's: "We do not ask for many

4. Alan de Lille, *De Arte Predicatoria*, cap. I, *Patrologia Latina*,
Vol. 210, col. 112. "Preaching of itself should have no jesting or childish words, nor any rhythmical numbers or metrical harmonies which
more caress the ears than instruct the spirit. That kind of preaching is
theatrical and farcical, and therefore ought to be condemned on all
sides."

5. For the texts of these tracts, which are little more than outlines,
see Harry Caplan, " 'Henry of Hesse' on the Art of Preaching," *Publications of the Modern Language Association*, 48 (1933), 340–61, and
Caplan, "A Late Medieval Tractate on Preaching," in *Studies in Rhetoric
and Public Speaking in Honor of J. A. Winans* (New York, 1926),
p. 71. Caplan discusses these and other tracts in *Historical Studies of
Rhetoric and Rhetoricians* (Ithaca, 1961), pp. 71–89. A full discussion
of medieval preaching techniques is to be found in Etienne Gilson's
Les Idées et les lettres (Paris, 1932), pp. 93–154.

orators, but we need those who are *useful*."⁶ Once again the
measure of eloquence is moral and the graces of art are subordinated to a larger end. A host of Humberts, however,
would have been unable to prevent the codification of sermon techniques, and the vices of the pulpit are predictably
the vices of late medieval poetry. Digressions are longer
and not at all to the point; exegesis becomes more elaborate
and arbitrary; authorities are brought in at the wrong time
to support the wrong arguments. In short, preachers turn,
as they do in all ages, from winning men's souls to winning
their admiration.

In the last analysis the rules of a *useful* rhetoric can be
reduced to Horace's doctrine of decorum. It is this that
rhetoricians, poets, and preachers alike failed to see, and it
is this, as recent criticism has emphasized, that Chaucer saw
so well. Again and again he tells us (indirectly) that rhetorical formulae are to be used rather than worshiped; that
stylistic effects depend upon a momentary relationship between modes of diction, characterization, and an audience
with a conditioned response; that this relationship is created
in the poem, through the poet's manipulation of rhetorical
signatures, and does not exist in a Platonic world of fixed
forms; that since style is what you make of it, the objectivity
of rules is deceptive and even dangerous; and that often the
poet is able to approach reality only by exposing the arbitrariness of correspondences which have passed for real. In
the *Pardoner's Tale,* he dramatically complicates a traditional equation by allowing a bad man to speak well. "I can

6. *Treatise on Preaching,* trans. the Dominican students, Province
of St. Joseph, ed. Walter M. Conlon, O.P. (London, 1955), pp. 43–44,
96. The italics in both passages are mine. "Sometimes it will be the
nature of the sermon which renders it inefficacious; for some preachers
in their discourses make use of authorities, or figures, or examples,
which are so inapposite and absurd that they are unable to produce any
effect on souls. . . . At other times sterility is caused by an absence of
divine grace" (p. 96).

tell a moral tale," says the Pardoner, and he does, in a context which implicitly denies the morality he preaches. But lest his readers should question the order which sermons support, assume, in other words, an identity between the "truths" of art and the "truths" of the universe, Chaucer makes a sharp distinction between the relativity of literary effects and the stability of the absolute; the latter reasserts itself as the Pardoner is mercilessly exposed. His command of the situation has been merely verbal and therefore illusory. It is not the form, but the substance of his sermon which is real. "The man whose clever tongue has seemed to give him control of every situation is reduced to furious silence. . . . The man who, like the revelers in his story, seems so firmly in control of his destiny has . . . demonstrated that avenging powers dwell close to a man's own home." The Pardoner's sermon, then, is true and not true; it changes before our very eyes, as Chaucer deliberatively perplexes us by suggesting that the laws of aesthetics are bound to human psychology, and are distressingly independent of immutable moral values.

The attack on rhetoric as a self-contained or rigorous discipline is even more pointed in *Sir Thopas;* here Chaucer as pilgrim attempts to tell a chivalric tale, and by mechanically and inappropriately trotting out convention after convention, he succeeds only in offering absurdity after absurdity; but in the context of the romance tradition, this is of course burlesque and as Talbot Donaldson remarks, "to the reader who knows . . . the culture . . . the result may seem hilarious."[7] Again our assessment of the performance wavers between contempt and admiration; and when we would turn for convenience to the distinction between poet and persona, we find that they are one, and the tale takes on another dimension in terms of the poet's attempt to define his art. If good art is

7. *Chaucer's Poetry: An Anthology for the Modern Reader,* ed. E. T. Donaldson (New York, 1958), pp. 929, 930, 935.

momentarily bad morality in the *Pardoner's Tale,* good art is somehow bad art, and the best poet the worst in *Sir Thopas.* Chaucer will not even allow us to rest in the arid security of a system complete within itself, as he suggests a universe where every system is only a partial description of reality and the correspondences between structures are ever expanding. Too many fifteenth-century poets write Sir Thopases unwittingly and tell truly moral tales only accidentally. Skelton's strength is that he sees this and is, before he leaves Diss, Chaucer's intellectual heir.

WARE THE HAWK

"Turning up at his church shortly before vespers, one 29th of August," Edwards conjectures, "Skelton was surprised to find the door bolted and barred against him."[8] Thus Edwards joins all other critics in accepting the historicity of the incident which provides the narrative line of Skelton's *Ware the Hawk.* That narrative is thin indeed. Probably peering through a window, Skelton discovers a neighboring parson who has entered the church in pursuit of a pigeon; he stands on the altar, urging his hawks to the kill. Although the doors are barred, Skelton manages to enter "with a pretty gin," and indignantly confronts a trespasser who is unaccountably and even riotously unrepentant. Enraged, the poet seeks satisfaction from an ecclesiastical court only to receive a further rebuff. He then writes the poem.

If we read it as fact, *Ware the Hawk* forces us to accept a Skelton who is pedantic, humorless, incompetent; and although his nationalistic pose is often unattractive, he is rarely incompetent. Edwards admits that the authenticity of the event is unverifiable; notwithstanding Skelton's invitation

8. *Skelton,* p. 89.

to look "In the officialles bokes" for an account of the matter, "no trace has been found of any such action";[9] along the same lines, the promise of a "tabull playne" peters out in a typically Skeltonic self-laureation. It is almost as if he were pulling our collective leg. Moreover, the situation itself is suspiciously conventional; the hawking parson, like the hunting monk, was a stock figure in anticlerical literature and Skelton somewhat ostentatiously refuses to name him. But these are all external considerations. The text itself is the strongest argument for a reinterpretation. Repeated interrogatio's ("delt he not like a fon") indicate that the speaker regards his poem as a second opportunity to plead his case; although he has lost in the courts he turns to his audience for a second hearing. In this situation, the pressures which in classical rhetoric demanded a performance that was organic are again operative, and it becomes the prosecutor's first task to win the sympathy of his audience, to persuade us that he is a good man before we will accept his speaking well. The speaker himself is very conscious of his position and of the resources at his command. He announces, in the language of formal rhetoric, that he will attempt to move us ("I shall you make relacion / By waye of *apostrofacion*");[1] and as if to underline the seriousness of his presentation, he adds the machinery of the artes praedicandi: the text is punctuated by eight hortatory exclamations (*Observate, Considerate, Deliberate, Vigilate, Deplorate, Divinitate*—probably for *Divinate*—*Reformate*, and *Pensitate*) which correspond to the development or distinction of the *thema* as taught in the manuals. The imperatives again emphasize the urgency of an appeal which is to be immediate as the reader is asked to respond both as auditor and Christian. But in the end, all this priming comes to naught, as Skelton systematically misapplies traditional techniques,

9. Ibid., p. 91.
1. Dyce, *1,* 156, lines 29–30. The italics are mine.

commits the very vices which assure hostility, and finally loses his case completely by losing his control. This could hardly be the best that Caxton's master rhetorician can muster.[2] While *Ware the Hawk* may not be Skelton's *Sir Thopas,* it is more than possibly a burlesque in the Chaucerian tradition.

The *exordium* is appropriately brief and admirable:

> This worke devysed is
> For such as do amys;
> And specyally to controule
> Such as have cure of soule,
> That be so farre abused,
> They cannot be excused
> By reason nor by law.   [1–7]

In his *De inventione* (a work Skelton knew very well) Cicero advises that the *"exordium* ought to be sententious . . . and of a high seriousness, and . . . should contain everything which contributes to dignity, because the best thing to do is that which especially commends the speaker to his audience. It should contain very little brilliance, vivacity or finish of style, because these give rise to a suspicion of preparation and excessive ingenuity."[3] Here our speaker follows the master's precepts faithfully; he invites confidence with his brevity and seriousness, and the urgency of lines 6 and 7 win attention. "We shall win good will," Cicero continues,

2. Skelton was undoubtedly a rhetorician. He was laureated by three universities, and there is reason to think that laureation signified a mastery of rhetoric. H. L. R. Edwards and F. M. Salter have shown in their introduction to his translation of the *Bibliotheca Historica* of Diodorus Siculus (Early English Text Society, orig. ser. 239, Oxford, 1957) that his poetry is studded with references to the standard rhetorical manuals of the late Middle Ages, Cicero's *De inventione,* the pseudo-Ciceronian *Rhetorica ad herennium,* and Geoffrey de Vinsauf's *Poetria nova.*

3. *De inventione, De optimo genere oratorum, Topica,* trans. H. M. Hubbell (Cambridge, Mass., 1949), pp. 51, 53.

"if we can bring them [our opponents] into hatred, un-
popularity or contempt . . . if some act of theirs is presented
which is base,"⁴ and Skelton responds with the statement of
the case or (in terms of sermonry) the *thema:*

> But that they play the daw,
> To hawke, or els to hunt
> From the aulter to the funte,
> With cry unreverent,
> Before the sacrament,
> Within the holy church bowndis,
> That of our faith the grounde is.
> That pryest that hawkys so,
> All grace is farre him fro;
> He semeth a sysmatyke,
> Or els an heretyke. [8–18]

This is perhaps the beginning of his difficulties. The audience
will remain sympathetic only "if we show that the matters
which we are about to discuss are important . . . or that they
concern all humanity or those in the audience . . . or the
general interest of the state."⁵ It seems improbable that this
incident can be made to bear the weight implied by the tone
of the exordium. Still, in many medieval sermons, the *thema*
(primary text) and the *prothema* (supporting text) seem at
first to be unconnected, the success of the performance depending on the skill with which the preacher brings them
together; and at this point our preacher might be expected
to manipulate his audience by playing on the word "here-
tyke," introduced in line 18. But, instead, he proceeds per-
versely to widen the gap between his rhetorical stance and
the effect of his recitation.⁶

4. Ibid., p. 45.
5. Ibid., p. 47.
6. See Gilson, *Les Idées et les lettres,* p. 151, for a sermon which depends for its effect on the bringing together of a *thema* and *prothema.*

Cicero warns that "one must refrain no less from an excess of superfluous facts than from an excess of words,"[7] and Humbert of Romans echoes this admonition in more specific terms: "there are preachers who . . . are afraid to omit the least detail, useful or not."[8] Skelton begins his narrative proper with a simple and acceptable *propositio:*

> For sure he wrought amys,
> To hawke in my church of Dis, [41–42]

but insists on appending a camera-like recreation of the scene which eventually makes it impossible to share his indignation. He invites us to consider the accused's every action—his entrance ("As priest unreverent, / Streyght to the sacrament / He made his hawke to fly"), his strategy ("The hye aulter he strypt naked; / There on he stode, and craked"), his blasphemy ("He shoke downe all the clothis, / And ʌware horrible othes") (45–52).

Two things are happening here. The speaker as always has a Ciceronian precedent for his technique: "by a vivid verbal picture the event is brought before the eyes of the audience so that they will think that they too would have done the same if they had been confronted with the same situation."[9]

Cicero explains that "in the case of the orator we may understand what is meant by function and end when we call what he ought to do the function, and the purpose for which he ought to do it the end" (p. 15). I shall argue that the speaker in *Ware the Hawk* confuses purpose and function.

7. Ibid., p. 59.

8. *Treatise,* pp. 33–34. In the same section, Humbert describes a preacher who might well be Skelton's protagonist, and predicts for him the kind of audience reaction which, I shall argue, is evoked by the egocentric bumbler of *Ware the Hawk:* "There are other kinds of preachers who diligently look for arguments irrelevant to their subject . . . in trying to reconcile them, the preacher runs the risk of exciting derision rather than producing edification" (p. 33).

9. *De inventione,* p. 243.

But in this case, if the situation is unfortunate it is also grotesque, and the audience reaction is not rage but laughter. One need hardly be a heretic to smile at this: "The hawke tyrid on a bonne; / And in the holy place / She mutid there a chase / Upon my corporas face. / Such *sacrificium laudis* / He made with suche gambawdis" (60–63). Mechanically following his models, the outraged cleric miscalculates badly, and as he obligingly offers an ever more frantic "vivid verbal picture," his urgings and our responses grow further apart. At the same time, as we become aware of this, the focus of attention shifts from the situation itself to his psychology; his antagonist's irreverence is balanced by his humorlessness. Immediately his case is lost, and somewhat forgotten, as we become too much interested in watching his mind work to allow him to work on us.[1]

After line 65 his every effort becomes a part of the case against him. Heiserman notes that the Latin imperatives which partition the poem "have little relation with the verses subsumed under them."[2] The division of the thema is discussed in detail in the preaching manuals (some list as many as nine methods), and in structural terms was more or less the entire sermon. Our preacher, however, ignores the

1. The remarkable thing about the critical history of this poem is that most critics take it all quite seriously. For Gordon, the poem is a prelude to *Colin Clout* and "expresses significantly his resentment at the license of the parish priest" (*John Skelton, Poet Laureate*, p. 105). For Edwards it is an illuminating reference to Skelton's years of exile at Diss (*Skelton*, pp. 89–92). To Lloyd the "capital fooling" of the poem indicates that "Skelton cannot remain angry for very long" (*John Skelton: A Sketch of His Life and Writings*, Oxford, 1938, p. 73). It seems to me a moot question whether Skelton was angry at all. There are two Skeltons in the poem. At an early point in *Ware the Hawk* the seriousness of its narrative situation is undercut by humor, but Skelton as speaker is not aware of that humor and becomes its butt. What must be kept in mind is that Skelton the poet is laughing at his fictional representative even as we do.

2. *Skelton and Satire*, p. 281.

oft-repeated injunction against arbitrary and irrelevant distinctions, and his commands (observe! consider! deplore!), little more than the machinery of pedantry, only call attention to his overwrought performance. His analysis of the hunt is even more damaging to an indictment which rests on the condemnation of hawking parsons.[3] We are granted a physiological explanation of the bird's sacrilege: "Her mete was very crude, / She had not wel endude; / She was not clene ensaymed, / She was not well reclaymed." He is, of course, unable to resist jargon: The hawk is "gery" (wild) and fails to cooperate when the falconer is "prest" (ready) with a "dow" (pigeon); when he pauses to turn veterinarian ("she loked as she had the frounce") the poem is fast becoming a manual of falconry; but he recovers his indignation and abandons his disquisition to recall his resolute course of action: "The church dores were sparred, / Fast boltyd and barryd, / Yet wyth a prety gyn / I fortuned to come in, / This rebell to beholde, / Wherof I hym controlde" (91–96). Whatever the "prety gyn" might have been, his entrance is hardly heroic (one can half imagine him scrambling awkwardly through some secret passage), and when he finally confronts the reprobate, the dignified posture of his opening lines has been forgotten.

To Skelton's amazement, his nameless trespasser is insolent rather than contrite: "But he sayde that he woulde, / Agaynst my mynde and wyll, / In my churche hawke styll" (97–99). In fact, this reprimand is the final indignity for the sportsman who has presumably suffered through a day of disappointment, and he defiantly stomps about the church, marshaling his birds in a mock service:

3. "The *narratio* is . . . useless when the audience has grasped the facts so thoroughly that it is of no advantage to us to instruct them in a different fashion. In such a case one must dispense with narrative altogether" (*De inventione*, pp. 61, 63).

> With, troll, cytrace, and trovy,
> They ranged, hankin bovy,
> My churche all aboute.
> This fawconer then gan showte,
> These be my gospellers,
> These be my pystillers,
> These be my querysters
> To helpe me to synge,
> My hawkes to mattens rynge.   [116–24]

Skelton's righteous anger heats to a new intensity, and he turns to the jury (the audience) for support: "Delt he not lyke a daw? / Or els is this Goddes law." But again his photographic recreation defeats him. The scene he describes is hilariously grotesque—two frenzied men of the cloth in the midst of a veritable aviary—but the humor escapes him completely, and as he leavens his report of an unsuccessful appeal to the ecclesiastical courts with cryptic suggestions of bribery and heresy ("mayden meed / Made theym to be agreed / . . . And the Pharasy," 149–50, 152) it is he who is the "daw."

The remainder of the poem is one long attempt at an *indignatio*, "a passage which results in arousing great hatred against some person, or violent offense at some action"[4] which predictably fails. Again Skelton follows his models faithfully, touching on each of the fifteen topics recommended under indignatio, and as always his perspective is faulty. In both the *De inventione* and the *Rhetorica ad herennium*, the prosecutor is advised to pay particular attention to the nature of the offense. Was the act an impulsive one or premeditated; is the crime grave or petty? Clearly the presentation of an argument will be greatly affected by the answers to these questions, and our plaintiff unfortunately

---

4. *De inventione*, p. 151.

96   SOME GRAVER SUBJECT

applies the topics for the gravest of offenses to a misdemeanor
which was hardly premeditated. Topics nine and eight ("a
comparison of the deed in question with other crimes," "the
crime has been committed not even by the boldest of men")[5]
provide him with his finest moments. Suddenly Diss is
Jerusalem, and the defecation of the hawks a greater crime
than the pollution of the great temple (165–77). Cicero
writes that an exemplum "supports or weakens a case by
appeal to precedent."[6] Here the appropriate verb is surely
weaken, for the insignificance of this affair is made only
more apparent by the allusion to the truly significant. He
concludes his formal argument by declaring the falconer's
offense more heinous than any in history:

> Of no tyrande I rede,
> That so farre dyd excede;
> Neyther yet Dioclesyan,
> Nor yet Domisian,
> Nor yet croked Cacus,
> Nor yet dronken Bacus;
> Nother Olibrius,
> Nor Dionisyus;
> Nother Phalary,
> Rehersed in Valery;
> Nor Sardanapall,
> Unhappiest of all.   [190–201]

This list which continues for some twenty lines (he mercifully decides to hold back the "much matter more" that he
has "in store") is both rhetorically unsound and pedantic.

5. Ibid., p. 155.
6. Ibid., p. 89. Humbert of Romans writes, "Examples should have
an obvious authority, so that they may not be received with scorn;
they should be at the same time truthful, so that they may be believed;
they should also be edifying, so that they may not be told in vain"
(*Treatise*, p. 136).

The choice of "tyrande" is obviously dictated by the exigencies of rhyme ("Unhappiest of all" is marvelously anticlimactic) and the whole is a surrender to the verbal ingenuity enjoined in the manuals. Remaining completely in character, he pauses to emphasize the scrupulosity of his scholarship: "I have red them poll by poll." "I have read them one by one." Passing from pedantry to obscurity (another kind of pedantry and the sin of all sins for rhetors and preachers), he devises a "tabull playne" which is, of course, incomprehensible,[7] and in the end abandons even the pretense of a public pose, descending for some ninety lines to pure abuse. As the cadences of his final taunt ring out—"For thoughe ye lyve a c. yere, ye shall dy a daw"—the promise of the opening exordium seems to mock him. "This worke devysed is / For such as do amys." Once again, he has lost.

For the reader, *Ware the Hawk* is an uncomfortable experience; although one can appreciate the intricacy of the burlesque, recognize Skelton's complete mastery of the system he parodies, smile at both the accuser and accused, the poem, like the *Bouge of Court,* raises more questions than it answers. Does Skelton (as poet rather than character) exonerate the defiler of the altar? His fictional representative may be a boor, but his concern for the place "Where Christis precious blode / Dayly offred is" is very real (179–81). What of pastoral care, judicial corruption, heresy, considerations too large, perhaps, for the incident in question, but nonetheless there? In short, there is in *Ware the Hawk* no clear moral focus; no position with which one can fully sympathize. Whether we read this curious poem as an expression of personal pique, or as a burlesque of an abused discipline, or even as a straightforward indictment, the misplaced in-

7. Henry Bradley in "Two Puzzles in Skelton," *The Academy,* 50 (1896), 83, offers a partial solution of the cryptogram. Predictably, the table is another of Skelton's self-celebrations.

tensity troubles. As he sits in Diss, Skelton may seem to have escaped the imperative of Dread's unanswered cry, but beneath the surface of these "personal" poems the old question is there. In a world like this what does one do?

PHILIP SPARROW

Philip Sparrow is perhaps Skelton's best-known poem. Countless readers have been enchanted by what C. S. Lewis calls "the lightest—the most like a bubble—of all the poems I know."[8] Yet it is one of the ironies of literary history that a good third of the poem is consistently ignored and sometimes deplored. Of its 1382 lines, only the first 833 (Jane Scrope's lament for her slain sparrow) are generally admired, while lines 834–1267 (the poet's extended commendation of Jane's beauty) and lines 1268–1382 (his reply to those who have objected on moral grounds to sections one and two) receive only passing attention. Ian Gordon remarks of the "Commendations," "It is a charming tribute, but of little importance beside the first part of the poem." "The structure of the 'Commendacions' is completely different from that of the lament and there is actually no great connection between the two parts."[9]

It seems to me that the critical silence on the third section is justified. Skelton had the disconcerting habit of attaching afterthoughts to his poems, and in this case the "adicyon made by maister Skelton" (which also appears in the *Garland of Laurel*) was probably written in 1523, some fifteen years after the composition of the main body of the poem. But with the dismissal of the middle section as "charming" (and, as Gordon implies, irrelevant), I cannot concur; for the very differences which separate it from the preceding 833 lines and lead Gordon, among others, to question its

8. *English Literature in the Sixteenth Century*, p. 138.
9. *John Skelton, Poet Laureate*, pp. 74, 131–32.

relevancy seem to me to provide the key to the poem's total meaning. Briefly, I see *Philip Sparrow* as a comparative study of innocence and experience, built around the contrasting reactions of its two personae to a single event, the death of the title figure. If we read only for the Skelton "whimsicality" celebrated by Robert Graves ("What could be dafter / Than John Skelton's laughter"), C. S. Lewis' partial encomium will seem wholly adequate; but the lightness which captivates Lewis is a single strain in a poem so complex that the resources of several disciplines are necessary for its interpretation.[1]

Once again Skelton builds his poem on the conventions of rhetoric. In *Ware the Hawk* the dramatic and the rhetorical are obviously incongruous, and a reader with no formal

---

1. This section has appeared in another form in *Studia Neophilologica, 34,* No. 2 (1962), 216–38. In *Philip Sparrow* the evidence that Skelton not only knew rhetoric but wrote with the rhetorical vocabulary in the forefront of his consciousness is overwhelming. As Edwards and Salter note (*Bibliotheca Historica*, p. xxxix), the leisurely examination of Jane's anatomy in lines 998–1193 is a direct imitation of de Vinsauf's first descriptio; and when the girl turns to curse Gib the Cat, she prefaces her outburst with a citation of the proper figure, exclamatio: "vengeaunce I aske and crye, / By way of *exclamacyon*" (273–74). Again, when she concludes her recital of the Troilus and Cresseide legend by summarizing the consequences of their actions, she points to the rhetorical ploy involved, conclusio: "Thus in *conclusyon* / She brought him in abusyon." (Italics are mine.) The most obvious instance of Skelton's conscious use of rhetoric is Jane's capsule recapitulation of the Punic War at line 668: "How Scipion dyd wake / The cytye of Cartage, / Which by his unmerciful rage / He bete down to the grounde." These four lines translate the very *circuitio* offered as an example in the *Ad herennium* (4.32.43): "Circumitio est oratio rem simplicem adsumpta circumscribens elocutione, hoc pacto: 'Scipionis providentia Kartaginis opes fregit'" (ed. Harry Caplan, Cambridge, Mass., 1954, p. 336). Since the unknown author of this most popular of rhetorical manuals makes a point of the originality of his examples (as opposed to other rhetoricians who plundered the poets), it seems clear that Skelton either wrote with the document by his side or had committed it to memory.

rhetorical training can respond fully to the humor. In *Philip Sparrow* Skelton makes more delicate discriminations, which can only be articulated against the background of a finely graduated formal system, and the reader must bring the system to the poem. As Skelton comes to see a relationship between the difficulty of making moral distinctions and the inadequacy of language, the index of innocence becomes verbal. Conveniently, the rhetoric of his day provides him with formulae to measure that index. The dissociation of rhetorical method from the organic theory which gave it relevance engendered many curiosities. In the *De inventione,* Cicero lists the personal attributes (characteristics) which could legitimately be cited either to support or discredit testimony: "Omnes res argumentando confirmantur aut ex eo quod personis aut ex eo quod negotiis est attributum. Ac personis has res attributas putamus: nomen, naturam, victum, fortunam, habitum, affectionem, studia consilia, facta, casus, orationes."[2] What is to Cicero one more area for legal argument becomes in medieval poetics a hard and fast rule of characterization. Both Marbodus in his *De ornamentis verbis*[3] and Matthew de Vendôme in his *Ars versificatoria*[4] advise aspiring authors to keep before them the natural characteristics of Cicero; John of Garland in the sixth chapter of his *Poetria*[5] provides a list of the same—with illustrations; and Geoffrey de Vinsauf's descriptio's became authoritative models.

The doctrine of the three styles (high, middle, plain) underwent a similar transformation. Where Cicero had

---

2. 1.24.34 (p. 70). "All propositions are supported in argument by attributes of persons or of actions. We hold the following to be the attributes of persons: name, nature, manner of life, fortune, habit, feeling, interests, purposes, achievements, accidents, speeches made."

3. Migne, *Patrologia Latina,* CLXXI, cols. 1687–92.

4. Edmond Faral, *Les Arts poétiques du XIIième et du XIIIième siècle* (Paris, 1924), pp. 118–19.

5. For text see *Romanische Forschungen, 13* (1902), 893–965.

seen them in relation to the efforts of the orator (the "plain" for presenting evidence, the "middle" for gaining the ear of the audience, and the "high" for swaying the audience),[6] they became in the poetry manuals of the twelfth and thirteenth centuries a means of indicating social norms. Atkins writes, "Classical doctrine had distinguished three main styles . . . which were differentiated . . . by their degrees of ornamentation. . . . By this date [the twelfth century] a new and strange meaning was often given to these terms. The distinctions were said to rest on the social dignity of the personages or subject matter concerned";[7] and goes on to note that of the sixty-four figures described in the *Ad herennium,* the ten tropes or "difficult ornaments" (*ornatus difficilis*) were allowed only to the high style, while poets were forced in the middle and plain registers to limp along with the fifty-four figures of speech (*verborum*) and thought (*sententiarum*). In short, by the thirteenth century, a hardening of the rhetorical arteries had combined with an imperfect understanding of Horace's doctrine of "decorum" to produce a highly stylized art of characterization. Tropes, not clothes, made the man (or woman) in the world of medieval poetic.[8] Through the manipulation of this poetic Skelton will create in a context of artificiality and innuendo, a personality whose

6. *Orator,* XXI, 69.
7. *English Literary History: The Medieval Phase,* p. 107.
8. Thus de Vinsauf writes: "Et tales recipiunt appellationes ratione personarum vel rerum de quibus fit tractatus. Quando enim de generalibus personis vel rebus tractatur, tunc es stylus grandiloquus; quando de humilibus, humilis; quando de mediocribus, mediocris." "The styles receive such names from a consideration of the persons and things with which the style is associated. When the style is associated with universal things or persons, then the style is lofty; when it is associated with low persons or things, then the style is low; when it is associated with middle persons or things, the style is the middle style." (Faral, *Les Arts poétiques,* p. 312). He goes on to stress the importance of consistency: "consideratum est ut stylum materiae non variemus, id est ut de grandiloquo stylo non descendamus ad humilem." "We must be careful

innocence and artlessness are overwhelming. In many ways, it will be his finest effort.

In the first section, Skelton's strategy is largely negative. From the opening interrogatio,

> *Pla ce bo*
> Who is there who?
> *Di le xi.*
> Dame Margery;
> Fa, re, my, my,
> Wherfore and why, why?
> For the sowle of Philip Sparowe
> That was late slayn at Carowe,   [1–8]

the fifteenth-century reader would expect (1) a parody of the Mass in the Goliardic tradition, (2) a play on the phallic possibilities of the sparrow in the tradition of Catullus and Ovid. As Skelton presents her, however, Jane is dramatically ignorant of either tradition, and the power of her monologue will depend on the disparity between the reader's (potential) sophistication and her naïveté. The possibility of blasphemy never occurs to her, nor, after the first hundred lines, to us. Although Jane does chant a Mass for Philip, she does not parody the service. Gordon, who has examined the services she draws upon—*Officium Defunctorum* (Breviary), 1–386, *Missa pro Defunctis* (Missal), 387–512, *Absolutio Super Tomulum* (Missal), 513–70, *Officium Defunctorum* (Breviary), 571–602[9]—notes the fidelity of her borrowings and the absence of parody:

---

not to vary the style of our matter lest from the lofty style we descend to the low." (Faral, *Les Arts poétiques,* p. 315). The initial section then is a *notatio* (character portrayal) and behind the girl's every word stands the poet, bound by the twin laws of decorum and consistency to put into her mouth a certain kind of rhetoric.

9. *John Skelton, Poet Laureate,* p. 132. Gordon also cites the *Ordo Commendationis Animae,* or "Commendations," as the basis of the

> The borrowed passages run in pairs—in every case an antiphon followed by the first lines of the following psalm, the whole rigidly keeping to the order in the Office—and never, strange though it appears, once parodying it, though the temptation to parody . . . was obvious enough.[1]

From the opening lines the only departure from orthodoxy is the service itself, and if this assumes a belief in the immortality of the animal soul, her youth and sincerity (it is *in*sincerity that characterizes the parodies) would seem to absolve her from the charge of heresy.

Although Skelton never allows us to question the reality of Jane's sorrow, he does undercut its significance. Lewis calls *Philip Sparrow* "our first great poem of childhood."[2] Jane *is* a child, and her perspective is childlike (but not childish); if Skelton is to succeed, he must allow his reader to be simultaneously condescending and sympathetic; for like the persona of *Ware the Hawk* she will bring the entire universe to bear on her problem, and where he offends, she must charm.

She begins in the best elegiac style with a demonstratio, "When I remember agayn / How mi Philyp was slayn" (17–18), which leads to a characteristically hyperbolic exclamatio: "I syghed and I sobbed, / For that I was robbed / Of my sparowes lyfe, / O mayden, wydow, and wyfe / Of what estate ye be, / Of hye or lowe degre, / Great sorowe than ye myght se, / And lerne to wepe at me!" (50–57). In these early lines the relationship between the figures is logical, even natural; recollection triggers reaction and the sense of formality is minimal. We hear echoes from medieval

---

second section; but this service presents a special problem to be considered later.

1. Ibid., p. 125.
2. *English Literature in the Sixteenth Century*, p. 138.

romance and even Marian lament;[3] but we feel that the
allusiveness of her complaint is accidental or unconscious
or somehow not her own, and it is the hyperbole of it all
rather than the erudition that captivates even as it amuses.
But at line 67 the comfortable pattern of demonstratio-
exclamatio is broken by the first of a series of Skeltonic lists
that are, in effect, formal digressio's: Jane prays that Philip's
soul may be saved from

> the marees deepe
> Of Acherontes well,
> That is a flode of hell;
> And from the great Pluto,
> The prynce of endles wo;
> And from foule Alecto,

and from a score of other horrors that fill the next fifteen
lines. What begins as a petition to Jesus becomes an ency-
clopedic recital of the mythology of the underworld, and it
is difficult (for both speaker and reader) to return at line
114 to tearful reminiscence. For some 150 lines, the alternation of demonstratio-exclamatio is once again regular; but
at line 273 a cry for vengeance "on all the hole nacyon / Of
cattes" grows into a wonderfully imaginative catalogue of
tortures:

> Of Inde the gredy grypes
> Myght tere out all thy trypes!
> Of Arcady the beares
> Might plucke awaye thynes eares!
> The wylde wolfe Lyacon
> Byte asondre thy backe bone!   [307–12]

---

3. " 'So my soon is bobbid / & of his lif robbid' / forsooth than
I sobbid, / Veryfying the wordis she seid to me. / Who cannot wepe
may lerne at thee." From *Religious Lyrics of the XVth Century*, ed.
Carleton Brown (Oxford, 1938), p. 18.

and it is with a distinct shock that we come back at line 323
to the inspiration of this impressive performance:

> Was never byrde in cage
> More gentle of corage.

What is happening is clear. Skelton is using a rhetorical
pattern to point up the central paradox of this section—a
genuine sorrow which cannot, however, be sustained. Although Jane's affection for Philip can hardly be questioned,
the natural recuperative powers of childhood will not allow
her an extended period of mourning. She is still very much
alive, very much enchanted with the wonders of the vital
world she lives in, and, as the poem develops, it becomes
more and more difficult for her to return from her excursions
(or digressions) into life to her self-imposed preoccupation
with the dead.[4] Her difficulty is also the reader's difficulty.
Trained to read "figuratively," he will recognize the demonstratio-exclamatio pattern and fall into its comfortable
rhythm. The catalogues will break that rhythm and force
him to construct a new pattern. In order to retain control of
the reading experience, he must *place* this additional
rhetorical component; and the name of the figure in question (digressio) will help him to see in its appearance and
gradual ascendancy a comment on the figures it supersedes.
The very demonstratio's she evokes to feed her sorrow defeat
her, for sorrow can hardly be sustained in the face of such
scenes as this:

> Sometyme he wolde gaspe
> Whan he sawe a waspe;

---

4. Edwards' (*Skelton*, p. 108) comment on this tension is especially
fine: "while the vespers are murmured around her, Jane's attention
flickers back over her memories . . . with all the vivid inconsequences
of her girlish mind until, mysteriously, the elegy becomes transmitted
into its opposite—a paean to life, its inexplicable loveliness."

> A fly or a gnat,
> He wolde flye at that
> And prytely he wold pant
> Whan he saw an ant;
> Lord, how he wolde pry
> After the butterfly!
> Lorde, how he wolde hop
> After the gressop!   [128–37]

The fact that Jane is now the natural rhetorician whose verbal gestures are the inadequate signs of an emotional reality, and now the sophist who offers to her audience endless exercises in amplificatio, tells us more about her than do her own statements and explanations. It is in the effort to understand the rhetorical movement of the poem that the reader comes to understand its heroine.

As her dirge continues, Jane returns to Philip only as a pretext for another digression. At line 387 she calls upon "all manner of byrdes in your kynd" to "wepe with me" and presides, for one hundred lines, over a Bird-Mass in which the solemnity of the occasion is lost in the vivacity of a virtuoso performance. This one large digressio contains a host of smaller ones as the girl enlivens her assignments to the feathered clerics with a little unnatural natural history:

> Chaunteclere, our coke,
> Must tell what is of the clocke
> By the astrology
> That he hath naturally
> Conceyved and cought
> And was never tought
> By Albumazar
> The astronomer,
> Nor by Ptholemy
> Prince of astronomy,
> Nor yet by Haly.   [495–505]

And at line 614 the necessity of an epitaph and Jane's admitted ignorance of "Elyconys well / Where the Muses dwell" lead to a 150-line recital of the literature she *does* know, a delightful collection of myth and folk tales:

> of the Wyfe of Bath
> That worketh moch scath
> When her tale is tolde
> Among huswyves bolde.   [618–21]

> of the love so hote
> That made Troylus to dote
> Upon fayre Cressyde,
> And what they wrote and sayd.   [677–80]

> the fable
> Of Penelope most stable.   [724–25]

> of great Assuerus,
> And of Vesca his queene,
> Whom he forsoke with teene
> And of Hester his other wyfe,
> With whom he ledd a plesaunt life.   [740–44]

These are an especially attractive illustration of what Skelton can do with the Skeltonic. By eschewing the feminine rhymes which go with the verse form in his flytings, Skelton draws attention to the couplets. In this way the Wife of Bath is delineated by the four rhyme words, "Bath," "scath," "tolde," "bolde," and Troilus and Cresseid by "hote" and "dote." At the same time the unusual pattern of run-on lines makes the basic unit of the passage (what the reader takes in between visual breaths) the capsule narrative itself rather than the line as in *Colin Clout* and *Why Come Ye Not to Court?;* and the closing line of each unit is somewhat fuller than its antecedents, forcing the reader to pause and consider what he has read. The end result of these effects is the characteriza-

tion of the speaker who becomes identified with the Ogden
Nash-like jingle of the rhymes (Bath, scath) and the charm-
ingly simplistic reduction of complex emotional and narrative conflicts (hote, dote). In order to provide a rhyme for
her couplet at line 744, Jane obviously seizes on the first
filler line that comes to mind ("With whom he ledd a
plesaunt life"), producing the kind of emphatic doggerel
Skelton so easily avoids. In any other context "a plesaunt
life" would be anticlimactic or bathetic or even suggestive;
here we smile as literary and social sophistication fall before
the naïveté of an innocent mind.

To appreciate *Philip Sparrow* one must recognize the
effort of will Skelton exercises in making the first 833 lines
Jane's. (Imagine, if you will, Marlowe writing both parts of
Hero and Leander.) The poem has been misread because
the girl has been denied her own opinions. When she comments critically on Gower, Chaucer, and Lydgate, literary
historians assume that it is Skelton who speaks with all the
authority of his profession; when she reflects on that medieval commonplace, mutability ("Of fortune this the chaunce
/ Standeth on varyaunce / ... No man can be sure / Allway
to have pleasure," 366–67, 370–71), we are to assume that
the poet thus indicates his philosophical position. Skelton
may or may not share Jane's opinion of the English poets
(lines 393–448 of the *Garland of Laurel* suggest that he
does), and he certainly is concerned with mutability; but as
these passages appear in the poem, they flow naturally from
the character of his persona as he has created it. Jane obviously delivers her critical clichés by rote, as a child might,
and when she supports her musings on mutability by citing
her own "tragedy" as an example, it is not difficult to see the
poet at work, skillfully (though not maliciously) pointing
up a childlike lack of proportion. Each block of digressive
material is longer than the preceding block; the connection
between them and the lament for Philip Sparrow becomes

more and more tenuous, and when Jane reaches the "turn" in her elegy and commends Philip's soul to God, we know that sorrow has passed:

> But whereto shuld I
> Longer morne or crye?
> To Jupyter I call
> Of heven emperyall,
> That Phyllyp may fly
> Above the starry sky.   [594–99]

In the final two hundred lines of her monologue, it is the technical problem of fashioning an epitaph that concerns Jane; and the rhetoric is, as might be expected, external to her as a thinking and feeling being. The entire section is a complex *expolitio*, the most elaborate of the amplificatory figures in which variations on a single theme are supported by *exempla*, reasons, illustrations, and framed by a formal introduction and conclusion. Here the theme is the inexpressibility *topos*, introduced by Jane at line 605:

> An epytaphe I wold have
> For Phyllyppes grave:
> But for I am a mayde,
> Tymerous, halfe afrayde,
> That never yet asayde
> Of Elyconys well,
> Where the Muses dwell.

This simple admission of ignorance is followed by the lengthy *digressio* noted above in which each myth or tale she refers to is, in a negative way, an example of the kind of literature to which she *cannot* refer. At line 754 the original declaration is rephrased,

> Yet I am nothing sped,
> And can but lyteil skyll,

and supported by an amazing catalogue of the authors unknown to her:

> Of Ovyd or Virgyll,
> Or of Plutharke,
> Or Frauncys Petrarke,
> Alcheus or Sapho,
> Or such other poetes mo,
> As Linus and Homerus,
> Euphorion and Theocritus,
> Anacreon and Arion,
> Sophocles and Philemon,
> Pyndarus and Symonides,
> Philistion and Phorocides;
> These poetes of auncyente,
> They ar to diffuse for me.   [756–68]

A third statement of self-disparagement,

> For, as I tofore have sayd,
> I am but a yong mayd,
> And cannot in effect
> My style as yet direct,   [769–72]

precedes an indictment of the English language as the source
(or in terms of the expolitio, the reason) for her difficulty:

> Our natural tong is rude,
> And hard to be enneude
> With pullysshed termes lusty . . .   [774–76]

> I wot not where to fynd
> Termes to serve my mynde.   [782–83]

This, in turn, suggests a survey of English poetry and a recital
of the critical clichés of the day—"Gowers Englysh is olde,"
"Chaucer, that famus clerke, / His termes were not darke,"
"Johnn Lydgate / Wryteth after an hyer rate" (784, 800–01,
804–05). With the word "Wherefore" in line 813, Jane

formally concludes the expolitio and offers a final variation
of the basic assertion:

> Wherefore hold me excused
> If I have not well perused
> Myne Englyssh halfe abused;
> Though it be refused,
> In worth I shall it take,
> And fewer wordes make.   [813–18]

For the reader, Jane's expolitio is simultaneously an indication of her recovery from the shock of Philip's death, and a
true statement of her intellectual limitations as they are
mirrored in, indeed *proven by,* her stylistic limitations; it
seals his attitude toward her. That attitude is, I think, compounded, in equal parts, of affection and condescension. As
her exclamations lose contact with their supposed inspiration (the death of Philip), we fasten on them as relevant to
what becomes the poem's real inspiration, the girl herself.
We accept her stories, her judgments, her reflections, not
because they tell us anything about birds, or myths, or poets
or language, but because they are hers. In other words, while
we reject her view of the situation as limited, we believe in
her completely. At the same time, our understanding of her
allows us to patronize her. We are so much wiser, so much
more mature; unlike her, we *do* have terms to serve our
mind; our English is aureate rather than rude; and we are
aware, as she is not, of the sexual implications of her
demonstratio's:

> And many tymes and ofte
> Betwene my brestes softe
> It wolde lye and rest.   [124–26]

> Wherwith he wolde make
> Me often for to wake,
> And for to take him in
> Upon my naked skyn.   [164–67]

> my byrde so fayre,
> That was wont to repayre
> And go in at my spayre,
> And crepe in at my gore
> Of my gowne before,
> Flyckerynge with his wynges!   [343–48]

It is perhaps difficult to read these lines without questioning her innocence, but we make the necessary effort and accept her demurral:

> What though he crept so lowe?
> It was no hurt, I trowe,
> He dyd nothynge perde
> But syt upon my kne:
> Phyllyp, though he were nyse,
> In him it was no vyse.   [169–74]

It is, however, a conscious effort, and Skelton insists that we make it. If his poem is to succeed, we must be continually aware of the distance between what Jane in her innocence would intend and what we would interpolate. As its first section ends, *Philip Sparrow* may seem little more than an invitation to the luxury of condescension: we smile gently at a grief which is disproportionate and at protests which are at least naive. But if we have forgotten Catullus' sparrow and the Venus masses of the Goliardic tradition, Skelton has not; and at line 834 he enters his own poem to disturb our self-satisfaction, to suggest that the wonderful directness of a girl who can wrap her being about a sparrow and believe momentarily in the immutability of her affections is infinitely superior to the triumphs of sophistication.

It would not be exaggeration to say that every man who reads Jane's lament falls in love with her. Skelton takes great care to establish a relationship between his heroine and her audience, but in the second half of the poem the focus is narrowed as her creator becomes our surrogate. C. S. Lewis writes, "The lady who is lamenting her bird may not really have been a child. . . . But it is as a child she is imagined in the poem—a little girl to whom the bird's death is a tragedy and who though well read in romances, finds Lydgate beyond her, and has 'little skill in Ovid or Virgil.' . . . Skelton is not . . . ridiculing. He is at once tender and mocking—like an affectionate bachelor uncle or even a grandfather."[5] He is far too conservative; the poet's affection is anything but grandfatherly. His entrance into the poem is unheralded; he merely continues the Latin hexameters of Jane's final farewell:

> Semper erunt nitido
> Radiantia sidera coelo;
> Impressusque meo
> Pectore semper eris.   [830–33]

(There will always be gleaming stars in the brilliant sky and you will always be engraven in my heart.)

> Per me laurigerum
> Britonum Skeltonida vatem
> Haec cecinesse licet
> Ficta sub imagine texta . . .   [834–37]
> Candida Nais erat,
> Formosior ista Joanna est;
> Docta Corinna fuit,
> Sed magis ista sapit.   [840–43]

(I Skelton, laureated, Poet of Britain, have been permitted to sing this under an imaginary likeness . . . Nais was dazzling, but this Jane is more beautiful, Corinna was learned but this Jane knows more.)

5. English Literature in the Sixteenth Century, p. 138.

Trumpets, however, are unnecessary. One realizes immediately that the style and tone of lines 826–33 and 834–43 are antithetical; from the moment he announces at line 872 "my pen hath enbybed / With the aureat droppes," artificiality and innuendo replace the ingenuousness of the first section, and in Skelton's characteristic fashion, the drama of *Philip Sparrow* is a drama of style.

Jane describes her epitaph for Philip as "Latyne playne and lyght," and in fact her entire monologue is conspicuously free of the studied stylization of aureate rhetoric. W. G. Crane divides rhetorical figures into three groups:

> The first consists of the figures of thought, which are based upon the process of dialectical investigation. . . . The second group consists of a number of varieties of exclamation, interrogation, and description, all of which direct their appeal to the emotions. The third class comprises about one hundred and fifty figures of a somewhat mechanical nature, produced by alteration from normal spelling, diction or syntax.[6]

If we retain Crane's classification but shift our focus from the figures themselves to the audience which responds to them, we shall be able almost to graph Skelton's method in *Philip Sparrow*. All rhetoric, like all art, is studied; artlessness is an illusory and hard-won effect. It is to Crane's second group that the poet who would create this illusion must turn; for "the exclamations, interrogations, and descriptions which appeal to the emotion" will seduce the reader into an intellectual languor, while the process of dialectic and the precision of syntactical configurations will make him very conscious of the effort behind the effect. In other words, one kind of rhetoric calls attention to itself, the other is in hiding.

Jane's monologue is a triumph of emotional rhetoric. Al-

6. *Wit and Rhetoric in the Renaissance* (New York, 1937), pp. 59–60.

though the educated reader is aware of its formality (the service itself is a formal situation), he would attribute the familiar apostrophes and the echoes of other, more stylized laments to the poet who stands behind his heroine and who speaks through her, but not with her, to his audience. (Skelton admits himself that it is he who writes this first section "under a feigned likeness." This is more than an admission of literary "unreality," for it complicates the relationship between the two voices in the poem which are now in some ways one.) Indeed, she seems uncomfortable with the literary machinery her situation requires (note her repeated declarations of incompetence, conventional, but in this case "sincere"), and is certainly unaware of either the suggestiveness of her exclamatio's or her own very real appeal. The poet, on the other hand, parades his rhetoric almost flamboyantly. When he announces that Nais is dazzling but Jane is more beautiful, Corinna learned, but Jane wiser still, he deliberately calls up the traditional body of love poetry in which such comparisons are made again and again. While in Jane's monologue the frequency and occurrence of the various figures exist in a describable relationship with her emotional development, the rhetorical pattern in the "Commendations" is static. The poet, as the master rhetorician, is always in control as he declares, "Now will I enterprise / Thorow the grace dyvyne / Of the Muses nyne / Her beauty to commende" (856–59). Exclamatio's in the form of tag lines from the *Ordo Commendationis Animae* follow a set refrain at regular intervals and call attention to themselves rather than springing (or seeming to spring) naturally from the poem:

> For this most goodly floure,
> This blossome of fresshe coulour,
> So Jupiter me socour.
> She floryssheth new and new

In bewte and vertew:
Hac claritate gemina
O gloriosa foemina
Retribue servo tuo, vivifica me!   [893–900]

This passage, with variations in the Latin, is repeated eleven
times in less than two hundred lines and establishes *pronominatio* (*antonomasia*) as the dominant figure of the section. Except for an extended attack on Envy (which, I shall
argue, is not digressive), the poet proceeds in an orderly
fashion with his markedly conventional descriptio, carefully
noting the lips as red as cherries, the skin as white as a swan,
the hands soft as silk, the hair golden as the sun. It is the
self-consciousness of his art which impresses, as we involun-
tarily contrast him with his creation. In other words, the
poet presents himself as everything Jane is not, cultivated,
learned, mature, aureate; and since we have come to understand the distance between ourselves and the girl in exactly
these terms, we feel a kinship with him. But as the poem
proceeds, our identification with this aureate voice will make
us increasingly uncomfortable.

The distance between them is obvious, even to the reader
who knows nothing of tropes and schemes, although the
social and intellectual codifications of tropes and schemes
will give that distance meaning. Characterization through
style is possible in any literature; one needs only the idiom
of conversation and a formal (in this case, aureate) vocabulary that can be parodied. Skelton is able, in addition, to call
on the resources of a system that measures style almost
mathematically. Of the 126 instances of twenty-two figures
in the first 833 lines, forty-five of these (or nearly forty per
cent) involve what de Vinsauf lists as methods of amplification—*circuitio, conformatio, correctio, digressio, exclamatio,
expolitio,* and *interpretatio.* Ten more instances (*conduplicatio* and *repetitio*) involve purely mechanical repetitions; and

a majority of the thirty-nine exempla are found in the cata-
logue-like digressio's of the last 300 lines. Over 75 per cent
of the figures in this first section are either repetitious or
amplificatory. There are only seven instances (less than six
per cent) of the "difficult figures." The statistics reverse themselves in the commendations: of 110 instances of twenty-two
figures, there are fifty-two (nearly 50 per cent) of the "difficult" ornaments (*denominatio, intellectio, pronominatio,
simile, superlatio*); conspicuously absent are the figures of
repetition (*conduplicatio, repetitio*) and amplification (*conformatio, digressio, interpretatio*) which dominate the earlier
section. The comparison, however, is more than statistical;
it becomes moral. When Jane repeatedly proclaims her
ignorance of rhetoric ("I wot not where to fynd / Termes
to serve my mynde"), a stale verbal formula (what Curtius
calls the modesty topos) seems fresh and disarmingly sincere,
because her speech *is* demonstrably free of syntactical in-
version, simile, word play; but when the poet writes, "My
pen it is unable, / My hand it is unstable, / My reson rude
and dull," the humility is a pose, and in the context of her
simplicity, offensive.[7]

The "Commendations" is one long essay on contrasting
sensibilities, as the reader is offered Jane's monologue from
a new perspective which is in comparison unattractive.
While Skelton pointedly avoids parodying the service in his
first section, he risks blasphemy in this one. The *Ordo Commendationis Animae,* the commendation of the soul to God,
becomes a courtly lyric in which the poet is the soul, "Now
wyll I enterpryse, / Thorow the grace dyvyne / Of the
Muses nyne, / Her beautye to commende," and Jane his
God, "O gloriosa foemina, / Quomodo dilexi legem tuam,
domina!" (1113–14). Every line is a potential double en-

7. For a more detailed statistical analysis see my "Aspects of Rhetorical Analysis: Skelton's *Philip Sparrow," Studia Neophilologica, 34,*
No. 2 (1962), 216–38.

tendre. Lines from Psalm 118, which examines the relationship between the law of God and man, are placed to suggest
a quite different relationship. "Deficit in salutatione tua
anima mea," the psalmist cries, acknowledging his dependence on the Grace of God. In *Philip Sparrow*, this same
petition (1090) is addressed to another deity who offers a
grace that is hardly spiritual:

> Who so lyst beholde,
> It maketh lovers bolde
> To her to sewe for *grace*,
> Her favoure to purchase;
> The sker upon her chyn,
> Enhached on her fayre skyn,
> Whyter than the swan,
> It wold make any man
> To forget *deadly syn*
> Her favour to wyn.
>
> [1073–82, emphasis mine]

The liturgical framework which, in the first section, under-
lines Jane's virtual humanization of her sparrow is here the
vehicle for a passion that can only be expressed through
innuendo.[8]

In the same way, the girl's demonstratio's are echoed
and even parodied; in his fantasy the poet replaces the sparrow, vicariously enjoying the no longer innocent delights
of their play. Jane's artless

> my byrde so fayre,
> ... was wont to repayre,
> And go in at my spayre,

---

8. Edwards (*Skelton*, p. 110) was the first to note that "nothing
could disguise the fact that the whole of the *Commendations* were a
supreme blasphemy. It was not only that Jane replaced the soul of the
defunct; more than that, she was quite literally deified."

> And crepe in at my gore,
> Of my gowne before,
> Flyckerynge with his wynges, [343–48]

is here a studied compliment:

> Her kyrtell so goodly lased,
> And under that is brased
> Such plasures that I may
> Neyther wryte nor say. [1194–97]

The "modest hiatus" is, of course, conventional, but with Jane's childishly frank outbursts ringing in our ears, it is not only trite, but faintly prurient.[1] The finality with which the girl's innocence has been established in Part One makes it difficult for us to accept her as even the passive object of a passion that is not at all innocent; and the careful patterning of detail forces us to do just that: if Jane recalls a daily scene,

> With his byll betwene my lippes;
> It was my prety Phyppes!
> Many a prety Kusse
> Had I of his sweet musse, [359–62]

the poet imagines an assignation:

> Her lyppes soft and mery
> Emblomed lyke the chery,
> It were an hevenly blysse
> Her sugred mouth to kysse. [1037–40]

Her disclaimers are natural:

> Phyllyp, though he were nyse,
> In him it was no vyse;

---

1. This passage is also a form of *praecisio* or *aposiopesis*, the technique of significant omission, i.e., insinuation, a figure of which the poet seems especially fond.

> Phyllyp had leve to go
> To pyke my lytell too;
> Phyllip myght be bolde
> And do what he wolde;   [173–78]

His are forced and coy:

> To tell you what conceyte
> I had than in a tryce,
> The matter were to nyse
> And yet there was no vyce,
> Nor yet no villany
> But only fantasy.   [1130–35]

The parallels are innumerable, and their effect is always the same, to force upon the reader an even greater awareness of the distance that separates them. He can never again capture the simplicity she brings to her every day. He can never express himself with the assurance and singlemindedness she commands. Experience has bound him to fetters of flesh, and sophistication has left him with only irony and innuendo. In the end it is almost obscene when Jane's plaintive cry, "Alas, my heart it stynges / Remembrynge prety thynges!" is absorbed into the sexual fantasies of a literary lover: "Yet though I wryte not with ynke / No man can let me thynke, / For thought hath lyberte, / Thought is franke and fre" (1199–1201).

When all is said and done, however, his affection is as real as hers, and perhaps even more poignant. From time to time the elaborate screen of convention the poet builds around him falls away and reveals a shrillness which belies his characteristic composure. His response (902–69) to a suggestion that his interest in the girl is less than impersonal is so overlong and overwrought that it becomes an admission of "guilt." And as his section of the poem closes, a final attempt at self-justification, a *subiectio,* is surprisingly non-aureate, a trifle desperate, and, I think, sincere:

> I have not offended, I trust,
> If it be sadly dyscust   [1249–50]
>
> Because I have wrytten and sayd
> Honour of this fayre mayd;
> Wherefore shulde I be blamed,
> That I Jane have named,
> And famously proclamed?
> She is worthy to be enrolde
> With letters of golde.   [1253–59]

Curiously enough, it is in the most artificial of contexts that an undercurrent of real emotion is most clearly heard. When the poet exclaims, "Clamavi in toto corde, exaudi me" (1192), the anguish rings true, despite the Chinese box-like structure of a parody (of the liturgy) within a parody (of Jane). "Servus tuus sum ego," I am your servant, he admits (1030), and we believe him. In terms of the dramatic crux of the poem, this is still another indication of the inverse relationship between maturity and the possibility of direct self-expression; but when we recall that Jane's "artless" lament is no less the result of complex rhetorical configurations, and is itself the product of this convention-bound mind, it becomes impossible to continue, since the terms of our comparison shift, Chaucer-like, before our eyes. The poet's admission that both parts of the poem are his (*Ficta sub imagine texta*) becomes a problem for the reader who is continually invited to distinguish between them. What is innocence, and can only the disillusioned recognize it? What is simplicity, and can only the artful produce its similitude? In *Philip Sparrow* Skelton is busily exploring the limits of his art, extending the intuition of "Knolege, aquayntance, resort"; language itself is incapable of mirroring reality; it is only through the juxtaposition of contrasting degrees of artificiality that man can suggest what *is*, or hint at what *may* be.

And the poet himself is aware of all this, even as he spins out his interminable compliment. It is Jane who has always fascinated, but to understand the poem is to realize that the truly complex personality is her (fictional) creator. For since it is he who has so painstakingly constructed the first section, he surely recognizes the hopelessness of his love. While Jane is capable of firing his passion, her monologue reveals her incapable of responding to it. When she presses his hand and his heart leaps ("Wherwyth my hand she strayned, / Lorde, how I was payned! / Unneth I me refrayned"), her heart no doubt beats on with a crushing regularity, and he is left to imagine a scene that will never take place:

> Unneth I me refrayned   [1124]
>
> Enbrasynge therwithall
> Her goodly myddell small
> With sydes longe and streyte;
> To tell you what conceyte
> I had than in a tryce,
> The matter were to nyse,   [1127–32]

There is no resolution as the poem ends, because, as the poet knows only too well, no resolution is possible. Amidst the hyperbole of the mock curses in the third section, Skelton re-establishes momentarily the poignancy of the first two; the poem, laments its author, is so complex and so delicate that even the girl herself misunderstands, or understands too well:

> Alas, that goodly mayd,
> Why shuld she be afrayde?

> Why shuld she take shame
> That her goodly name,
> Honorably reported,
> Sholde be set and sorted,
> To be matriculate
> With ladyes of estate?   [1282–89]

Alas, indeed, for all fallings away from innocence, for all impossible loves, for all misunderstandings and failures of communication. We leave the poet, as we left Dread, with little more than a verbal command of his situation. In retirement, Skelton improvises another variation on a constant theme—the insoluble dilemma of a world whose complexities do not yield to man's attempt at analysis. Henry VIII will soon recall him to the activity of London where a solution becomes a necessity.

Something of his temper at the time of his return can be seen in "Calliope," written, Pollet suggests, in 1513.[2] It is Skelton's answer to the question, "Why were [wear] ye *Calliope* embrawdred with letters of golde?"[3] In the first of three stanzas Skelton replies simply that he wears Calliope's livery because she has designated him her servant:

> Calliope,
> As ye may se
> Regent is she
>   Of poetes al
> Which gave to me
> The high degre
> Laureat to be
>   Of fame royall.   [1–8]

2. *Skelton,* p. 88.
3. Dyce, *1,* 197.

Stanza two continues in this mood as Skelton admits that it is
an act of boldness on his part to go thus attired:

> Whose name enrolde
> With silke and golde
> I dare be bolde
>   Thus for to were.
> Of her I holde
> And her housholde;
> Though I waxe olde
>   And somdele sere.   [9–16]

The lines "Though I waxe olde / And somdele sere," introduce a new note. Immortality is earned in the struggle
of the human situation, and the poet, chosen though he may
be, is nonetheless only human, and subject to all the frailties
and misfortunes which beset other men. Far from overturn-
ing the calm strength of the opening lines, the sobering
recognition of his mortal limitations only strengthens the
poet's reliance on his craft and its ultimate source. He is
grateful for the sense of purpose poetry accords him even
as he acknowledges his inevitable involvement in the
processes of an unstable world:

> Yet is she fayne,
> Voyde of disdayn
> Me to retayne
>   Her serviture:
> With her certayne
> I will remayne,
> As my soverayne
>   Moost of pleasure,
> *Maulgre touz malherueux.*   [17–25]

The final line, "Maulgre touz malherueux," "despite all un-
happiness," is an indication of the sober considerations be-

hind this little poem. Against the reassuring "certayne" in line 21 stands the specter of uncertainty, of "malherueux," of "disdayn," of age, of decay. It is to Skelton's credit as a man that he does not rationalize this specter, and it is his salvation as a poet that he seeks in his art a bridge between the appearances which surround him and the reality he believes in.

4   The Poet as Hero

WOLSEY

WHEN SKELTON LEFT LONDON in 1504, Thomas Wolsey was a chaplain in the train of Sir Richard Nanfan; when he returned in 1512 or 1513, the butcher's son was the youngest member of the King's Council; three years later he became a Cardinal, and Lord Chancellor, and by 1520 many considered him the de facto ruler of England. Through one of those curious junctures of political and literary history which sometimes threaten to make them indistinguishable, the arc of Wolsey's career was paralleled by the accelerated growth of certain tendencies which would eventually destroy Skelton's world, and at some point between 1515 and 1520 the Cardinal became for the aging poet the symbol of all that was dangerous in the contemporary scene. Not only to Skelton, but to the great families whose unofficial propagandist he was in the 1520s, Wolsey seemed to be the architect of the centralizing process that was steadily undermining their feudal position.[1]

In a society where power is concentrated and hierarchical,

---

1. Otto Gierke, *Political Theories of the Middle Ages,* trans. F. W. Maitland (Boston, 1958), writes: "Medieval theory endeavoured to establish a definite scheme descriptive of this articulation, and the graduated hierarchy of the Church served as a model for a *parallel* [italics mine] system of temporal groups. . . . But as time goes on we see that just this federalistic construction of the Social Whole was more and more exposed to attacks which proceeded from a centralizing tendency. This we may see happening first in the ecclesiastical and then in the temporal sphere" (p. 21). This is a perfect description of the danger Skelton discerns in Wolsey's rise to power.

spiritual and political allegiance become one, and in the
process of absorption which almost certainly follows, the
concerns of the political, of the things of this world, become
primary. In England, a strong nationalism and a corresponding resistance to foreign intervention (which extended to the
Papacy) joined with the rise of the middle class to make
centralization, the secular state, and the crisis of the 1530s
(from our point of view) inevitable. Skelton and his patrons,
however, were not Nostradamuses, although they may accurately be described in the early decades of the century as
Jeremiahs. What they saw, and it is improbable that they
saw beyond this, was the gradual deterioration of their influence, the erosion of their traditional privileges, the circum-
scription of their spheres of action, the abandonment of
their policies, the steady influx of new men—all in all the
repudiation of their way of life; and since Henry's personal
popularity was overwhelming, they centered their resentment and animosity on the man who seemed to control him
—Wolsey, who obligingly fed their hatred by being conspicuously ubiquitous, by continually consolidating his
sources of power, by transforming the star chamber into a
throne room, by parading his pomp and circumstance before
a nobility which would see in his display a vain attempt to
obliterate the ignominy of a low birth.

As a churchman, Wolsey was no less peremptory and
autocratic than he was as Lord Chancellor: the rapidity of
his advancement bred dark rumors of betrayals and even
crimes; his confiscations of monasteries, although defensible
in administrative terms, would seem to his enemies an un-
warranted disruption of centuries of tradition; when he
"formed a liaison with 'the daughter of one Lark' "[2] the way
was open to more personal attacks, and Skelton gives us an
unforgettable if exaggerated portrait of a lecherous, glutton-

2. A. F. Pollard, *Wolsey* (London, New York, and Toronto, Long-
mans, Green, 1929), p. 306.

ous, vain (in short, worldly) cleric. And above all, the remarkable concentration of power which was repeatedly
noted by ambassadors to the English Court, must have
seemed to the nobility an open assault on the clearly defined
lines of feudal society; in Wolsey the three estates merged
in a particularly unholy alliance, as the commoner who had
become a cardinal threatened to become the "one man who
would rule the realm," replacing the allegiances of the old
system with a single allegiance. Wolsey was certainly not
the first prince of the Church in England to wield political
and ecclesiastical power, nor the first whose "virtue" was
questionable; but a disturbed and confused aristocracy, committed to monarchy and the monarch, needed a scapegoat,
and the Cardinal, ostentatious, imperious, conspicuous, was
available. Finally, history was against him; in 1517 Luther
published his theses on *Indulgences,* and by the early 1520s
the "horrible fly of heresy" was spreading throughout Europe. The assumption of authority involves the bearing of
responsibility for all ills; in the minds of his enemies, and
certainly in Skelton's poetry Wolsey becomes a kind of
antichrist, a prince of the Church whose ambitions and
spiritual aridity subvert the faith and endanger every man's
salvation.

For Skelton these troubled years brought a more personal
challenge. In 1519–20 the academic community was split
by what has become known as the Grammarians' War. The
issue was the method of Latin instruction: William Horman,
headmaster of Eton, and Robert Whittington, a disciple of
the grammarian John Stanbridge, published rival grammars
and initiated a literary quarrel that predictably descended to
personal abuse. The lines of battle are familiar to a generation once again debating the relative merits of progressive
and "preceptive" education. Whittington insists that a
mastery of fundamentals precede reading; he systematically
describes the structure of the language, supporting his rules

with examples that are often his own. Horman minimizes grammar and concentrates on the imitation of the ancients. His position is essentially Colet's:

> to understande latyn bokes, and to speke and to wryte the clene latyn . . . besyly lerne & rede good latyn authours of chosen poetes and oratours, and note wysely how they wrote and spake, and studi alway to followe them: desyring none other rules but theyr examples.[3]

Horman was seconded by William Lily, headmaster of St. Paul's and a disciple of Colet's; Whittington, by Skelton. Only a single epigram (Lily's) remains of their exchange, but it is enough to illustrate the distance which now separated the new humanists and the man whom Erasmus had praised as "England's Homer."[4] Lily closes with this line, "Doctrinam nec habes, nec es poeta,"[5] and anticipates the tag ("beastly Skelton") that was to follow the poet into the twentieth century.

Modern scholarship, however, has repeatedly demonstrated that Skelton was not at all beastly, and his rejection of humanistic values can hardly be explained as ignorance or even willfulness. What Skelton saw in the Grammarians' War (and this is documented in *Speak, Parrot*) was another front in the increasingly clear-cut struggle between those who would maintain the old ways and the world view they reflected and the new men who in their advocacy of new methods (unwittingly) repudiated that world view. M. Pollet explains that "A vrai dire, la querelle des *Vulgaria* n'était

3. From Colet's *Aeditio*, quoted in Nelson, *John Skelton, Laureate*, p. 153. Nelson's discussion of the Grammarians' War (pp. 148–57) is excellent, as is Pollet's analysis of its importance for Skelton (*John Skelton*, pp. 135–46).

4. See *Erasmus* by Preserved Smith (New York, 1923), p. 62, for a full text of Erasmus' tribute to Skelton.

5. See Dyce, *I*, xxxviii. "You would style yourself learned and a poet, but you have no learning and are not a poet."

qu'un cas particulier du conflit général engagé à la même époque autour du New Learning, un simple remous dans la grande marée de la Renaissance qui rejetait de part et d'autre les partisans du mouvement nouveau et les partisans de l'ordre établi."[6] Horman's pedagogical strictures rest on an assumption Skelton could not accept—the primacy of eloquence. In Colet's emphasis, the usefulness of the language becomes less important than its beauty. Skelton had come more and more to realize that language was man-rather than God-made and he would have regarded the attempt to canonize the stylistic characteristics of any age (especially a pagan age) as a foolish and even sinful preoccupation with the products of the human mind. His grammatical conservatism is curiously avant garde: he would maintain the rules because they provide a public (if artificial) framework which could accommodate the ever-changing elements of an imperfect medium. Intelligibility and accessibility, not elegance, are his linguistic criteria, and his repeated defense of the vernacular is far ahead of the time. Again the new emphasis on scholarship and philology would have seemed to him a reversal of the relationship between human knowledge and the knowledge of God, and he may even have seen in the humanist's claims for the civilizing potential of literature a dangerous confidence in man's ability to minimize or at least neutralize his inadequacies. There is a significant difference between Whittington's traditional "Alakke this hevy world," and Horman's more optimistic and modern, "I rejoyce in the encresse of cunnynge: that is now a dayes."[7]

Myron Gilmore writes that "medieval justifications for

6. *John Skelton*, p. 142.
7. Quoted by Pollet (*John Skelton*, p. 141). Horman's use of the phrase "now a dayes" is especially interesting as it is firmly associated with the complaint tradition which *denies* the idea of progress and the possibility of the "encresse of cunnynge."

the study of classical literature . . . were now given a new
emphasis and contained perhaps unconscious admissions of
the growth of secular tastes. All these assumptions found
concrete expression in the theories of education of the Christian humanists. The nature of man, fundamentally good although corrupted by original sin, was capable of improve-
ment by an intellectual discipline."[8] The youthful translator
of Diodorus Siculus might well have shared this faith and
would certainly have agreed with the conservative statement
of a Hawes:

> This is the costome that the poetes use,
> To tell theyr tale with al due cyrcumstaunce,
> The vylayne courage they do moche refuse
> That is boystous and rude of governaunce,
> And evermore they do to them avaunce
> Nurture, maner, and al gentylnes.
> In theyr behavynge with all semelynes.
>
> And thus the gentyll rethorycyan,
> Through the labour of his ryall clergy,
> The famous nurture orygynally began
> Oppressynge our rudenes and our foly,
> And for to governe us ryght prudently,
> The good maner encreaseth dignyte,
> And the rudenesse also inyquyte.[9]

The years, however, had brought disillusionment; when
Skelton returns to the Court, he rededicates the didactic
Speculum Principis and fashions the equally didactic *Mag-*

8. *The World of Humanism* (New York and Evanston, 1962), p.
206.
9. *The Pastime of Pleasure,* ed. W. E. Mead, p. 51, lines 1212–25.
See also lines 876 ff., "Before the lawe in a tymblynge barge / The
people fayled without parfytenes / Throughe the worlde all aboute at
large / They hadde none ordre nor no stedfastnes / Tyll rethorycyans
found Justice doubtles / Ordenynge kynges of ryghte hye dygnyte."

nificence; but his former pupil, now his monarch, is not at all responsive. In the poems of 1521–23 he is increasingly skeptical of the persuasive power of eloquence, and the pronouncements of the new humanists must have seemed naive. These of course are speculations; we cannot transform our hindsight into Skelton's perceptions. Surely, however, he would recognize in the inductive methodology of Horman's treatise the abandonment of a scholastic metaphysic which did not depend on, but ordered, the data of experience. In 1527, Bilney and Arthur (see p. 4) are reviled for failing to master the "principles silogistical," for relying on mere observation; they generalize from particulars and negatives, make no distinction between ordinary men and saints, disregard the discriminations of formal theology; in short, they turn from a given which would arrange their world for them to the deceptive solidity of the factual and their empirical reasoning. Although Skelton comes to distrust rhetoric, scholastic logic remains for him the foundation of all right-thinking precisely because it juxtaposes clearly defined intellectual categories (which are divine) on the contradictions of the human situation.

Thus Skelton places himself in a long line of philosophers and theologians, from Plato to the logical positivists, for whom reason, God's viceroy in man, is the way to truth, and rhetoric, an instrument of self-deception.[10] Of course this op-

10. Hawes furnishes a concise statement of the relationship between logic and man's efforts to make his way in a fallen world: "Who wyll take payne to folowe the trace / In this wretched worlde of trouthe and ryghtwysenes / In heven above he shall have dwellynge place / . . . So by logyke is good perceyveraunce / To devyde the good and the evyll a sondre." (*Pastime,* 11.624–27, 631–32.) The Fall is often allegorized as a surrender of the rational to the affective faculty of the soul, and fallen man's capacity for logical reasoning is seen as a reflection, however dim, of the clarity of perception he enjoyed in Paradise. See D. W. Robertson, *A Preface to Chaucer* (Princeton, 1962), pp. 69–77, and Perry Miller, *The New England Mind: The Seventeenth Century* (Boston, 1961), pp. 111 ff.

position does not apply for poets who are granted a more direct intuition than either can provide. Skelton cannot be corrupted by the secular emphasis of the new education; his fears are for others; had Bilney and Arthur submitted their minds to the discipline of reason (logic), they would not have strayed.

Inevitably, Wolsey is in the background, for it was the "progressive" Cardinal who in 1520 established a professorship of Greek at Oxford and placed the enormous weight of his prestige behind the new educational theories. In the *Replication,* Skelton interrupts his castigations of the abjurers to suggest that those who encouraged their studies must share their guilt. That Wolsey did in fact contribute ten pounds to Bilney's maintenance is a nice historical postscript to a passage whose relevance is clear without it:

> Some of you had ten pounde,
> Therwith for to be founde
> At the unyversyte,
> Employed whiche myght have be .
> Moche better other wayes.
> But, as the man sayes,
> The blynde eteth many a flye: [Heresy]
> What may be ment hereby,
> Ye may soone make construction
> With right lytell instruction;
> For it is an auncyent brute,
> Suche apple tre, suche frute.   [146–57]

By 1521, then, the pressures of history (political and intellectual) were forcing Skelton toward a final re-evaluation of the role of the poet-prophet in a fallen world, and in that year Wolsey produced and starred in a diplomatic farce which allowed the poet to polarize his many grievances. From August to November, Wolsey was at Calais, ostensibly to mediate the rival claims of Francis I of France and the

Emperor Charles V. Characteristically, the Cardinal brought with him a huge train and, for good measure, the great seal, without which much of the business of the realm went undone. Hall remarks that "duryng the continuance of the Cardinall in Calayce all writtes and patentes wer there by him sealed and no sheryffes chosen for lacke of his presence."[1] Wolsey was playing a double game, offering the Princess Mary, promised in 1517 to Francis, to the Emperor; carrying out a foreign policy that was nominally Henry's and in reality his own.

The negotiations were long and expensive, and the fiscal conservatives, who were Wolsey's natural enemies, pressed for his return. Moreover, the alliance with Charles was a questionable one in view of the advantages of indefinite vacillation. Pollard notes that the "motives of his policy puzzled his contemporaries. We have it on Sir Thomas More's authority that when the question of peace or war was discussed in council . . . 'some thought it wisdom to sit still and leave Charles and Francis alone.' "[2] It was not until December that Wolsey's motives became clear, though some would have surely guessed at them earlier; in return for England's active intervention, Charles had promised to support the Cardinal at the next Papal election,[3] and Leo X's

1. *Chronicle*, p. 627.
2. *Wolsey*, p. 125. In another context (*Henry VIII*, London, 1919) Pollard is more forceful. "No possible advantage could accrue to England from such a destruction of the balance of power; her position as mediator was only tenable so long as neither France nor Charles had the complete mastery" (p. 151).
3. Pollard, *Wolsey*, p. 126: "neither Leo X nor Sir Thomas More was aware of the special inducement which turned the scale in favour of intervention. The French, wrote Charles V's ambassador in London on 7 April 1520, 'have promised, what we might have done much better, to make Wolsey pope.' The emperor took the hint and Wolsey accepted the bait; Charles undertook at Bruges to do his best to secure Wolsey's election as pope, whenever a vacancy occurred. It came with unexpected rapidity."

unexpected death on December 2 brought Henry's secretary to Rome to press the English claim. Charles had no intention of keeping his promise, and the conclave eventually chose Cardinal Adrian of Utrecht, who had been the Emperor's tutor. But for several months the possibility of Wolsey as Pope must have seemed very real to his enemies; and to Skelton, who had for a decade watched the once hard lines of his feudal universe crumble away, the danger was not political or ecclesiastical, but universal. In the two years that follow, he will nearly equal the production of sixty, as he forges one of the most complex statements of moral and poetic responsibility in English literature.

SPEAK, PARROT, PART ONE

Nothing is more indicative of Skelton's artistic maturity than his choice of the legendary Psittacus as his fictional spokesman in 1521. He is able to draw, of course, on the tradition that begins with Ovid's lament for Corinna's Psittacus, where the parrot is presented as the master mimic, dear to his mistress, incessantly but uncomprehendingly vocal, unconcerned with, and uninvolved in, the horrors of the world. In bestiaries and encyclopedias, the bird is roughly comparable to the court jester who offers garbled scraps of wisdom in snatches of foreign tongues, an outspoken revealer of confidences, indulged because he is not responsible for his sometimes telling juxtaposition of random phrases:

> Suche shredis of sentence, strowed in the shop
> Of auncyent Aristippus and such other mo,
> I gader togyther and close in my crop.   [94–96]

> I pray you, let Parot have lyberte to speke.   [100]

And as the medieval version of the tape recorder or camera eye, he becomes a useful satiric device, the accurate but de-

tached reporter whose criticism is triggered by a purely
physiological mechanism:

Colostrum now for Parot, whyte bred and swete creme!

[84]

Mete, mete for Parot, mete, I say, how!   [104]

And finally, as a ladies' pet, he is, like Catullus' sparrow, a
convenient surrogate for a courtly poet's passion, what Jean
Lemaire de Belge calls in 1505 the Green Lover ("L'Amant
Verd").[4]

In another tradition, however, the same Parrot boasts a
genealogy which contradicts the more conventional image
of mimic-fool. As Boccaccio summarizes it, in a passage
Skelton surely knew,

> Psyttacus, son of Deucalion and Pyrrha (so Theodontius
> says) having been steeped in the learning of his grand-
> father, Prometheus, went to Ethiopia where he was
> much venerated. When he had reached a great age, he
> prayed that he might be removed from human affairs.
> Yielding to his entreaties, the gods transformed him
> into the bird which bears his name.[5]

Here, then, is a parrot who is the semidivine and immortal
heir of an heroic tradition. His grandfather, Deucalion reminds us in the *Metamorphoses,* breathed the breath of life

4. In his "Premiere Epitre de l'Amant Vert." See *Jean Lemaire de
Belge,* ed. Paul Spaak (Paris, 1926). Heiserman (*Skelton and Satire,*
p. 154) summarizes the literary Parrot's attributes: "Parrot's conventional attributes serve neatly the purpose of Skelton's poem. Parrots
command all tongues; parrots are wine-bibbers and nonsense chatterers;
parrots, being green, are symbolic of masculine potency; as such, they
are exempt from decay." Heiserman surveys Parrot's literary history
before 1521 on pp. 174–77.

5. *Genealogia Deorum,* Book IV, chap. xlix. The translation is Nelson's (*John Skelton, Laureate,* p. 183); Nelson was the first to connect
the legend with Skelton's hero.

into clay, "animas formatae infundere terrae"⁶ (the analogy
with Christ does not escape Skelton), and Deucalion himself, who with his wife survives the flood, saved the human
race through faith and action. English tradition places the
metamorphosed Psittacus in Paradise, where he is, like his
less respectable Ovidian counterpart, detached from the
vicissitudes of humanity; his detachment, however, is self-
imposed, and not a condition of his nature.

Skelton's parrot is an amalgam of both traditions; or to be
more accurate, he is the wise son of Deucalion who for his
own reason adopts the role of the pampered pet. The ambiguity of his situation is apparent in the opening stanza:

> My name is Parrot, a byrd of paradyse,
> By nature devysed of a wonderous kynde,
> Dyentely dyeted with dyvers dylycate spyce,
> Tyl Euphrates, that flode, dryveth me into Inde;
> Where men of that countrey by fortune me fynd,
> And send me to greate ladyes of estate:
> Then Parot must have an almon or a date.   [3–9]

Here Parrot identifies himself as a resident of Paradise, and
his frequent allusions to Deucalion and the great flood assure us that we are listening to the Ethiopian Seer. His entrance into the world of human affairs, he explains, was quite
accidental. One of the four rivers of Paradise (Pison, Gehon,
Euphrates, Tigris) has somehow transported him into India,
where he was by chance ("by fortune") captured and sold
to an English lady. As a Paradisian, he is uncomfortable in
sixteenth-century England, where he must beg for almonds
and dates; and in the course of the poem he will repeatedly
remind his audience of his uniqueness. But while Parrot re-
sents the indignity of his terrestrial prison, he is quite willing

6. Book I, 1.365. Citations from the *Metamorphoses* are to the Loeb
Library Edition, trans. F. J. Miller (London, 1916).

to use the traditional associations which surround the literary
parrot-as-pet to shield himself from his environment. Ironically, the Psittacus who had asked the Gods to remove him
from human affairs is now forced to observe the sphere he
left behind so many ages ago, and what he sees is the anarchy
of a world which would seem to invite a new flood. Whenever his questioners attempt to involve him in the problems
of contemporary Europe, he withdraws, as he does in the
first stanza, into the relative security of his more conventional
identity, crying "Parrot must have an almon or a date," "To
dwell amonge ladyes Parrot is mete." Moving effortlessly
from one role to another, Parrot will deliberately taunt his
auditors as he first evokes their responses and then disap-
points their expectations. Repeatedly he allows us to assume
that his "wanton parable" can be understood in terms of one
or more of his traditional guises—reportorial satirist, master
linguist, indulged fool, green lover—only to dart away to
a new tack as he reminds us that he is none of these, but the
parrot who "dothe not putrefy" (218). By playing with these
literary conventions, he implicitly ridicules them, and suggests that those who see them as effective modes of combating
evil are naive. Yet he refuses to offer an alternative, retreat-
ing with apparent unconcern into the Paradise-like detachment of his cage. Still Parrot's aloofness is, itself, a pose; his
metamorphosis has not bereft him of his humanity, and the
mounting intensity of his involuntary responses to the abuses
of the day betrays his inability to detach himself from a race
that is still his. Of all Skelton's heroes, Parrot is the most
complex and the most reluctant, and the main movement of
the poem is his transformation from satirist-observer to
participant.[7]

7. Although Nelson made the connection between Parrot and Boccaccio's Psittacus in 1936, no one has seen the possibilities of a Parrot
who is half-human, half-divine; and this fact is, I believe, at the center
of the poem.

Again, in *Speak, Parrot,* it is the *internal* conflict of a carefully delineated persona that polarizes an apparently impossible confusion into accessible and relevant patterns. This is Skelton's most baffling poem, an obscure mélange of proverbs, oaths, songs, allusions, which finally yields to a more or less straightforward complaint against the times, and the difficulties of explication are compounded by the uncertainties of chronology and text. Berdan, assuming that the numbers scattered throughout the poem refer to the number of years since Henry VIII's accession, fixes on 1517–18 as the time of composition.[8] Nelson, resting his case on internal evidence and the hypothesis that the same numbers refer to the time of Skelton's laureateship (also of questionable date), prefers 1521–22.[9] Both scholars present reasonable and reasoned analyses based on the events of the years they respectively favor. Edwards and Heiserman also argue for the 1521–22 dates, but disagree with Nelson and each other on many of the details. The problem is compounded by the text. The sixteenth-century editions contain only the first 237 lines of the poem. In a manuscript in the Harleian collection lines 60–237 of the printed version are omitted, but line 59 is followed by what became in Dyce's collation the second part of the poem (238–514).[1] It has been inferred from the existence of two versions and from references in the second section to the reception of the first that *Speak, Parrot* was considerably revised and lengthened following the circulation of lines 1–237. A minor controversy also rages over the sudden introduction in lines 238–79 of Galathea, an unheralded interlocutor to whom Parrot sings an apparently irrelevant song. Nelson is inclined to

8. *"Speke, Parrot,* An Interpretation of Skelton's Satire," *Modern Language Notes,* 30 (1915), 141.

9. "Skelton's *Speke Parrot,*" *Publications of the Modern Language Association,* 51 (1936), 59–82.

1. MS Harleian 2252, fols. 133–39.

regard the passage as unassimilated material; Edwards insists on a consistent interpretation; both admit, in a joint series of articles, that some additional lines which would explain and anchor the "floating" section may have been lost.[2] In short, the critic is hampered by conditions—intentional obscurity, a disputed date, a doubtful text—which would seem to render any reading provisional; but if, as I believe, the focal point of *Speak, Parrot* is, characteristically, the psychology of the speaker, unanswerable questions of history and scholarship may at least be rendered less urgent, and a more or less satisfactory reading becomes possible.

In the first fifty-eight lines, Parrot himself provides us with the pattern which organizes the detail of his poem. In rapid succession he strikes each of the traditional poses: he toots in a "myrrour of glass," which is, by extension, the parrot-satirist's mirror of reality; he accepts the attention of admiring and indulging mistresses ("These maidens ful mekely with many a divers flowre / Freshly they dresse and make swete my bowre," 13–14); he displays his linguistic versatility ("In Lattyn, in Ebrew, Araby, and Caldey; / In Greke tong Parrot can bothe speke and say," 27–28); and mockingly undercuts his performance by recalling classical strictures on his stupidity ("Quis expedivit psittaco suum chaire," 30). All this is offered against the background of a domesticated playfulness, as Parrot performs only, it seems, for rewards: "With, Speke, Parrot, I pray you, full curtesly they say; / Parrot is a goodly byrd, a prety popagey" (15–16); but the imperative (Speak, Parrot), which is casual here, will become a trumpet call before the poem closes.

As Parrot continues to parade his accomplishments, he

2. "The Dating of Skelton's Later Poems," *Publications of the Modern Language Association,* 53 (1938), 601–22. The suggestion of a "lost" transitional passage is advanced by Edwards (p. 616) and taken up by Nelson (p. 622). Both view this only as a possible alternative to their own respective theories.

draws perilously close to specificity: when his apparently random proverbs ("trust in yourself," "without wisdom, strength falls," 41–42) follow a conventional "God Save the King," the juxtaposition suggests the didacticism of *Magnificence,* and in the eighth stanza a trilingual condemnation of immoderation precedes an almost certain allusion to Wolsey:

> But reason and wyt wantyth theyr provyncyall
> When wylfulnes is vycar generall.   [55–56][3]

At this point the sixteenth-century reader (with his fifteenth-century mind) who would expect an extended indictment of the contemporary scene is disappointed by a retreat: *"Ticez vous,* Parrot, *tenez vous coye"* (58). The sequence will be repeated again and again—the gradual emergence from a tissue of obscurity of a coherent and relevant criticism and the immediate withdrawal into "discretion," into hedonism ("An almon now for Parrot," 50), and obscurity. Parrot's determination to remain detached is paralleled on the verbal level by his unwillingness to speak "playnely." For the last time, Skelton translates a moral dilemma into a drama of style, as he recreates a crisis that is at least partially autobiographical.

At line 59 Parrot begins his commentary again: "Besy, besy, besey, and besynes agayne!" The key word is "agayne," and it is here that Parrot (as the son of Deucalion) begins to justify his reticence. To the worldly wise and world-weary seer, this "besynes" is an old, old story; he has seen it all before. His immediate reaction is a compound of indifference and disgust, but unexpectedly, one of the ladies who surround his cage refuses to accept his silence, pressing her

---

3. *"Moderata juvant,* but *toto* doth excede; / Dyscression is moder of noble vertues all; / *Myden agan* in Greke tonge we rede" (52–54).

inquiry in a tone that will become increasingly urgent: *"Que Pensez voz,* Parrot? what meneth this besynes?" (60). And Parrot answers with an eighty-line outburst of proverb, song, and biblical allusion so obscure that for four hundred years commentators found it indecipherable. It is only since 1936 that Nelson, Edwards, and Heiserman have identified a majority of the allusions, and although their readings differ in detail, we may now with some confidence describe the several themes to which Parrot repeatedly returns:

(1) The abdication of duly constituted authority before the arrogance of an ambitious adviser. Parrot avoids a direct criticism of Henry and Wolsey by using only biblical names. In a line like "Melchisedeck mercyfull made Moloc mercyless" (62), he merely establishes a causal relationship between the mildness of a ruler and the unopposed growth of evil, leaving the reader to draw his own conclusions. (A further irony may reside in the reference in Hebrews [7:4–18] to Melchisedeck as a type of Christ whose priesthood is superior to Aaron's.) He makes the same point proverbially ("Bo ho doth bark wel, but Hough ho he rulyth the ring," 132), but again, as he will remind us in a later passage, one can hardly accuse him of libel. His "reasoning," however, is inescapable: the King who can act and will not ("an arrow unfethered and without an hed, / A bagpype without blowynge standeth in no sted," 76–77) invites usurpation and a disruption of order.

(2) The absence in the modern world of heroism. Parrot quotes extensively from the Eighty-Second Psalm, which laments the passing of Gideon who would have been able to defend Israel against the enemies that now surround her.[4]

---

4. "O God, do not remain unmoved; be not silent, O God, and be not still. / For behold, your enemies raise a tumult / . . . Yes they consult together with one mind . . . the tents of Edom and the Ismaelites, Moab and the Agaranes, Gebal and Ammon and Amalec, Philistia with the inhabitants of Tyre; the Assyrians, too, are leagued with them;

The psalmist dramatizes the crisis by recalling the campaigns of Moses, Deborah, Barak, Jael, Gideon, and Jephthah which now must be refought. Parrot as our Jeremiah adds his own lament:

> *Ulula,* Esebon, for Jeromy doth wepe!
> Sion is in sadness, Rachell ruly doth loke;
> Madionita Jetro, our Moyses kepyth his shepe;
> Gedeon is gon, that Zalmane undertoke,
> Oreb *et* Zeb, of *Judicum* rede the boke;
> Now Geball, Amon, and Amaloch,—harke, harke!
>
> [115–20]

Our Moses (Henry?) is tending his sheep for Midianite Jethro (since the Midianites as Gideon's foes are also cited in Psalm 82, Jethro may be Wolsey who, in a reversal of roles, employs our Moses), and does not answer the call; again, Gideon is gone and Jephthah is dead, and Geball, Amon, Amaloch, and "Og, that fat hog of Basan" (124) (the collective enemy and, of course, Wolsey) threaten to retake "Esebon," the city won first by Moses and later by Jephthah in battles which traditionally symbolized the triumph of the spirit over the flesh.[5] The allegory is both political and ecclesiastical; Psalm 82, Nelson points out, is described in the Douay and Authorized versions "as a prayer against them that oppress the Church,"[6] and Parrot claims

---

they are the forces of the sons of Lot. Deal with them as with Madian; as with Sisara and Jabin at the torrent Cison / who perished at Endor. . . . Make their nobles like Oreb and Zeb."

5. "But Parrot hath no favour to Esebon" (113). "O Esebon, Esebon! to the is cum agayne / Seon the regent Amorraeorum, / And Og, that hog" (122–23). "Ulula, Esebon, for Jepte is stark ded!" (128).

6. "Skelton's *Speke Parrot,*" p. 78. "Two Heshbons are sharply distinguished in medieval allegory. The first is the city under the rule of the heathen. . . . The victory of Gideon is a victory of the sword of the Spirit and the darts of the Word of God. A new city rises on the

that while Esebon, sad Zion, and Rachel (types of the
Church) are weeping over the violation of sanctuary and
the dissolution of the monasteries, the high priest plays Judas
(Anti-Christ).[7]

(3) The inevitability of corruption and the futility of
action. The majority of Parrot's exempla are taken from
Judges ("of *Judicum* rede the boke") which from one point
of view is a depressing chronicle of endless backslidings re-
lieved only by the sporadic appearance of a chosen hero.
Parrot's guarded allusions to European politics are pointed
enough to indicate that he sees the sixteenth century as an
extension of that chronicle. And from the vantage point of
history, heroism is ultimately ineffective. Heiserman insists
that "We need not precisely identify biblical persons with
contemporary ones."[8] I would go further: Parrot is determined to avoid precise identifications. While the sixteenth-
century reader may have been able to make connections
which seem esoteric to us, no audience could be expected to

---

ashes of the old. . . . In Skelton, this second Heshbon has given way
to the first. Alas, cries Parrot, Gideon and Jephtha and Moses are here
no longer to defend the forces of the good. The lack of such heroes has
turned the city 'that was Sihon's' again into the hands of that evil king."
Nelson supports his interpretation by quoting from the commentaries
of Josephus, Rabanus Maurus, and Wolbero.

7. "*asylum, whilom refugium miserorum, / Non fanum, sed pro-
fanum,* standyth in lyttyl sted / . . . Esebon, Marybon, Wheston next
Barnet; / A trym tram for an horse myll it were a nyse thing; / Deyntes
for dammoysels, chaffer far fet. . . . *Quod magnus est dominus Judas
Scarioth*" (126–27, 129–31, 135). The point is made more intelligibly
in *Colin Clout:* "Relygous men are fayne / For to tourne agayne / *In
secula seculorum*" (376–78). "My lady nowe she ronnes, / Dame Sybly
our abbesse, / Dame Dorothe and lady Besse, / Dame Sare our pryoresse,
/ Out of theyr cloyster and quere" (392–96). "Howe ye brake the dedes
wylles, / Turne monasteris into water milles, / Of an abbay ye make a
graunge" (419–21).

8. *Skelton and Satire,* p. 141. Although Heiserman is aware of the
difficulty of precise identification, his own analysis of this section is a
brilliant survey of all the possibilities.

have understood what is in effect a private idiom. Nelson
rejects one of Edwards' readings as too bewildering,[9] but
bewilderment is exactly the effect Parrot desires, bewilderment and awe, for he plays parrot-like games with just
enough virtuosity to remind us that he is not at all an ordinary bird, "Above all other byrdis, set Parrot alone" (114).
The breadth of his allusions and the ease with which he
moves between centuries are proof of his lineage; but when
his "shredis" of sentence become less arbitrary and identification is a possibility, he breaks off with a laugh ("Now
Geball, Amon, and Amaloch,—harke, harke! / Parrot
pretendith to be a bybyll clarke," 120–21), or returns to
the purely physical world of sweetmeats and kisses:

Colostrum now for Parot, whyte bred and swete creme!

[84]

Mete, mete for Parrot, mete, I say.   [104]

My delyght is solas, pleasure, dysporte, and pley.   [110]

And as he "pretendith to be a bybyll clarke," Parrot, with a
studied irrelevance, strikes his most unbiblical pose—the
Green Lover. He is, of course, privy to his mistress' toilet,
and responds to the stimulus of feminine ceremony with
this boast:

Our Thomasen she doth trip, our Jenet
     she doth shayle:
Parrot hath a blacke beard and a
     fayre grene tayle.   [85–86]

Edwards traces Parrot's beard and tail to the image of Lust
in the *Court of Love,*

9. "The Dating of Skelton's Later Poems," p. 613.

oon in grene, full large of brede and length,
His berd as blak as fethers of the crow,[1]

and goes on to exclaim,

And what is his brilliant tail but the dream of every
old man from the time of Chaucer's Reeve: "For in
our will there sticketh a nail / To have an hoar head
and a greene tail."[2]

As an animated phallic symbol in a world of ladies, Parrot
is a potential lover. This is not an overinterpretation; at line
72 Parrot remarks, "In Popering grew peres, whan Parrot
was an eg," and Farmer and Henley list "poperine-pear" as
a slang word for phallus.[3] If it is coupled with the "blacke
beard and . . . fayre grene tayle" of line 86 and the very
possible pun on mete in "To dwell amonge ladyes Parrot
is mete," this otherwise obscure allusion can be read as part
of a deliberate pattern. Characteristically, the sexuality is
merely verbal and the cage he voluntarily withdraws into
abets his determination to give nothing of himself, to remain
uninvolved.

The single thread that unifies this amazing passage is
Parrot's refusal to accept the burdens of morality, what
Heiserman calls his "profound aloofness,"[4] and this deliber-

1. *Chaucerian and Other Pieces*, a supplement to *The Complete
Works of Geoffrey Chaucer*, ed. W. W. Skeat (Oxford, 1897), p. 437,
lines 1059–60.
2. *Skelton*, pp. 189–90. Cf. number 46 in Robbins' *Secular Lyrics
of the XIVth and XVth Centuries*, "My Gentle Cock": "I have a gentyl
cock, / comyn he is of kynde; / his comb is of red corel, / his tayl is of
Inde" (9–12).
3. *Slang and Its Analogues Past and Present* (7 vols. London, 1890–
1904), 5, 256. Heiserman (*Skelton and Satire*, p. 140) points out that
"Poperinghe was a village in Flanders and not far from Calais," and
reads the line quite properly as a reference to the Calais conference. My
interpretation does not preclude this reading, but merely adds a new
dimension to it.
4. *Skelton and Satire*, p. 149.

ate distancing of the self from the battlefield of experience
is philosophically justified (in several languages) by a kind
of tolerant fatalism:

> But *moveatur terra,* let the world wag;
> Let syr Wrig wrag wrastell with syr Delarag;
> Every man after his maner of wayes,
> *Pawbe une arver,* so the Welche man sayes. [90–93]

Man stumbles through history, repeating his mistakes, back-
ing himself into the same impossible corners. Parrot sees
nothing but futility in this endless drama, and in the stanza
that calls a halt to his tour de force, he redefines his position
in terms his audience would be sure to recognize:

> Tholomye and Haly were cunnyng and wyse
> In the volvell, in the quadrant, and in the astroloby
> To pronostycate truly the chaunce of fortunys dyse;
> Som trete of theyr tirykis, som of astrology,
> Som *pseudo-propheta* with chiromancy:
> Yf fortune be frendly, and grace be the guyde,
> Honowre with renowne wyll ren on that syde. [136–42]

For the first time since the opening lines the confused reader
is graced with a stanza that forms a comprehensible syntactical unit; although some depend for guidance on the
"tyrykis" (an illusory or deceptive appearance) of science
and astrology, some on palmistry (fortune-telling), fortune
and grace operate independently of man's feeble devices.
The resignation of the final couplet is thoroughly conventional and would have immediately brought to mind the innumerable "complaints" which poured forth from the well
of fifteenth-century piety. With this tag, then, Parrot informs
his auditors that what they have been straining to understand is merely another complaint; but in true Parrot fashion

his revelation is one more obfuscation, for this "complaint" is unlike any other in the tradition. There is no single complaint theme, but a series of themes which together are an expression of a more or less uniformly negative attitude toward the world. In a list which is hardly exhaustive we might include: (1) the transitoriness of mortality; (2) the vanity of human wishes; (3) the capriciousness of fortune; (4) the imminence of judgment day; (5) the decline of virtue; (6) the sinfulness of man; (7) the glories of a former age. Obviously some of these are complementary, others somewhat incompatible: (1) and (4), (2) and (3), (5) and (7) are possible pairings, while the assumptions of (5) and (7) would seem to have only an oblique relationship to the concerns of (1)–(3) and contradict the Augustinianism of (6). (Carleton Brown's distinctions between Songs of Mortality, Songs against Fortune, Songs of the Decadence of Virtue in his *Religious Lyrics of the XVth Century* can be seen as a recognition of these differences.) Parrot, however, revels in contradiction: he laments the passing of heroism, but his view of history and human nature, cyclic and pessimistic respectively, would seem to rule out the possibility of heroism; he is alternately nostalgic for the Old Testament era and disposed to find in it the pattern of contemporary abuses. And in the end he dismisses the problem of heroism by denying its efficacy, as he bows to Fortune with a deference that is mockingly flippant. But it is the form of his "complaint" more than its theme which puzzles. John Peter maintains "that . . . Complaint is usually conceptual. . . . Satire tends rather to work in the concrete particularity of real life. . . . Complaint is impersonal, Satire personal,"[5] and while these definitions ignore the interaction of the two modes, his distinction between the topical and often private criticism of the satirist and the more anonymous moralizing

5. *Complaint and Satire in Early English Literature* (Oxford, 1956), p. 9.

of the complainer is useful. Parrot, of course, will not commit himself in either direction. At times he seems to be moving toward a satiric indictment of Wolsey, but he repeatedly withdraws before the straining reader can make the necessary connections. In Peter's terms (which, I emphasize, are conveniences), what Parrot does is offer the framework of complaint and taunt us with the promise of satire.

In medieval literature the complaint attitude is sometimes suspect as a convenient rationale for inaction. Philosophy chides Boethius in the opening pages of the *Consolation:* "It is rather time to apply remedies than to make complaints." And Chaucer's Host echoes her in his criticism of the *Monk's Tale:* "no remedie / It is for to biwaille ne compleyne" (fragment B, 2784–85); Troilus uses complaint to justify his unwillingness to break out of the paralysis which, he would like to believe, passion has forced upon him. In the *Testament of Cresseid,* Cresseid's self-pitying complaint is undercut by the reaction of the "Lipper Lady" who listens to her:

> quhy spurnis thow aganis the Wall,
> To sla thy self, and mend nathing at all?
> Sen thy weiping dowbillis bot thy wo,
> I counsall the mak vertew of ane neid.   [475–78]

It is this kind of counsel, adding to the awareness of difficulties the determination to act, that Parrot does not offer.

Against the series of biblical allusions he places contemporary proverbs, songs, and place names which hint at the connection between the ancient times and ours, but he never elaborates his intimations into a comprehensive treatment of the modern scene. In the end the juxtaposition of detail from two worlds serves only to evoke the cyclical pattern which leads to the resignation of complaint. In the same way Parrot is now the conventional and familiar bird of a familiar tradition, now the distinct personality for whom the entire poem is a reflection of a personal and unique dilemma.

Yet, while Parrot mocks us, he unwittingly mirrors his confusion in ours, for the inconsistencies which block any attempt to ascertain the poem's moral focus are basically the inconsistencies of his position: he chides the potential Moses and Gideons of the day, the heirs of an heroic Judaeo-Christian tradition, for merely tending their sheep, but is himself content to retreat into the security of his gilded cage, although as the son of Deucalion and the grandson of Prometheus, his response to crisis should be immediate. He questions the efficacy of the satiric conventions associated with his literary identity, but puts forward in their place only the negative morality of complaint; he assiduously cultivates an air of unconcern, but the real anger behind his almost inaccessible allusions to Wolsey and Henry is betrayed by the nervous energy of the verse, and his periodic return to the carefree hedonism of "Parrot wants an almon or a date"[6] is less and less a deliberate effort to tease, and more and more a defensive reaction to the realization that centuries of noninvolvement have not insulated him from the shock of recognition. In lines 143 to 187 Parrot launches a final attack on the abuses of the English scene, which in its vehemence and directness brings closer the moment when he will no longer be able to hide behind contradictions. His targets are the humanists whose educational program, Parrot insists, contributes to the political and ecclesiastical irresponsibility elliptically described in the preceding section. In their emphasis on elegance in scholarship, they leave their pupils incapable of carrying on the everyday business of life ("they cannot say in Greke, rydynge by the way, / How hosteler, fetche my hors a botell of hay!" 151–52); again their erudition is useless when they would "frame a silogisme"; in

6. See lines 84, 106–07.

their intellectual pride (and this is a hit at Erasmus), some presume to correct even Scripture, "For they scrape out good scrypture, and set in a gall, / Ye go about to amende, and ye mare all"; they lose themselves in the petty distinctions of syntactical propriety ("Whether *ita* were before *non* or *non* before *ita*," 163), forgetting that the spirit saves, the letter killeth; they abandon old authorities for the sake of novelty and encourage children who "can skantly the tensis of . . . conjugacyons" to "medyll with Quintylyan." With fine irony Parrot prefaces his criticism with a proverb in the very language the new men worship: "Monon calon agaton / Quod Parato / in Graeco." The only beauty is goodness; the entire humanist program, Parrot implies, substitutes a dilettantish appreciation of the beauties of language for a recognition of the moral beauty (goodness) of a medium that allows man to confront (if only inadequately) the recurrent problems of this vale of tears, and in his concluding couplet he makes that very point with a conciseness we have not seen before:

> Settynge theyr myndys so moche of eloquens,
> That of theyr scole maters lost is the hole sentens.
>
> [186–87]

If we recall that, in medieval exegetical theory, "sentence" is interchangeable with "fruit" and "kernel," the couplet can be read as a more explicit statement of what has been hinted at before: the new men are in the bondage of the letter, and perhaps of heresy.

But again Parrot's reactions only undercut his assumed position. He castigates modern man for failing to understand that language is a means of communication, even as he constructs a private idiom to prevent man from communicating with him. He is, we note, becoming progressively less obscure, and it is perhaps the shock-like impact of the eloquens-sentens couplet, in sharp contrast to his self-proclaimed aloofness, which prompts him to a final withdrawal ("Now a nutmeg, a nutmeg, *cum gariopholo,* / For Parrot to pyke upon, his brayne for to stable," 188–89) and a lament for the simplicity of "Paradyce, that place of pleasure perdurable."

Before retiring for the last time, Parrot offers a traditional, and, in his case, mocking defense of his method:

> The myrrour that I tote in, *quasi diaphanum,*
> *Vel quasi speculum, in aenigmate,*
> *Elencticum,* or ells *enthymematicum,*
> For logicions to loke on, somewhat *sophistice:*
> Retoricyons and oratours in freshe humanyte.
>
> [195–99]

This allies him with the rhetoricians and orators of the fifteenth century whose aesthetic is fairly represented by Hawes:

> It was the guyse in old antiquyte,
> Of famous poetes ryght ymaginatyfe,
> Fables to fayne by good auctoryte;
> They were so wyse and so inventyfe,
> Theyr obscure reason, fayre and sugratyfe,
> Pronounced trouthe under cloudy fygures,
> By the inventyon of theyr fatall scryptures.[7]

In theory, the cloudy figures of aureate poetry are identified with prophecy ("fatall scryptures"), but in practice they are part of a stylized poetic of obscurity supported by a circular but unanswerable defense:

> But rude people, opprest with blyndnes,
> Agaynst your fables wyll often solysgyse,
> Suche is theyr mynde, such is theyr folyshnes;
> For they beleve in no maner of wyse

---

7. *Pastime,* lines 715–21.

That under a colour a trouth may aryse.
For folysshe people, blynded in a matter,
Will often erre whan they of it do clatter.

The word, then, is for the "elect" and Parrot goes so far
as to equate his "riddle," his mirror-like presentation of human confusion, with the glass through which St. Paul tells
us we see only darkly.[8] It is with this allusion to I Corinthians 13 that Parrot and Skelton betray and reveal themselves respectively. In that epistle, specifically in chapters 13
and 14, the apostle diagrams the relationship between the
personal sense of inspiration, the public character of prophecy, and the primacy of charity. Paul admits that the gift of
tongues ("a power to speak in foreign languages, previously
unknown") is perhaps an echo of the tongues of angels, and
therefore a sign of inspiration, but insists that charity ("the
supernatural virtue comprising love of God above all things
and love of neighbor for God") demands that inspiration
be "translated" into prophecy, into communication: "Aim
at charity, yet strive after the spiritual gifts, but especially
that you may prophesy."[9] He recognizes the distinction
between God's language and man's, but stresses (and Milton

8. Hawes' aesthetic of intentional obscurity is a late medieval mis-
interpretation of Augustine's discussion of figurative language. In his
Christian Doctrine (2.6) Augustine notes that figurative language is
valuable because it evokes an *intellectual* response from a reader. That
is to say, a metaphor (or trope) presents a puzzle to the reader and
the mental effort of solving that puzzle assures the effective communication of the truth it offers. A figure also serves to reduce the speed of a
reading experience, thus allowing the mind time to consider what is
put before it. Augustine's observations are a legitimate extension of
Aristotle's comparison of a good metaphor to a good riddle (*Rhetoric*,
3.1405b). For Hawes, the difficulty of a figure is a social rather than a
moral or an intellectual matter; it protects poetry and poets from the
unworthy. This position is present in embryonic form in Boccaccio's
Genealogia Deorum Gentilium (14.12), and fully articulated by Lydgate,
Hawes' acknowledged master. Ibid., lines 792–98.
    9. I Cor. 14:1–2.

follows him here) the necessity of accommodation. "For he
who speaks in a tongue does not speak to men but to God;
for no one understands, as he is speaking mysteries in his
spirit. But he who prophesies speaks to men for edification,
and encouragement, and consolation. He who speaks in a
tongue edifies himself, but he who prophesies edifies the
Church. Now I should like you all to speak in tongues, but
still more to prophesy; for he who prophesies is greater
than he who speaks tongues, unless he can interpret so that
the Church may receive edifications."[1]

The Church here, of course, is the whole body of believers,
and Paul's injunction to edify the Church is an injunction
to charity. It is not that the speaker in tongues is to be rejected but that the limitations of his gift require a further
step; and there is the possibility that the same man may
both speak in tongues and interpret. Paul does not consider
the man who could interpret and will not, but his exhortation, "Let all things be done unto edification,"[2] allows us to
assume his reaction to such a man, as does the most famous
verse in this section of Corinthians: "If I should speak with
the tongues of men and of angels but do not have charity,
I have become as sounding brass or a tinkling cymbal."[3] I
will not labor the similarity between tongues and the aureate
aesthetic of the obscure and the elect; but it seems to me
clear that Skelton's doctrine of inspiration, his awareness of
the distance between intuition and communication, and his
insistence on the involvement of the poet are drawn from
this source, and the *provisional* victory of the plain style at
the end of *Speak, Parrot* is a measure of his understanding
of Paul's argument. At this point in the poem, Parrot's
silence is uncharitable in the Pauline sense of the word,
and his citation of the epistle is from his point of view (not

1. Ibid., 2–5.
2. Ibid., 27.
3. 13:1.

Skelton's) a mistake. The apostle warns that he who speaks
in tongues shall be to the one to whom he speaks "barbarus,"
a foreigner. Parrot thinks himself exactly that, and remains
isolated behind his private and paradisial idiom, but he will
in time discover that his removal from humanity can never
be final, and that charity is required even of him.

Parrot is hardly consistent in his self-justification, turning
from the teasing description of his words as a divine riddle
to the more "practical" explanation of prudence:

> But of that supposicyon that callyd is arte
> *Confuse distributive,* as Parrot hath devysed,
> Let every man after his merit take his parte,
> For in this processe Parrot nothing hath surmysed,
> No matter pretendyd, nor nothyng enterprysed,
> But that *metaphoria, allegoria* with all,
> Shall be his protectyon, his pavys, and his wall.
>
> [202–08]

Parrot has said nothing—how unfortunately true—and he
again invokes the catch phrases of the aureations to justify
the wall he builds, not as a protection from physical harm[4]
but from a possible encounter with problems he knows to
be insoluble. The penultimate thrust is completely in char-

---

4. As an immortal he can hardly fear death. It may be too much to
say that Parrot is close here to the sin of Despair, but William Harris
points out that in *Magnificence,* Skelton's hero moves from overweening
pride to a complaint-like cry and toward an attempted suicide: "Allasse!
to lyve longer I have no delyght; / For to lyve in Mysery, it is harder
than Dethe. / I am wery of the worlde, for unkindnesse me sleeth."
Harris argues that the theme of the play is fortitude rather than
"measure." His position is a corroboration of my own, since he shows
Skelton treating the problem of suicide and despair much as I think
he does in the *Bouge of Court,* and undercutting the adequacy of complaint as I see him undercutting it in *Speak, Parrot.* See "The Thematic
Importance of Skelton's Allusion to Horace in *Magnyfycence,*" *Studies
in English Literature, 3,* No. 1 (1963), 9–18.

acter—one more reminder of what he might have said, one
more claim that beneath his confusion is method:

> But Parot is my owne dere harte and my dere derling;
> Melpomene, that fayre mayde, she burneshed his beke:
>
> [213–14]
>
> When Parrot is ded, she dothe not putrefy:
> Ye, all thyng mortall shall torne unto nought,
> Except mannes soule, that Chryst so dere bought;
> That never may dye, nor never dye shall:
> Make moche of Parot, the popegay ryall.   [218–22]

And he closes with the clichéd resignation that precludes
further conversation:

> Pompe, pryde, honour, ryches, and worldly lust,
> Parrot sayth *playnly,* shall tourne all to dust.
>
> [228–29, emphasis mine]

Thus far, this is the only thing he is willing to say "playnly."

These thirty lines have moved commentators to a single
question: Who is Parrot? Nelson couples this passage with
the earlier "Parot is my owne dere harte,"[5] and decides that
this is Skelton's way of identifying himself with the bird.
Edwards rejects this as restrictive and argues that Parrot
represents the poetic faculty, "that strange inspiration which
descends upon a man and makes him utter that which will
not putrefy."[6] The text itself links Parrot, as an immortal
bird, with the soul of man, the one imperishable. (In line
218 Parrot suddenly changes sex: "When Parrot is ded, she
doth 'not putrefy.' " The only "she" available is the traditionally feminine soul of line 220.) Which is it to be? Who is
Parrot? It seems to me that in the context developed in the
first 237 lines, Parrot can sustain a multilevel interpretation.

5. *John Skelton, Laureate,* p. 183.
6. *Skelton,* p. 191.

SPEAK, PARROT, PART TWO   157

If he is in any way Skelton, he is Skelton the poet as distinct
from Skelton the man; for poets, as Skelton never tires of
telling us, are, like Parrot, both human and in touch with
the divine. It is not difficult to see that every poet faces
exactly the same choice as Parrot, whether to spurn a world
he knows by divine inspiration to be hopelessly fallen or to
take arms against its sea of troubles. (Colin Clout will give
Skelton's final answer when he vows to write till the day
he dies.) On another level Parrot is indeed everyman, who
although he has not the special knowledge of the immutable
granted to the poet, is intensely aware of what is not immutable. He, too, must decide in the face of that awareness
whether to act or retire in anticipation of judgment day.
Parrot easily holds all identities in his own; he is the poet,
everyman, and on the narrative level, Psittacus. In each
guise he is suspended, in Eliot's words, between the emotion
and the response. In each guise he chooses not to respond as
the first half of the poem closes. As man he throws himself
at the mercy of Christ, pleading the vanity of the world as
an excuse for his inaction; as poet he refuses to use language
as a means of effective communication; as the son of Deucalion he hoards his wisdom in a narrow cage; as a lover
he remains inactive. Paradoxically, the virtuosity with which
he plays his complex games has forced him partially to re-
enter the world he rejects. Even as he falls silent, the stage
has been set for a total re-entry, for neither his auditors (who
include all mankind), nor that part of humanity Parrot retains, will allow him the luxury of an unearned peace.

SPEAK, PARROT, PART TWO

The second half of the poem opens with the emergence of
a single interlocutor who calls herself Galathea and chal-
lenges Parrot with a mind that is almost the equal of his
own:

Speke, Parotte, I pray yow, for Maryes saake,
Whate mone he made when Pamphylus loste hys make.

[238–39]

With Galathea's injunction, Skelton begins to transform the
stasis of the first half of his poem into conflict. In the first
237 lines he has set up the relationship between protagonist
and environment in terms of opposition, but not of collision.
Parrot's desire for retirement, his willingness to remain the
vicarious lover, and his use of language as a noncommuni-
cating medium are balanced against the need for remedial
action, the potential power of love (charity), and the responsibility of the poet to make himself understood. In the last
275 lines protagonist and environment collide, as all the
forces that act to draw Parrot into the human situation become concentrated in the figure of Galathea. Her repeated
exhortation (Speak, Parrot) becomes the driving force of
the poem as the whole question of withdrawal and involvement is bound up in Parrot's willingness to offer the wisdom
of the poet-prophet to a world badly in need of it.

Her strategy is simple; she accepts his philosophical and
literary "supposicyons" (or appears to) and meets him on his
own terms. Playing on his predilection for complaint, she
asks him to recite the complaint ("mone") of Pamphilus,
the hero of the twelfth-century pseudo-Ovidian *Pamphilus
de Amore*,[7] for his love, who is, of course, Galathea herself.

7. La *"Comédie" latine en France au XII siècle*, ed. Gustave Cohen
(Paris, 1931), 2, 169–223. What follows is the first attempt to examine
the *Pamphilus* closely in order to determine its relationship to Skelton's
poem. Edwards is the only critic to discuss it at all, and it seems that
he has seen only the Old French version by Jehan Bras-de-fer, ed.
Joseph de Morawski (Paris, 1917). The *Pamphilus* was undoubtedly
popular in the late Middle Ages: there are several references to it in
Chaucer's *Franklin's Tale*, and the *Oxford English Dictionary* attributes
the emergence of the word "pamphlet" to the popularity of this "little
book," an etymology Skelton alludes to at line 356 of *Speak, Parrot*.

If we assume that Galathea has detached herself from the crowd around Parrot's cage, from the audience he has so thoroughly confused, her request can be seen as a stratagem which would reverse their roles, would make the reluctant Green Lover the pursuer. And a reading of the *Pamphilus* reveals that she not only operates within the framework of Parrot's earlier statements but appropriates his allusiveness (which to the ordinary reader is elusiveness) in order subtly to criticize his stance. The *Pamphilus* is a simple tale of seduction with the emphasis on strategy rather than morals; the only sin in the universe of this bourgeois drama is inaction, and from the first, hero, heroine, intermediary, and reader know that the conclusion of the poem will find Pamphilus and Galathea in bed.[8] What amuses is the unanimous fidelity to the rhetorical machinery, which implies a morality no one of the characters believes in. Pamphilus sets the tone in the opening lines:

> Quam prius ipse viam meliorem carpere possum?
> Heu michi! quid faciam? non bene certus eo.
> Conqueror estque mee iustissima causa querele,
> Cum sit consilii copia nulla michi.[9]   [7–10]

This is the conventional attitude of romance complaint, and would remind English readers of a later lover, Chaucer's Troilus: but unlike Troilus, Pamphilus is his own Pandarus and is immediately ready with a counter-attitude to which he is obviously more committed: "Sed quia multa nocent, opus est michi quaerere multa: / Nam solet ars dominum

---

8. An earlier editor, A. Baudouin (*Pamphile,* Paris, 1874) is rather ill at ease with the piece, because he insists on taking Galathea's protests at their face value. Pamphilus knows better.

9. "How could I earlier have taken a better path? Alas, what am I to do? I move about uncertainly. I complain passionately because of the justest grievance, since there is no supply of advice for me."

sepe iuvare suum" (11–12).[1] As the poem proceeds to its
inevitable end, the machinations of Pamphilus and an aged
procuress are set in motion to the incongruous accompani-
ment of moralizing laments and virginal protestations:

> Hac in re nullam video michi prosperitatem,
> Non habet et tutum mens mea propositum.
> Obstitit interdum factis fortuna virorum,
> Propositumque suo non sinit esse loco.[2]   [265–68]

> Per Veneris morem virgo cito perdit honorem:
> Igneus ille furor nescit habere modum;
> Non leve vulnus habent violenta Cupidinis arma.[3]
>
>   [413–15]

> Heu michi: quo fugiunt vires et corporis usus!
> Mens mea non servit, nec mea lingua michi,
> Heu miser! in nostris est nulla potencia membris.[4]
>
>   [451–53]

John Peter comments on the possibility of parody in the
complaint tradition: "it cannot have been only by degener-
ates that the complaints were sometimes dismissed as moral
babble . . . it is not, after all, very difficult to imagine contemporaries of Mannyng and Langland who . . . while accepting Complaint's general premise of an unstable and
unpredictable world were more disposed to respond with a

---

1. "Yet, because many things harm, it is my task to seek some helps
for me. For industry customarily comes to the aid of those who have it."
2. "I see no success for me in this situation; nor has my mind any
safe plan; Fortune has been known to oppose the deeds of men and not
allow a plan to be successful."
3. "Through the law of Venus, a maiden quickly loses her honour.
That fiery flame knows nothing of regulation. Nor do the violent
weapons of Cupid know anything of slight wounds."
4. "Woe is me! Where flee the strength and use of my senses?
Neither my mind nor my tongue serves me. Miserable! There is no
power in my limbs."

Carpe diem! than with *contemptus mundi.*"⁵ Fortune, fate,
the impossibility of action, retirement before the omniscience
of unknowable deities—the commonplaces of complaint—
these are jokes in the *Pamphilus* as they are less obvious
jokes in the first half of *Speak, Parrot.* The negativity of
complaint is silently rejected and ridiculed by a narrative
whose moral is, finally, if you don't succeed at first, try, try
again:

Tunc Venus hec inquit: Labor improbus omnia vincit,
Quolibet et poteris ipse labore frui.⁶   [71–72]

Concipit ingentes animos immanis egestas,
Et facit artificem sepius hoc hominem.
Ars hominis magnum superat studiosa periclum,
Et labor arsque vigil forte iuvabit adhuc.⁷   [467–70]

Cursus fatorum nescit mens ulla virorum,
Solius est proprium scire futura Dei.
Desperare nocet, votum labor improbus implet,
Arsque vigil magnas sepe ministrat opes.⁸   [499–502]

In short, do not despair, for a small effort, no matter how
imposing the difficulties, may initiate great things. In the
world of the *Pamphilus* these admonitions are a part of the
strategy of seduction; in another context, one closer to Parrot,
they are more: When Deucalion finds himself the only man
on earth, he despairs for the survival of the race: "o utinam
possim populos reparare paternis / artibus atque animas

5. *Complaint and Satire,* p. 57.
6. "Then Venus said, 'A great effort conquers all obstacles. Whatever you wish you will be able to accomplish through effort.' "
7. "A large necessity leads to great passions and often makes a man
industrious. The zealous industry of a man will overcome a great
danger. Labor and watchful industry will aid chance to a point."
8. "The mind of man does not know the course of the Fates. To
know the future is the property of God alone. To despair is harmful; a
great effort will fulfill a desire."

formatae infundere terrae! / nunc genus in nobis restat
mortale duobus."⁹ Still, he has the presence of mind to pray
for guidance and offer himself as the instrument of restoration: "dic, Themi, qua generis damnum reparabile nostri /
arte sit, et mersis fer opem, mitissima, rebus!" (379–80).¹
Commanded to throw behind them the bones of their great
mother, the couple stand uncertain until Deucalion reasons
that the earth may be their mother and the stones her bones.
Distrusting his conjecture and skeptical of the heavenly imperative, he nevertheless decides to act—at this point Ovid
interjects the obvious "sed quid temptare nocebit" (397)²—
and he saves humanity—"quis hoc credat" (400)³—through
what seems a wholly inadequate gesture. Centuries later his
son looks out on an equally hopeless scene and he too doubts
that any effort he might make could be appreciably effective.
Parrot ignores not only family precedent but the example
of the men he nostalgically celebrates in the first half of the
poem. When the Lord tells Moses to lead the Israelites out
of Egypt, he makes a triple protest: "Who am I that I should
go to Pharao and lead the Israelites out of Egypt?" " 'But,'
objects Moses, 'suppose they will not believe me, nor listen
to my plea?' " "If you please, Lord, I have never been eloquent, neither in the past, nor recently, nor now that you
have spoken to your servant." And the reply to this complaint-like admission of inadequacy is "Who gives one man's
speech. . . . It is I who will assist you in speaking."⁴ Again,
when Gideon is commanded, "Go with the strength you

9. *Met.*, Book I, lines 363–65. "Oh, would that by my father's arts I
might restore the nations, and breathe, as did he, the breath of life into
the moulded clay."
    1. "O Themis, tell us by what means our race may be restored, and
bring aid, O most merciful, to a world o'erwhelmed."
    2. "But what harm will it do to try?"
    3. "Who would believe it?"
    4. Exodus 3:11–12; 4:1; 4:10; 4:11, 12.

have and save Israel from the power of Madian," he too
demurs: "Please, my lord, how can I save Israel? My family
is the meanest in Manasse, and I am the most insignificant in
my house." The response is immediate: "I shall be with
you." Gideon marshals the Israelites in the Valley of Jezrael,
where God has him reduce the host first to ten thousand
and then to three hundred, saying, "By means of the three
hundred . . . I will save you."[5] The soldiers of God, then, may
conquer despite overwhelming odds and unfavorable appearances, or to return to the words of Pamphilus and a source
that is far from biblical, "Let God be the guardian and
guide of my Labors / and direct all my work and design"
(273–74).[6] Perhaps not even Skelton would expect us to
recognize in Galathea's request for Pamphilus' lament an
allusion to figures who appear only fleetingly in another
section of his poem; but the relevance of the *Pamphilus* is
undeniable and in Parrot's world, where allusiveness is a
way of life, the associations become at least possibilities.

However "cloudy" this may seem to the ordinary reader,
Parrot knows perfectly well what is being asked of him (the
abandonment of the negativity of resignation), and he answers Galathea in kind, not with Pamphilus' complaint, but
with an amorous lyric in which he rejects her invitation to
become the pursuer and introduces still another dimension
to the poem's multiple perspective:

> My propire Besse,
> My praty Besse,
> Turne ones agayne to me:
> For slepyste thou, Besse,
> Or wakeste thow, Besse,
> Myne herte hyt ys with the   [240–45]

5. Judges 6:14, 15, 16; 7:7.
6. "Sit Deus ergo mei custos rectorque laboris, / Omne gubernet
opus propositumque meum."

I wylbe ferme and stabyll,
And to yow servyceabyll,
And also prophytabyll,
Yf ye be agreabyll
To turne agayne to me,
My propyr Besse   [251–56]

Be love I am constreyned
To be with yow retayned,
Hyt wyll not be refrayned:
I pray yow, be reclaymed,
And torne agayne to me,
My propyr Besse.   [262–67]

This certainly does not belong to the *Pamphilus,* but it does
have affinities with the lament Ovid's Polyphemus makes
for his Galathea[7] which in its detail would recall for the
Christian reader the *Canticle of Canticles* interpreted by
St. Bernard as "the union between Christ and the individual
soul." Again we are moving into a web of allusion which
seems inaccessible unless we assent to Edwards' reading of
Parrot's ditty as "a clear allusion to . . . a moralized ballad":[8]

Come over the burne, Besse,
Thou lytyll prety Besse,
Come over the burne, Besse, to me!
The burne ys this worlde blynde
And Besse ys mankynde,
So propyr I can none fynde as she;
She daunces and she lepys,
And Crist stondes and clepys:
Cum over the burne, Besse, to me![9]

7. *Met.,* XIII, lines 789–869.
8. *Skelton,* p. 193.
9. The text is from Ritson's MS, British Museum, Additional MS
5665, a fifteenth-century collection of songs and carols, as printed in an

"The burne ys this worlde blynde / And Besse ys mankynde."
If Parrot's Galathea-Besse is mankind, Parrot-Pamphilus
(in Greek, the all-loving) is Christ, and his answer to her
entreaty (Speak, Parrot) is, as Edwards puts it, "pious allegory—Christ's lament over the fickleness of humanity." In
short, Parrot is once again playing variations on his favorite
themes. The song becomes (1) a *de contemptu mundi* statement from an impeccable source (Christ), (2) a "come live
with me and be my love" appeal in which the promised land
is allegorically the union of the soul and Christ, and literally
the aloofness of Parrot's cage. If we preserve the distinction
between Parrot and Christ, the phallic imagery of the third
stanza ("I wylbe ferme and stabyll, / And to yow servyceabyll") is an echo of the poperine pear and green tail of
lines 72 and 76 and a reminder that while Christ is willing
(and able) to pour out his love of the world, Parrot is not.
If Parrot sees himself as a Christ figure, he forgets that, in
the complaint-of-Christ tradition, the Savior calls to mankind from the cross, having put on mortality willingly and

---

appendix to John Stevens, *Music and Poetry in the Early Tudor Court,*
pp. 338–50. Stevens noted that "the song, in various forms, was widely
current in the late xv and xvi centuries" (p. 348). In the early sixteenth
century, secular and moralized versions existed side by side, making the
allusion possible and probable for Skelton's reader. It was later turned
into a political song, and is sung in *King Lear,* III.6.27. A full text of the
moralization is printed in *A Little Book of Songs and Ballads, gathered
from Ancient Musick Books,* ed. E. F. Rimbault (London, 1851), pp. 71–
76. The last stanza reads, "Nowe, Besse redresse the, / And shortly
confesse the / Of synnes that opres the, let see; / The water hit fallyth, /
And Crist stondyth and callyth, / Come over the burne, Besse to me."
Sternfeld, in *Music in Shakespearean Tragedy* (London, 1963), p. 169,
cites Parrot's song as the only surviving secular version of the ballad.
The moralization belongs to the complaint-of-Christ tradition. For
further references to this song in its religious and secular versions, see
R. L. Greene, *The Early English Carols* (Oxford, 1935), p. 192, and
R. T. Davies, *Medieval English Lyrics* (London, 1963), pp. 256–57,
359–60.

offered himself as a sacrifice. And finally, on the literal level
(specifically in the pun on "prophytayll"), we hear the familiar boast of prophecy, and the promise of wisdom to
those who are able to come to him. Parrot has long ago
passed over the "burne" ("this worlde blynde") and while he
will welcome his auditors to Paradise, he is not about to
return.

As the collective voice of a mankind which lives in the
"burne," Galathea will not accept the illegitimate extension
of a legitimate attitude. Parrot quite properly prefers the
stability of another world to the uncertainty of this one, but
as a captive of mortality (and we all are that) he shares the
responsibility of Everyman in the endless effort to maintain
as close a relationship as possible to the divine patterns of
order; and as a poet, as a prophet, as the son of Deucalion
his responsibility is that much greater. Galathea decides to
press the attack from the flank, by simultaneously exposing
the reality behind Parrot's mask of unconcern and undermining the *metaphoria* and *allegoria* he has taken for a
shield. In a series of envoys which, although they parody
Parrot's riddling style, would have been intelligible to the
well-informed Englishman, she confronts him with a detailed account of Wolsey's movements at the Calais conference of 1521, and asks him to speak:

Lenvoy primere
Go, litell quayre, namyd the Popagay,
Home to resorte Jerobesethe perswade.   [280–81]

Secunde Lenvoy
Passe forthe, Parotte, towardes some passengere,
Require hym to convey yow ovyr the salte fome.
                                                       [301–02]

Le dereyn Lenvoy
Prepayre yow, Parrot, brevely your passage to take.
                                                       [324]

Lenvoy royall
Go, propyr Parotte, my popagay,
That lordes and ladies thys pamflett may behold.

[356–57]

This last request to "propyr" Parrot to go forth so that "lordes and ladies thys *pamflett* may behold" recalls Pamphilus' lament for his "propyr" Bess, and in effect transforms Christ's cry to mankind ("Cum over the burne . . . to me") into mankind's cry to Parrot.

As Galathea documents Wolsey's abuses for the still reluctant Parrot, the enormity of the danger he symbolizes becomes ever clearer. For eighty lines and, as the inserted dates show,[1] over a period of three months, she makes point after point. Wolsey's efforts to reconcile the Empire and France are useless:

For Jerico and Jerssey shall mete togethyr assone
As he to exployte the man owte of the mone.

[307–08]

While Wolsey gluts himself "with purpose and graundepose" (309), the absence of the Chancellor's great seal disrupts the realm, causing the "pore suters" to "have many a hongry mele" (312). Wolsey's activities go against every dictate of reason:

To bryng all the see into a cheryston pytte,
To nombyr all the sterrys in the fyrmament,
To rule ix realmes by one mannes wytte,
To such thynges ympossybyll reason cannot consente.

[331–34]

Through December, Parrot seems unmoved, and his only response is a familiar (but increasingly suspect) declaration

1. According to Nelson's calculations (*John Skelton, Laureate*, p. 163), the envoys refer to a period between October 30, 1521, and early 1522. This raises a question concerning the composition of the poem. Was it written after the fact, and are the inserted dates part of

of faith and resignation: "God amend all, / That all amend
may! / Amen, quod Parrott, / The royall popagay" (352–
55). But as Galathea assaults Parrot with the facts of a situation he finds increasingly difficult to ignore, she slyly reports
to him the attitude of a public which is hardly admiring:

> Yet some folys say that ye arre ffurnysshyd with knakkes,
> That hang togedyr as fethyrs in the wynde.   [294–95]

> sum dysdayne yow, and sey how ye prate,
> And howe your poemys arre barayne of polyshed eloquens.
>   [316–17]

Of course, she assures him, his critics are unreasonable, and
carefully remaining within the context of his earlier pronouncements she constructs a defense which echoes the
propaganda of the rhetoricians:

> lewdlye ar they lettyrd that your lernyng lackys,
> Barkyng and whyning lyke churlysshe currys of kynde,
> For whoo lokythe wyselye in your warkys may finde
> Muche frutefull mater.   [296–99]

> For trowthe in parabyll ye wantonlye pronounce.   [363]

In Skelton's terms (and, as we shall see, in Galathea's), this
is no defense at all, for while truth may rest under Parrot's
parable, it is his "wanton" (in the now obsolete sense of
irresponsible) speech that deprives him of approbation and
attention. Man can hardly be blamed for disregarding the
incomprehensible. As the confrontation between Parrot
and humanity becomes more direct, Galathea skillfully
unites the physical (political) and verbal (aesthetic) lines

Skelton's attempt to recreate in the reader's mind the sense of being
privy to the sudden revelation of news? Or are the intervals indicative
of the method of composition? Whatever the answer the result is an
extremely effective use of a kind of journalistic technique, similar, in
some respects, to Skelton's earlier *Against the Scots.*

of her strategy, and at line 370 she pointedly follows her
mock defense with a more open appeal, urging him to modify
his style:

> Parrotte, tuam moderare Minervam:
> Vix tua percipient, qui tua teque legent.² [370–71]

For the first time, Parrot's reaction is involuntary rather than
studied; with the suggestion that his wisdom is mere parrot-
like nonsense, he bursts into the traditional prophetic and
Hawesian condemnation of blindness and cowardice:

> Helas I lamente the dull abusyd brayne,
> The enfatuate fantasies, the wytles wylfulnes
> Of on and hothyr at me that have dysdayne. [376–78]

> O causeles cowardes, O hartles hardynes!
> O manles manhod, enfayntyd all with fere [383–84]

> For drede ye darre not medyll with suche gere. [387]

Parrot is indeed on shaky ground when he throws stones at
those who, like him, prefer glass houses to the responsibilities
of commitment. Gone are both the obscurity and the pretense of aloofness; Galathea has lured him from his cage.
Instinctively, he attempts to return and retreat to parable:

> Lyacon lawghyth there att, and berythe hym more bolde;
> Racell, rulye ragged, she is like to cache colde. [393–94]

At an earlier point this couplet would have confused and
annoyed, but *Speak, Parrot* is a poem that educates its reader. Here, if the reader has managed to grasp even dimly the
poem's allusive pattern, it gathers up many of the themes

2. "Parrot, moderate your wit; your readers will scarcely understand
you."

he has seen before, and anticipates the conclusion. Rachel is of course the Church, and Lyacon, the priest-king, is her oppressor. Jupiter punishes Lyacon's impiety by transforming him into a wolf (this is, significantly, the first metamorphosis),[3] the animal which characterized Wolsey to his enemies partially because of the play on words. Lyacon's impiety provokes Jupiter to visit the flood on man which leads to the heroism of Deucalion and the second metamorphosis. (The excesses of humanity under Lyacon have also forced the maiden Astrea to leave the Earth.) Parrot's allusiveness is of a new order as an awareness of the inevitability of involvement dictates his choice of detail and points to his unavoidable responsibility. Galathea senses this and plays her trump card. Pace, Henry VIII's secretary, has been sent by Wolsey to Rome where the College of Cardinals is meeting to elect a new Pope. Slyly she asks,

Whate sequele shall folow when pendugims mete togethyr?
Speke, Parotte, my swete byrde, and ye shall have a date.
[409–10]

Parrot explodes at the possibility of Wolsey as Pope, seeing in it a potential for disorder equal to the great flood:

He tryhumfythe, he trumpythe, he turnythe all up and
    downe   [426]

Hys wolvys hede, wanne, bloo as lede, gapythe over the
    crowne:
Hyt ys to fere leste he wolde were the garland on hys
    pate,
Peregall with all pryncs *farre passyng hys estate.*
[428–30]

For a split second he attempts to withdraw once again into the world of dates and kisses, "Now Galathea lett Parrot,

3. *Met.,* Book I, 176 ff.

I pray yow have hys date" (433), only to realize that in the
threat of a complete collapse of order, even his existence as
a lady's pet offers no security:

> Yett dates now ar deynte, and wax verye scante,
> For grocers were grugyd at and groynyd at but late.
>
> [434–35]

Sensing that Parrot's resistance is completely broken, Galathea asks him to set aside his sophistry,

> Nowe Parrot, my swete byrde, speke oute yet ons agayne,
> Sette asyde all sophysms, and speke now *trew and playne.*
>
> [440–41, emphasis mine]

And without any demurrer he complies:

> So many morall maters, and so lytell usyd;
> So myche newe makyng, and so madd tyme spente;
> So myche translacion into Englyshe confused;
> So myche nobyll prechyng, and so lytell amendment;
> So myche consultacion, almoste to none entente;
> So myche provision, and so lytell wytte at nede;
> Syns Dewcalyons flodde there can no clerkes rede.
>
> [442–48]

> So many complayntes and so smalle redresse;
> So myche callyng on, and so smalle takyng hede,
> So myche losse of merchaundyse, and so remedyles;
> So lytell care for the comyn weall, and so myche nede;
> So myche dowghtfull daunger, and so lytell drede;
> So myche pride of prelattes, so cruell and so kene—
> Syns Dewcalyons flodde, I trowe, was nevyr sene.
>
> [463–69]

Parrot has decided to embrace mankind, to abandon parable for plainness, to speak.

In *Speak, Parrot,* it seems to me, there can be no question of Skelton's artistry. The dialogue between Galathea and Parrot gains its relevance from the opposition between persona and environment developed in the first 237 lines, while the possibility of a resolution of that opposition is realized only when the focus is narrowed by the introduction of Galathea. The contrast between the studied brilliance of Parrot's "wanton" parable and the conventionality of this final statement parallels on the verbal level the tension between withdrawal and involvement. If the poem is read (reductively) as Skelton's mature consideration of the problem of diction, it proclaims the victory and superiority of the plain style. But as always the victory is provisional and the superiority is relative, not absolute. (This will be made explicit in *Colin Clout.*) The search for a "true" style is abandoned rather than rewarded. Ironically, the earlier stanzas in their fantastic jumble of fragments, their deliberate confusion of ancient and modern, are truer (in a mirror-like way) to the fact of the human situation than the stately lines of the lament; but this is fidelity not to a transcendent reality but to the appearances of man's limited perception, the kind of faithful reproduction offered by the ordinary parrot. Words are not things, they merely allow us to make visible and tangible (in a way that is deceptive) our ultimately subjective ordering of the world around us. Language is a plastic medium and the poet-prophet realizes that all verbal descriptions of what *is* are necessarily descriptions of what *seems* to be and that the only way even to suggest reality is to force the reader to proceed from a sense of the limitations of the visible and tangible (linguistic and physical) to a conviction of things not seen. This is, of course, too large a conceptual burden for *Speak, Parrot.* The question here is not the nature of language (although that is certainly a peripheral consideration) but the place of language in the world of lines 1–237. Although language cannot be ac-

curate in the sense we would have it be so, it can be responsible, and the triumph of the plain style is the triumph of
responsibility, the triumph in Parrot's personal history of
commitment. Again and again, Skelton argues that in a
world as difficult as this, the adoption of a private non-
communicating idiom is an evasion of responsibility and a
perversion of one of the few tools with which man can confront its difficulties. The poet-prophet, as Parrot finally
acknowledges, is a man gifted with the intuition of another
world who has been chosen to communicate, as best he can,
God's message to his fellow man.

The commitment to communication, however, does not
ensure success. While Skelton rejects the morality of complaint, the sophistic rationalization of a Harvey Hafter who
piously exclaims, "Halve up the helme, loke up and lete
God stere" (*Bouge,* line 250), he rejects it as partial rather
than as invalid.[4] Parrot's "plain" complaint does not qualify,
but makes explicit, and therefore more relevant, the assumptions of his earlier, private lament. (It is one more indication of the complexity of Skelton's aesthetic and moral vision
that terms like "explicit" fail us here; the obfuscating explicitness of Parrot's "wanton" lament makes it vague and
private, while the more general nature of his final statement
makes the entire poem a specific—explicit?—and public
one.) In 1521 Skelton finds that the intrusion on a hitherto
closed universe of heresy and secularism demands something
more than resignation. What that something is he does not
say, but his insistence on balancing the valid morality of
complaint with the recognition of terrestrial obligation is at
least a beginning. The very syntax of the stanza shows how
he both accepts and goes beyond the tradition. In his *General
Satire* (often cited as a probable source for the concluding

4. Skelton's placing this clichéd statement of resignation in the
mouth of the obviously negative Harvey supports my thesis that he
undercuts the attitude in *Speak, Parrot.*

section of *Speak, Parrot*), Dunbar tags his criticism with this refrain, "Within this land was never hard nor sene," and in the background of his indictment we sense that misty Golden Age to which the satirists of every age would return. But Parrot's indictment is more devastating and more honest. Underneath his lament for the times is a lament for all times of which this is but a moment. The forces of darkness threaten always, and it is the responsibility of every man to hold them back in the moment which is his. ("Syns Dewcalyons flodde the world was never so yll.") Deucalion may have saved mankind once, but a new flood seems imminent, and Psittacus must carry on his father's work. By juxtaposing this most traditional of literary forms with its cyclical implications on the identifiable evils of a specific age, Parrot at once admits the inconclusiveness of the battle against disorder and accepts the fact that it must be waged.[5] The very absence in Parrot's lament of any grand design for victory is proof of an acceptance that is truly heroic. Unlike the satirist, Parrot does not pay lip service to the memory of any Golden Age; he knows that the "good old days" never were, except in Paradise, and that to rewin Paradise, we must first hold earth.

5. In an interpretation which is, surprisingly, more biographical than my own, Heiserman regards the lament-for-the-times as an admission of failure: "it begins as an experiment with the conventions of the Complaint Against the Times, seeking to press them to their limits, and . . . it is finally forced in defeat to become merely one more such Complaint after all. *Speak, Parrot* is a unique exhibition of the satirist contending with his tradition and his art. In it we can observe the poet being driven back to his beginning point . . . we hear his bitter complaint against his own failure" (*Skelton and Satire*, pp. 128–29). This is, however, Parrot's poem, just as the first half of *Philip Sparrow* is Jane's. Skelton is usually very good about indicating just how much of him we can read into his speakers. In *Philip Sparrow, Colin Clout, Bouge of Court,* and *Speak, Parrot* he is careful to give his personae such unique characteristics that we see them as fully realized characters who engage us for their own sake. (In *Philip Sparrow* he even expatiates

In the last analysis, *Speak, Parrot* is not an apocalypse, but a definition of an attitude. In a way, the poem fails, for it offers no solution to the problem it poses—the endemic advance of evil; it merely proclaims a disposition (Skelton's as well as Parrot's) to continue a difficult and perhaps hopeless rearguard action with whatever means (unidentified in the text) are available. With the promise that Parrot will speak again (513) we look forward to the accommodation of the *Replication* where Skelton can defend his faith and his art and at the same time admit that "heresy will never die." If this reduces *Speak, Parrot* to spiritual autobiography, I can only suggest that it is clearly Skelton's most exhaustive consideration of a conflict (between aspiration and possibility, faith and fact, prophetic wisdom and an unhearing humanity) which had obsessed him since the 1490s. The current distinction between poet and persona can hardly be as absolute as some would have it; perhaps we can say (guardedly) that there is more of Skelton in Parrot than in any of his other spokesmen. *Speak, Parrot* is a personal poem, which is directly relevant to the few whose situation can be

---

on the distinction between himself and his heroine.) In the *Garland of Laurel, Why Come Ye Not to Court?* and the *Replication,* on the other hand, he insists on no such distinction. When Skelton does bother to construct a fictional representative, it is because he wants the reader to consider the issues of the poem as they relate to a character for whom they are especially relevant. At times a Parrot or a Colin or a Dread or even a Jane will think, speak, or act as John Skelton might, but these points of contact are natural, and suggest a relationship that should not be conceived of as an identity. Parrot's problem is Skelton's, in a way, but we shall understand either of them only if we are willing to begin with the poem, and accept its fiction. In the poem, the question is not how to write satire, but whether to write (speak) at all. Of course, Skelton uses Parrot's unique problem to say something about writing satire, but this is not, I think, the focus of the poem. Somehow we have trapped ourselves into thinking that a poet must either be one with his persona or be completely separable from him; the truth of the matter is much more complex.

compared to that of its unique protagonist (most of us are
not fortunate enough to feel the temptation of retiring with
Truth); but it seems to free Skelton to adopt a more public
pose, and in *Colin Clout* it is Everyman who asks and finds
an answer to the old questions. In both poems, I believe, we
hear the voice of the poet, reminding us that while the
struggle against evil may never be conclusive, we can all be
soldiers in the legion of the good.

My Name Is Colin Clout

In *Colin Clout* Skelton builds on *Speak, Parrot,* using the
insights of the more private poem to fashion a statement of
responsibility that is available to Everyman. Again, Skelton
gives voice to the dilemma of the poet. In *Against the Scots*
he had cried, "Si veritatem dico, quare non creditis mihi?"
"If I am telling the truth, why don't you believe me?"
Colin Clout asks the same question with a different emphasis: "Why do I speak if no one will listen?"

> What can it avayle
> To dryve forth a snayle,
> Or to make a sayle
> Of an herynges tayle;
> To ryme or to rayle,
> To wryte or to indyte,
> Eyther for delyte
> Or elles for despyte;
> Or bokes to compyle
> Of dyvers maner style,
> Vyce to revyle
> And synne to exyle?   [1–12]

With the lines "Vyce to revyle / And synne to exyle" we
return to the *Bouge of Court* and the confused poet who
would like to spare "not vyce to wryte" and "indyte" of

"moralyte." To this is added the stylistic antithesis of *Philip Sparrow* and *Speak, Parrot* as Colin in an almost ritualistic way laments the frustrations of writing. The aureate poet, the people complain, "clytters and . . . clatters / . . . medles and . . . smatters / . . . gloses and . . . flatters"; on the other hand, "yf he speake playne, / Than he lacketh brayne, / He is but a fole"; and finally, were the poet's diction "accurate," a relativist world would dismiss him peremptorily:

> And yf that he hyt
> The nayle on the hede,
> It standeth in no stede;
> "The devyll," they say, "is dede,"
> "The devyll is dede." [33–37]

Colin prefaces his poem with a verse from the Ninety-Third Psalm, "Quis consurget mecum adversus malignantes? aut quis stabit mecum adversus operantes iniquitatem?" And he answers, "Nemo, Domine!" Once again, a Skelton hero finds himself in a world whose demands seem greater than his resources, but where an earlier protagonist would have moved from an over-reaction to an awareness of the complexity of his situation, Colin *begins* with that awareness and proceeds to the kind of consideration that looks beyond the personal. Colin is unique among Skelton's heroes in that his recognition of temporal instability and uncertainty is balanced almost from the first by a reserve of confidence in the ultimate efficacy of faith and fortitude; but, like his fellows in the canon, he offers no easy answers.

Criticism of *Colin Clout* has been bound up in the question of sources and literary conventions. The one thousand-odd lines that follow this introduction appear on the surface to be a denunciation of the clergy in the Lollard tradition of the anonymous *Plowman's Tale* and *Pierce the Ploughman's Crede*. Colin is usually seen as the lineal descendant of Langland's Piers, honest, simple, a modern Peter, a solitary

figure in a world gone awry, and on this basis Skelton was
regarded by the reformers of the next generation as a
kindred soul. But all modern commentators agree with
Gordon, who insists that "the second great movement of the
Renaissance shifted Skelton never an inch from his orthodoxy. Towards the Reformation he showed nothing but
repugnance, and towards the reformers nothing but impla-
cable hatred."⁶ Gordon supports his point by citing passages
in which Colin seems to turn on himself and attack his own
attack. After 330 lines that graphically describe clerical
abuses, Colin unexpectedly speaks out in defense of the
clergy:

> This is a farly fyt,
> To here the people jangle,
> Howe warely they wrangle:
> Alas, why do ye not handle [ye = the clerics]
> And them all to-mangle?
> Full falsely on you they lye,
> And shamefully you ascrye.   [331–37]

Gordon distinguishes between those who would reform the
Church completely and those who would work for reform
within the orthodox framework, and places Skelton in the
latter category. Thus for him, *"Colin Clout* reveals how
Skelton could attack his own Church in exactly the same
terms as the reformers, and yet turn on these reformers in
still bitterer satire." But, why the elaborate subterfuge of
pretending to defend the group (the willful Bishops) he
indicts? Heiserman asks this question and decides that Gordon's explanation does not exonerate Skelton's persona from
a charge of schizophrenia; he suggests that, in Colin, Skelton
attempts unsuccessfully to fuse two conventional heroes, the
neutral reporter and the searcher for truth. (It might more

6. *John Skelton, Poet Laureate,* p. 102.

accurately be said that Skelton writes a Lollard and anti-Lollard poem simultaneously.) Since Colin is already certain of the truth and only pretends to defend the clergy, he goes on, "the result is an inadequate fiction, a split in dramatic structure which remains visible in spite of the close organization of the poem's matter."[7]

In our age when almost every hero or nonhero is not at all certain of the truth, the critic is hardly nonplussed when he encounters inconsistency, but in this case the biases of a socio-intellectual and an historical approach, respectively, have prevented Gordon and Heiserman (and others) from considering the apparent contradictions in Colin Clout's stance as an integral part of the poem's structure. Gordon and Heiserman assume that since the world described in the poem languishes in doubt and disorder, Colin is necessarily the representative of the stability it has abandoned:

> Doubts were for weaker spirits; for him the faith that never questions.[8]

> As the personification of stability Colyn could attack disorder in the whole commonwealth.[9]

7. *Skelton and Satire*, p. 240.
8. *John Skelton, Poet Laureate*, p. 107.
9. *Skelton and Satire*, p. 192. This section was written and rewritten several times before I was privileged to see, in manuscript, Robert Kinsman's recently published "The Voices of Dissonance: Pattern in Skelton's *Colyn Cloute*," *Huntington Library Quarterly*, 26, No. 4 (1963), 291–313. In some ways, Kinsman's interpretation complements my own. His description of the "dissonant voices" which the reader must discern in order to "understand what the dimensions and qualities are of the object attacked" (p. 293) corresponds to my description of the possible authorities Colin considers in his mental journey through the three estates. I am directly indebted to him for his analysis of the way in which Skelton prepares for what I call the climactic "anti-speech" at line 1152. "One should become aware that a very specific and formidable foe is emerging from the ranks of the higher clergy so generally attacked. An actual and grammatical singular, as it were, is

But a reading of the poem reveals that Colin does indeed doubt, and that far from a personification of stability, he is, with Dread and Parrot, a spirit who yearns for stability. Thus, he begins, as we have seen, with a statement of his uncertainty in terms of the problem of communication, and hints that man's disbelief in evil ("The devyll they say is dede") and its consequences, implying as it does a corresponding disbelief in good and its potential, is the root of the problem. What must be emphasized is that as a man, and a minor cleric, Colin cannot escape the implications of his criticism and confusion. He does not contradict the "they" who claim the devil is dead; he too indicates a lack of confidence in the existence of ultimates in a world of ultimate disorder:

> "The devyll," they say, "is dede,"
> "The devyll is dede."
> It may well so be,
> Or els they wolde se

<hr />

more and more clearly discerned among the blurred plurals of Skelton's general comments. He is readying us for the grating voice of that swelling but hitherto voiceless presence" (p. 302). Before reading this I had been aware of the impact and significance of this speech, but I had not seen how carefully Skelton sets the stage for it. Kinsman and I differ, however, in our conception of the title figure. In order to account for some of the inconsistencies which puzzle other critics, he makes a distinction between the poet and Colin, the former acting as the *pathos* which stirs "his hearers to sympathy for his stand," the latter as the *ethos* "that makes his [the poet-prophet of the first thirty-six lines] original stand credible" (p. 300). "The reader," he maintains, "first hears the heroic voice of the poet in the first person, then the documentary drone of Colin Clout" (p. 293). I shall argue that there is no such distinction, that the entire poem, including the drama of the voices, takes place in Colin's mind, a mind the reader comes to know. Kinsman maintains that "from time to time, the poet steps from behind the mask of Colin" (p. 301), but Colin quite explicitly identifies himself "from time to time" as a cleric who writes and reports (see lines 1083–90), in short, as the only first-person voice in the poem.

> Otherwyse, and fle
> From worldly vanyte.   [36–41]

Allied with neither the corrupt clergy nor the shrill voice of
reform, he is caught between the two and, more important,
between the conflicting "truths" they represent:

> the temporalte
> Accuseth the spiritualte;
> The spirituall agayne
> Dothe grudge and complayne
> Upon the temporall men:
> Thus eche of other blother
> The tone agayng the tother:
> Alas, they make me shoder!   [61–68]

It is not the Bishops or the lay people who make him shudder, but the implications of the dispute between them.
Colin's first concern is the state of his own soul, and if what
the people say is true, if the clergy is corrupt, wayward, and,
even as he suggests at the close of the poem, heretical
(Sadducees), then how are they to guide him in his efforts
to obey God's law? His plight is the plight of every man
who is asked to believe in the existence of an unknowable
truth, but sees in the world he inhabits (the only world
available to his limited perception) innumerable contradictions of that truth. Whom shall he believe, the people, who
point to facts that cannot be denied, or the Bishops who in
the midst of corruption invoke an authority which transcends
the factual? As a man who feels, he is drawn to the former;
as a man who desperately desires to be a son of God, he is
drawn to the latter. Once again a Skelton poem gains co-
herence when its surface issues—Lollardry, Church reform,
the suppression of the monasteries—are seen as backdrops
for the internal drama of the protagonist.

Significantly, Colin's first positive verbal action is one of

self-assertion as he attempts to create an island of identity
in the midst of the chaos that confronts him on every side.

> My name is Colyn Cloute.
> I purpose to shake oute
> All my connyng bagge,
> Lyke a clerkely hagge.   [49–52]

This is a part of the tradition; Jack Upland prefaces his series
of questions with "I, Jack Uplande, make my mone." But in
the Lollard poem the name is only a courtesy to the reader,
affording him a partisan identification that is not repeated.
Colin will return periodically to his name, reminding us
that this is *his* poem before it is a polemic tract. He will
"shake out" his entire stock of knowledge as a prelude to the
search for a pattern of cause and effect. There is no hint that
he has decided what that pattern will be before he begins,
and his defense of his style adds to the tentativeness of his
stance:

> For though my ryme be ragged,
> Tattered and jagged,
> Rudely rayne beaten,
> Rusty and moughthe eaten,
> If ye take well therwith,
> It hath in it some pyth,
> For as farre as I can se,
> It is wrong with eche degre.   [53–60]

This is not an absolute defense of the "ragged" style. Like
Parrot, who achieves this equilibrium only at the close of
his poem, Colin chooses the plain style as the best of the
media available to him. It has in it "some pyth"; but as everything else in the human situation, it is ultimately inadequate.

As soon as one understands that Colin is not a rhetorical
device upon which Skelton mounts an attack on the abuses of
the age, but is, rather, the center (structural and conceptual)

of the poem that bears his name, the inconsistencies that trouble some critics fall into place. The great mass of detailed indictment which makes up the body of the poem is informed by four simultaneously orchestrated movements: (1) The battle in Colin's mind between the two "truths" available to him, which is a part of (2) the never-ending documentation of the irresponsibility of conflicting authorities, an irresponsibility which is symbolized in the emerging figure of a single man, an irresponsibility so pervasive that it leads to (3) a recurring examination of the problem of salvation and to the tentative identification of another single figure, Christ; for 980 lines the negativity of (1), (2), and (3) is challenged only by (4) Colin's repeated attempts to establish his identity. In the final 300 lines the dissonances are dissolved (or dismissed) by a direct confrontation between the single figures of (2) and (3).

(1) The battle in Colin's mind between the two "truths" available to him is reflected in his inability to maintain the fiction that he is only a reporter of the criticism of others. Instead of being an indication of Skelton's failure to integrate certain conventions, Colin's indecisiveness is the rhetorical manifestation of a troubled soul. He prefaces his first extended attack with a disclaimer of responsibility, "Laye men say indede" (75). He, Colin, is saying none of these things, and after a fifteen-line review of clerical abuses, he turns on his sources of information the lay:

> Forsothe they are to lewd
> To say so, all beshrewd!   [90–91]

This pattern is repeated again and again; Colin begins by disassociating himself from the information he gathers:

> The temporalyte say playne   [132]

> wandrynge as I walke,
> I here the people talke.   [289–90]

> the communalte yow call   [639]
>
> Squyre, knyght and lorde,
> Thus the Churche remorde.   [982–83]

He then proceeds to report at length the accusations he has
heard, only to turn on those who make them:

> What hath lay men to do
> The gray gose for to sho?   [197–98]
>
> Full falsely on you they lye
> And shamefully you ascrye.   [336–37]
>
> With language thus poluted
> Holy Churche is bruted.   [488–89]
>
> Theyr tonges thus do clap.   [1060]

But the increasing length of Colin's reports tends to destroy
the force of his sporadic disclaimers, much as the digressions
in *Philip Sparrow* qualify Jane Scrope's periodic exclamations of sorrow. As the evidence of clerical corruption
mounts, the claim that this is all the fabrication of a maliciously slanderous populace becomes unsupportable. The
reader instinctively realizes that the charges are all too true
and, what is more important, so does Colin. His attempts to
disassociate himself from the criticism of the people always
follow a particularly damning accusation. At line 321 he
climaxes a description of the Bishops' addiction to luxury
with a couplet that anticipates Butler and Swift in its force
and conciseness:

> Theyr moyles [mules] golde dothe eate,
> Theyr neyghbours dye for meate.   [321–22]

Immediately, almost as if he were reacting to what he has
just said, Colin springs to the Bishops' defense:

> This is a farly fyt,
> To here the people jangle,
> Howe warely they wrangle:
> Alas, why do ye not handle
> And them all to-mangle?   [331–35]

The use of the personal pronouns is significant. "Ye" in line 334 refers, of course, to the Bishops, and it is to that body of men that Colin addresses his poem; each new section of the poem begins, as we have seen, with a qualifying phrase, i.e. "men say that ye"; but as the pace quickens and the accusations accumulate, the qualifying "men say" tends to recede into the background; the rhetorical "ye" is retained, but the construction it belongs to (in Latin, indirect discourse) has been left behind. Consequently, the accusing voice with its repetitions of "ye," "ye," "ye" seems to be solely Colin's. Once again Skelton makes his point by imposing a structural pattern on the assertions of his persona. What must be kept in mind is that Colin's obvious inability to distance himself from the criticism he repeats does not render his efforts toward that end meaningless. Poetry is not logic. Contradictory movements within a poem do not cancel each other out and are often an indication of complexity rather than artistic confusion. In this case Colin's tendency to undercut his assumed stance is a central motif in the structure of the poem, a rhetorical manifestation of his dilemma.

(2) The contradiction which allows us to chart the topography of Colin's mind is itself but one of the many contradictions which in combination suggest the topography of the poem's universe. In brief, everything is contradictory, or as Colin himself observes in the traditional language of the "three-estates" literature, "hoder moder" (69). Not only is all confusion, but those who might be expected to point the way to stability are unwilling to discharge their responsibilities. Colin's reportorial eye systematically records an

apparently endemic evasion of responsibility, and the traditional (and formal) dissection of the three estates serves as
a framework for his personal problem.

The willful irresponsibility of the Bishops and the presumptuous assumption of responsibility by the lay are of
course constant and intertwined themes. It is the Bishops
who bear the brunt of the frontal attack, and the apparently
haphazard documentation of their sins of omission is reinforced periodically by a damning dramatization:

> With golde all betrapped,
> In purple and paule belapped;
> Some hatted and some capped,
> Rychely and warme bewrapped,
> God wot to theyr great paynes,
> In rotchettes of fyne Raynes,
> Whyte as morowes mylke;
> Theyr tabertes of fyne silke,
> Theyr styrops of myxt gold begared;
> There may no cost be spared;
> Theyr moyles golde dothe eate,
> Theyr neyghbours dye for meate.   [311–22]

> And as farre as they dare set,
> All is fysshe that cometh to net:
> Buyldyng royally
> Theyr mancyons curyously,
> With turrettes and with toures,
> With halles and with boures,
> Stretchynge to the starres,
> With glasse wyndowes and barres;
> Hangynge aboute the walles
> Clothes of golde and palles,
> Arras of ryche aray,
> Fresshe as flours in May;

> Wyth dame Dyana naked;
> Howe lusty Venus quaked,
> And howe Cupyde shaked
> His darte, and bent his bowe
> For to shote a crowe
> At her tyrly tyrlowe.   [934–51]

These tableaux serve to indicate the larger divisions of the poem and to fix (for the reader) the major seat of irresponsibility. Within these divisions, Colin regularly digresses to examine contingent or subordinate spheres of action, and his reports are distressingly similar. Although there exist clergymen ("two or thre") who, unlike the Bishops, are "Full worshypfull clerkes, / As appereth by theyr werkes, / Lyke Aaron and Ure, / The wolfe from the dore, / To werryn and to kepe / From theyr goostly shepe" (150–55), their acceptance of responsibility is only partial; they are afraid to speak out against their less conscientious brethren: "But they are loth to mell, / And loth to hang the bell / Aboute the cattes necke, / For drede to have a checke" (162–65). As "men say" (176) they do not wish to be "combred with care" (178) and their silence is perhaps more reprehensible than the obvious sins of their superiors.

Indeed, as we become acquainted with the world of *Colin Clout,* it is obvious that no one (*Nemo Domine*) will assume the burden of "care." If the prelates are derelict and the lesser clergy cowards, the nobles are betrayers of their own interests:

> For the lordes temporall,
> Theyr rule is very small,
> Almost nothyng at all.
> Men saye howe ye appall
> The noble blode royall:
> In ernest and in game.   [610–15]

In a system that operates in terms of checks and balances, a refusal to exercise jurisdictional authority necessarily opens the way to centralization and the breakdown of the system. In the society to which Skelton is committed, bishop and noble theoretically control independent areas of authority. Although they share an allegiance on a higher level, it does not determine the scope of their administrative functions (which are neither comparable nor interdependent). When usurpation is not resisted, the usurped assume at least half the guilt:

> But noble men borne
> To lerne they have scorne,
> But hunt and blowe an horne,
> Lepe over lakes and dykes,
> Set nothyng by polytykes;
> Therefore ye kepe them bace,
> And mocke them to theyr face.   [621–27]

The second estate offers Colin nothing.

The tyranny of the Bishops and the surrender of the lords, leading eventually to centralization, lead immediately to minor and major displacements. The monasteries are appropriated, as the monks are forced to "tourne agayne / *In secula seculorum,* / And to forsake theyr corum" (377–79). And since the Bishops appropriate "things" rather than functions, "pseudo-authorities," who are unable to assure the stability they promise, rush in to fill clerical power vacuums. Ignorant clerks set themselves up as exegetes only to "blaber, barke, and blother, / And make a Walshmans hose / Of the texte and of the glose" (779–81). "The foure ordores of fryers" roam the countryside, offering to "shryve, assoyle . . . reles," succeeding only in leading their victims astray:

> they provoke
> Both Gyll and Jacke at Noke

> Their dewtyes to withdrawe,
> That they ought by the lawe.   [856–59]

Confused and poor, the people lash out at those who repeatedly fail them, and their cries (heralds as Skelton knows only too well of rebellion and anarchy) are the final confirmation of Colin's opening lament:

> as farre as I can se,
> It is wronge with eche degree.   [59–60]

As the vision of a world turned upside down becomes more and more oppressive, a single figure gradually attracts to itself the various indictments which make up the poem. He first appears in the passage tagged as "Skelton's prophecy":

> Ptholome tolde me
> The sonne sometyme to be
> *In Ariete,*
> Ascendant a degre,
> Whan Scorpion descendynge,
> Was so then pretendynge
> A fatall fall of one   [469–75]

> Lay salve to your owne sore,
> For els, as I sayd before,
> After *gloria, laus.*   [482–84]

But Colin returns immediately to his general criticism of the Bishops, and the mysterious "one" seems forgotten. At line 640 and following, however, the documentation of prelatical pride involves details which point unmistakably to a specific offender: "ye were wonte to drynke / Of a lether bottell / With a knavysshe stoppell, / Whan mamockes was your meate, / With moldy brede to eate; / Ye cowde none other gete" (651–56). Maintaining a distracting ambiguity, Colin again gives us the plural ("Couching your drousy heddes /

Sometyme in lousy beddes") only to follow with an allusion
to Paul's condemnation of the overconfident and a repetition
of the earlier prophecy with its single villain:

> But *qui se existimat stare*[1]
> Let hym well beware
> Lest that his fote slyp,
> And have suche a tryp;
> And falle in suche dekay,
> That all the worlde may say,
> Come downe, in the devyll way!   [666–72]

It is only at line 934, where the strains of the poem coalesce,
that this grammatical blur, so effective as a structural reflection of Colin's vacillation, resolves itself to an unambiguous
singular; and significantly the identification of our man of
mystery and the pictorial climax of the indictment of the
Bishops coincide. The detailed description of the Hampton
Court tapestries dispels any doubt; this is Wolsey's home,
and the "one man" who would "rule all thynges alone,"
who plays at checkmate "with lordes of great estate" (1015),
who controls the access to the King, who, in short, bears the
ultimate responsibility for the instability of Colin's world is,
of course, the Cardinal.

(3) We need not look to a personal quarrel for an explanation of Wolsey's prominence in *Colin Clout;* Skelton
is here a master craftsman, and had the Cardinal not existed,
he would have been invented if only for this poem. His
presence "works" in many ways; but we can begin with the
obvious. As the head of the Church in England (Archbishop
of York as well as Cardinal), Wolsey's personal inadequacies
suggest and reflect the inadequacy of the ecclesiastical hierarchy; whenever Colin periodically abandons the guise of

---

1. I Cor. 10:12. "Therefore let him who thinks he stands take heed
lest he fall." Prophecies like this are common in anticlerical literature.

impartial reporter to speak directly, it is to hurl an imperative at the Bishops.

> Ye bysshops of estates
> Shulde open the brode gates
> Of your spirituall charge,
> And com forthe at large,
> Lyke lanterenes of lyght.   [692–96]

The tone is peremptory, but the undertone is desperate: what
seems a demand for action is in fact a plea. The appeal is,
like everything else in the poem, conventional. In a sermon
which Owst terms "perhaps the darkest account of the
Church and some of the fiercest denunciation of fellow-
clergy to be found in all English sermon-literature,"[2]
Master William de Rymyngton asserts, "Set prohdolor hiis
diebus huius modi lux multociens extinguitur in curatis, qui
nec verbo doctrine nec exemplo bone vite lucent suis sub-
ditis, quin pocius quasi per Egipti tenebras eos obnubilant
et involvunt."[3] But where de Rymyngton is angry, Colin is
defensive. Only "lyght" will dispel the confusion of the
battle between the "truth" he sees (the corruption of the
clergy) and the "truth" he would acknowledge (the Church
as mediator between man and God); only "lyght" will illumi-
nate the path to salvation. "Come forth," Colin calls, "help
me!" He wants desperately to believe in the consecration of
the clergy, and his rejection of their critics is reflexive, anguished, and shrill. "Full falsely on you they lie" (336) he
cries and the reader seems almost to hear a whispered "don't
they?" There is a note of "say it isn't so" running through

2. Owst, *Literature and Pulpit in Medieval England* (New York,
1961), p. 273.
3. Ibid. "It might be said in these days that light of this kind is
often extinguished in curates who neither in the words of their teaching
nor in the example of a good life enlighten their sheep, but are inclined,
rather, to veil and envelop them in the darkness of Egypt (Anti-Christ)."

this poem; for if it is so and if, as the people maintain, the
Bishops are Sadducees, heretics who have "determyned
playne / We shulde not ryse agayne / At dredeful domis
day" (1233–35), Colin is lost.

And lost he is, in the world of his poem. Like Dread he
literally knows not where to go; his attempt to order the
chaos that surrounds him leads as we have seen to contradiction and even self-accusation; his criticism of the lay ("And
thus they hurte theyr soules / In sclaunderyng you," 343–
44) is almost a denial of his poem; and since Colin himself
cannot but respond to the "sclaunder" he rejects, his soul
too is "hurte." When he makes his only sustained attack on
the lay (488–594), it is to brand them heretical: "And some
have a smacke / Of Luthers sacke, / And a brennyng sparke
/ Of Luthers warke, / And are somewhat suspecte / In
Luthers secte" (542–47). And if this is true, his obvious involvement in their grievances pulls him toward heresy in
spite of himself. Counterpointing his quest for salvation is
the relentless documentation of the irresponsibility which
assures its failure. Irresponsibility on any level leads not
only to anarchy, but to damnation. The confiscation of the
monasteries is more than a social and administrative problem, for

> theyr founders soules
> Have lost theyr beade rolles,
> The mony for theyr masses
> Spent amonge wanton lasses.   [422–25]

Colin refuses to speculate on the fate of the neglected souls,
but the rhyme pattern of his *praecisio* (dwell, mell) makes
speculation unnecessary: "where theyr soules dwell, / Ther-
with I wyll not mell. / What coulde the Turke do more /
With all his false lore, / Turke, Sarazyn or Jew?" (429–33).
Could Turk, Saracen, or Jew do more than condemn the
Christian soul to hell? In the same way, the ignorance of

those who are (through default) allowed to interpret the sacred text is more than a philological problem; for commentators who barely know "how farre Temple barre is / From the seven starrys" (828–29) but continue to "amend the gospell / And . . . preche and tell / What they do in hell" (823–25) will lead their auditors exactly there. And, although the great army of wandering friars, preaching for "grotes" and "flatterynge" for "cotes," are no more a physical danger than our door-to-door salesmen, their product is, after all, salvation; their claim to authority, empty, their wares worthless: "Agaynst curates they repyne; / And say propreli they ar *sacerdotes,* / To shryve, assoyle, and reles / Dame Margeries soule out of hell: / But when the freare fell in the well, / He coud not syng himselfe therout" (875–80). In short, they can offer no "lyght," and as we have seen again and again, those who could will not:

> For bysshops have protections,
> They say, to do corrections,
> But they have no affections
> To take the sayd dyrections   [893–96]
>
> To occupye suche places,
> To sowe the sede of grace.   [899–900]

This is another instance of the control Skelton has over his unique verse form. Dyce rejects the manuscript reading of line 900 and substitutes "the sede of grace*s*"[4] (italic mine); but Skelton is fully aware of what he is doing. "Grace" is the last rhyme in a series of four ("cases," "faces," "places"), and Skelton knows that the singular will force his reader to pause and consider this very important word. The "sede of grace" is, of course, the object of Colin's quest, and in his despair he turns almost reflexively from earthly to heavenly sowers: "I reporte me to you / O mercyfull Jesu" (434–35).

4. Vol. 1, p. 346.

While Colin attempts to chart a course in troubled waters, Skelton allows the reader to anticipate his arrival in the harbor of faith. If "Quis consurget mecum adversus malignantes? aut quis stabit mecum adversus operantes iniquitatem?" is a justifiable question on the basis of the scene Colin so painfully explores, in the psalm the response is inevitable and immediate: "Were not the Lord my help, I would soon dwell in the silent grave. / When I say, 'My foot is slipping,' your kindness, O Lord, sustains me; / when cares abound within me, your comfort gladdens my soul."[5] To line 1250, Colin's allusions to Christ are either involuntary cries of pain ("O mercyfull Jesu") or the basis of an ironic juxtaposition—"He dranke eysell and gall / To redeme us withall; / But swete ypocras ye drynke" (456–58)—before he moves on to another area in his never-ending dissection of fifteenth-century England. For the reader, however, they promise the appearance of another single figure, who will literally *make* Skelton's prophecy come true: "How could the tribunal of wickedness be leagued with you, which creates burdens in the guise of law? Though they attack the life of the just and condemn innocent blood, / yet the Lord is my stronghold, and my God the Rock of my refuge. And he will requite them for their evildoing, and for their wickedness he will destroy them; the Lord, our God, will destroy them."[6]

(4) While the promise of Christ suggests a resolution of Colin's problem in terms of another world, he is still very much in this one—alone, unoriented, confused. Ironically, the only thing he can cling to is his sense of isolation from the forces that pull at him, his sense of identity. The critics who identify Colin with any of the classes or estates which vie for his allegiance in the poem are, I think, mistaken. This is a poem of quest and the quester stands apart from

5. Psalm 93:17–19.
6. Ibid., 20–23.

the various systems of value he meets, examining each in turn, pulled now by one, now by another, continually seeking a point of rest. Although his search necessarily involves an examination of the world and all mankind's position in it, it is his own position that most concerns him. As the confusion and uncertainty he finds on every side threaten to overwhelm him, his only recourse is to reassert his existence as an entity. At regular intervals, almost as if he were trying to maintain his sense of selfhood through a ritual incantation, Colin repeats his initial statement of introduction, "My name is Colyn Cloute":

> Thus I, Colyn Cloute   [287]
>
> What Colyne, there thou shales!   [401]
>
> let Collyn Cloute have none
> Maner of cause to mone.   [480–81]
>
> I wryte after this facion;
> I, Colyn Cloute,
> Among the hole route.   [1082–84]

The wages of self-assertion are, however, responsibility. Being Colin Clout is its own problem. Colin begins by questioning the efficacy of poetry, and an awareness of the inadequacy of its medium never leaves him: "O mercyfull Jesu, / You supporte and rescue, / My style for to dyrecte, / It may take some effecte" (435–38). This is, of course, a rhetorical formula (an invocation to a Christian muse), but in a poem where "dyrection," and "supporte" are missing, and "effecte" in question, it is much more. As a human tool whose significance at any one moment depends on subjective association, language can neither communicate nor (outside of a prayer) invoke a reality which is suprahuman. (A remark of Percy Bridgman's may be relevant here: "Whenever we have a system dealing with itself we may expect to encounter mal-

adjustments and infelicities, if not downright paradox.")[7]
Poetry, then, only clarifies the subjective, and the subjective
is sometimes terrifying:

> For I abhorre to wryte
> Howe the lay fee dyspyte
> You prelates, that of ryght
> Shulde be lanternes of lyght.   [439–42]

Capturing the pattern of one's observations on paper seems
to make them official. Colin's sensitivity as an observer and
chronicler only leads him in circles to a clearer understanding of his impossible situation rather than to a solution, and
his sporadic attempts to disassociate himself from his observations is a reflection of his dilemma. Committed to poetry
as a vehicle for self-assertion, but trapped by the limitations
of his medium into documenting his possible damnation—
one can hardly blame him for "abhorring to wryte."

Yet Colin seems to gain strength from the very negativity
of his poem, and if his style has neither efficacy nor "accuracy," it is all he has; it is truth as he knows it. Writing
is ever painful for him ("Sory therfore am I," 486) but, on
the other hand, "trouth can never lye." He may be "loth to
tell all" (638); but he will. He has made his peace with the
human situation and becomes one of a line which includes
Sophocles' Oedipus ("Let my fate go where it will"),
Chaucer's dreamer ("I wot myself how best I stonde"),[8] and
Hamlet ("The readiness is all")—men who, though almost
crushed beneath the "weight of all this unintelligible world,"
remain true to their own selves and persevere in activities
which seem futile, even self-defeating, and in terms of the
divine, insignificant. As another poet-prophet[9] was to say,

---

7. *The Limits of Language,* ed. Walker Gibson (New York, 1962),
p. 46.
8. *House of Fame,* line 1878.
9. Milton, "On His Blindness."

"God doth not need / Either man's work or his own gifts"; but God's self-sufficiency (which is, of course, axiomatic) does not absolve man from the responsibility of continuing in his work or exercising his gifts ("Well done good and faithful servant"); for Colin the moral decision is the verbal decision and it is clearly a recognition of limitation as well as an affirmation:

> I, Colyn Cloute,
> Among the hole route
> Of you that clerkes be,
> Take nowe upon me
> Thus copyously to wryte,
> I do it for no despyte.
> Wherefore take no dysdayne
> At my style rude and playne.   [1083–90]

J. Robert Oppenheimer has written: "It is style which complements affirmation with limitation and with humility; it is style which makes it possible to act effectively, but not absolutely . . . it is style which is the deference that action pays to uncertainty."[1] Assertion is possible, and necessary, despite uncertainty; at line 1090 the problem of style (and of "dyrection") is finally solved by a recognition of its insolubility. Colin will no more be able to forge the "perfect" diction than he will be able to discover (in this world) the perfect authority. The only response to the human dilemma (and the artistic) is a provisional one; "words, words, words," cries Hamlet; "deeds, deeds, deeds," we might add as we see movement deflected, purpose obscured, cause and effect illusory. "Our thoughts are ours, their ends none of our own," laments the Player King. Perhaps, but they *are* ours, and in the limited field of our perception all we have; while as Christians we may (indeed must) hope for the time when

1. Quoted in *The Limits of Language*, p. 51. The sentence is from Oppenheimer's series of lectures, *The Open Mind*.

our thoughts (acts) and their ends are one ("O that great Sabbaoth God graunt me that Sabaoths sight!"),[2] as mortals we must endure:

> Tyll my dyenge day
> I shal bothe wryte and say.   [508–09]
>
> Wherefore take no dysdayne
> At my style rude and playne.   [1089–90]
>
> I wryte trewly.   [1118]

The convenient schematizations of the preceding pages are deceptive. No one of my four "movements" operates in isolation; at any one moment in the poem, more things are happening than the critic can record; we gain the clarity of analysis at the expense of complexity, and the only excuse for the critical process in terms of a poem like *Colin Clout* is the possibility that some readers will go from these pages to the original with heightened expectations. Even the casual reader, however, will be somewhat aware of the coalescence, in the last 300 lines, of themes which are woven through the poem. The "tapestry" passage climaxes the indictment of the prelates who are once again urged (begged) to reform:

> Stande sure, and take good fotying,
> And let be all your motying,
> Your gasying and your totying,
> And your parcyall promotyng;   [1074–77]

those who have the power to force a reform are reminded indirectly of their cowardice:

> some of you but late
> Hath played so checkemate
> With lordes of great estate,   [1013–15]

2. The last line of Spenser's *Mutabilitie Cantos.*

> That they shall mell nor make,
> Nor upon them take,
> For kynge nor kayser sake;   [1017–19]

and "virtuous" clergymen are assured simultaneously of
Colin's friendship and (through the repetition of "no" and
"nor") of their virtual nonexistence:

> Of no good bysshop speke I,
> Nor good preest I escrye,
> Good frere, nor good chanon,
> Good nonne, nor good canon,
> Good monke, nor good clercke,
> Nor yette of no good werke.   [1097–1102]³

Always counterpointing the confusion (anarchy) of the scene
is Colin's own confusion, as he pits self-assertion against an
uncertainty which a thousand lines of "exploration" can only
intensify:

> Whether it be wrong or ryght,
> Or els for dyspyght,
> Or howe ever it hap   [1057–59]

> And whether they say trewly
> As they may abyde therby,
> Or els that they do lye,
> Ye knowe better then I.   [1063–66]

3. Cf. Kinsman. "Within the space of 35 lines we have 'no man'
repeated, with variations . . . eleven times. Besides making the ironic
suggestion that the good are scarcely to be found in any religious organization, the poet's rhetorical device is preparing us for one bad man"
("The Voices of Dissonance," pp. 310–11). The source is, I think,
Barclay's first eclogue or Aenius Silvius' *Miseriae Curialium*, Barclay's
source: "That no prince I blame deliting in goodness / . . . I would
not have that ascribed to them all / . . . As for my part, I blame no
man at all, / Save such as to vice be subject, bounde and thrall" (*The
Eclogues of Alexander Barclay*, lines 660, 669, 711–12).

Finally, in a master stroke, Skelton allows (or forces) the
shadowy "one man," whose ambition to "governe over all"
has brought about the decay of true government, to speak
in his own voice. The tone is unmistakably Wolsey's and
the inference is clear: here is the "official" reply of the
ecclesiastical establishment to Colin's (and, twenty-five years
later, Dread's) cry for help, and as a direct rather than a
reported declaration, it is crushingly effective. Each of the
anonymous charges is repeated by the accused:

> The vyllayne precheth openly,
> And declareth our vyllany.   [1175–76]

> He sayes that we are rechelesse,
> And full of wylfulnesse . . .   [1178–79]

> And howe at a pronge
> We tourne ryght into wronge.   [1196–97]

And the answer—a rhetorical realization of the worst of
Colin's fears. First, force,

> Take hym, wardeyne of the Flete,
> Set hym fast by the fete!
> I say, lyeutenaunt of the Toure,
> Make this lurdeyne for to loure, [1167–70]

and ultimately, damnation:

> Renne God, renne devyll,
> Renne who may renne best,
> And let take all the rest!
> We set not a nut shell
> The way to heven or hell.   [1224–28]

Once again an examination of a possible source reveals the
distance between Skelton and other late medieval satirists.
I do not find that anyone has traced this speech to Barclay's

Eclogues or to Aeneas Silvius' *Miseriae Curialium*, but the
similarity is there:

> He sayes that we are rechelesse,
> And full of wylfulnesse,
> Shameles and mercylesse,
> Incorrigible and insaciate;
> And after this rate
> Agaynst us dothe prate.   [*Colin Clout*, 1178–83]

> They carpe us lyke crakers,
> Howe we wyll rule all at wyll
> Without good reason or skyll;
> And say how that we be
> Full of parcyalyte;   [*C.C.*, 1191–95]

> Delay causes so longe
> That ryght no man can fonge;
> They say many matters be born
> By the ryght of a rambes horne.
> Is not this a shamfull scorne,
> To be teared thus and torne?   [*C.C.*, 1198–1203]

> No, but harke man what sayth the good pope Silvius
> Lo, this same is he which by his bad councell
> Causeth our prince to be to us to fell.
> This same is he which rayseth deme and taxe,
> This same is he which strayned men on rackes.
> This same is he which causeth all this warre,
> This same is he which all our wealth doth marre.
> This is of Commons the very deadly mall,
> Which with these charges thus doth oppresse us all.
> Who him displeaseth he beateth all to dust,
> This same is he which killeth whom him lust,
> That all the devils of hell him hence cary,
> That we no longer endure his tiranny.
>   [Barclay, *Eclogue* 1, lines 802–14]

The difference is that in Aeneas Silvius' epistle and Barclay's pastoral dialogue, the "he" who offends and abuses is attacked from a safe distance: indeed the point of Cornix's speech at line 802 is to reveal to Coridon what the people say *behind the back* of a great man. In *Colin Clout* the words that "men say" find their way to the defiant prelate himself, who acknowledges the criticism of the traditional anticlerical satirists, and moves not to answer but to suppress it: "Take hym, wardeyne of the Flete," "We set not a nut shell / The way to heven or hell." And in *Colin Clout* there is no epistolary or bacchic (Barclay's shepherds leaven their dialogue with wine) buffer between the enemy and the vir bonus. Colin begins by "shodering" between the conflicting claims of lay and clergy, and he ends listening to the one voice who unites the irresponsibility of each, Wolsey the parvenu, Wolsey the ambitious prelate, Wolsey, as republican and absolutist, the symbol of a force that would destroy Colin's (and Skelton's) world. Skelton's intuition (poetic and moral) is unerring. In this world the voices of disorder often have the "last word" and if Colin's reply to this rhetorically magnificent anti-speech is defiant it is hardly triumphant:

> Lo, this is the gyse, now a dayes!
> It is to drede, men sayes,
> Lest they be Saduces.   [1229–31]

If the people are Lutherans and the clergy Sadducees, where is he to turn? The temporary answer is—to rest:

> Now to withdrawe my pen,
> And now a whyle to rest,
> Me semeth it for the best.   [1250–52]

But rest where? As a pilgrim who seeks an ultimate stability within the limits of the human situation, Colin's search is endless and apparently hopeless. Almost a Byronic hero, he shuttles between exploration and disillusionment, ever seeking, unable to rest; but if Childe Harold and Don Juan salvage only the experience of the search itself, Colin does reach his safe harbor. While the Byronic hero has no faith and Dread, who has lost his, surrenders to the pride that is despair, Colin turns to the one refuge for the weary travelers of this world, to the shelter of a comfort whose very existence negates the threat of Wolsey and all he stands for:

> The forecastell of my shyp
> Shall glyde, and smothely slyp
> Out of the wawes wod
> Of the stormy flod;
> Shote anker, and lye at rode,
> And sayle not farre abrode,
> Tyll the cost be clere,
> And the lode starre appere:
> My shyp nowe wyll I stere
> Towards the porte salu
> Of our Savyour Jesu,
> Suche grace that he us sende,
> To rectyfye and amende
> Thynges that are amys,
> Whan that his pleasure is.
> Amen! [1253–67]

The image of a ship sailing through the sea of mortal troubles is one to which Skelton always returns. It is of course conventional, but its conventionality is only a reflection of its timeless applicability. Spenser, who takes more than his nom de plume from Skelton, will use the image to equate the journey of his Saint George with the journey of Everyman (Colin Clout). These final lines, scarcely noted in some interpretations, are a perfect statement of Colin's triumph over himself and his world. He has explored that world in a vain search for the immutable; in twelve hundred

ragged, violent, "realistic" lines he has recorded the chaos
and instability he has found; and now, his passion spent, he
reveals the fruits of that exploration—the realization that
the immutable is the benign. Faith in God's infinite grace,
in his willingness to "rectyfye and amende / Thynges that
are amys" stills all the fears that torture him throughout;
and although he must end by admitting his own inadequacy
before the problems of his poem, there is consolation in the
effort; for it is his willingness to confront those fears that
leads him to a faith so much more real than the easy resignation Parrot offers in the early stages of the poem that bears
his name. In these companion poems, Skelton considers the
relationship between the human and divine spheres from
contrasting angles; and both move from their respective
vantage points of paradisial arrogance and terrestrial ignorance to a position of equipoise where all the contradictions
of all spheres are more than balanced by the acceptance of
a Saviour, and man can see his way to limited action. But
Colin Clout speaks to us with the impact that attends only
the shock of recognition, and is for all its "plainness" the
greater poem. Colin is, too, a poet-priest, but his priesthood
has little to do with prophecy or inspiration and everything
to do with responsibility (pastoral care) and endurance. We
even forget, until he reminds us, that he is himself a clerk,
for his vocation is in this case less important than his
humanity.

Skelton is often praised, as I have noted, for his realism,
for reintroducing into English literature a concreteness unknown since Chaucer and Langland; but if realism implies,
as it does for the late nineteenth century, being true to life,
then Skelton is hardly a realist; for the mass of concrete
description and detail in *Colin Clout* operates primarily to
emphasize the impossibility of knowing what being true to
life is. It is because he is confronted in the range of his immediate perception with contradictory statements of what
is true to life that Colin turns finally to another world: the

fact that the Bishops eat meat at Lent and feed their mules gold while men starve is not so much a criticism of the Church as it is one instance of the radical inconsistency of temporal sources of authority which claim to be absolute; the fact that the arguments of the lay border on heresy, even while Colin is forced to acknowledge their cogency, is not so much a comment on those arguments as it is a comment on man's inability to make sense of his world. P. W. Bridgman suggested in 1950 that "the structure of nature may . . . be such that our processes of thought do not correspond to it sufficiently to permit us to think about it at all."[4] To Skelton and Colin this is obvious.

Colin Clout, then, is not so much a satire on classes or ideas as it is an assessment of the human situation, and the journey through the three-estate motif in all its concreteness is a backdrop against which Skelton demonstrates for us and for Dread the necessity of turning to God. The very familiarity of the topoi from sermons, controversial tracts, and complaints against the times allows the reader to ignore them as real issues and to concentrate on the mind which marshals them in review. Of course, Skelton is sincere in his attack on clerical abuses, and on one level the poem can certainly be read as a satire; but much more than an effective indictment of aberration—and that is what pure or near pure satire is—*Colin Clout* is a consideration and evaluation of all of experience as man knows it. What happens to Colin is hardly unique. Every man undergoes this process of discovery, and many turn at last from the uncertainty of this world to a reality whose existence they know only by intuition. But it is the glory and burden of humanity that each of us is born to make his own discoveries and that the moment of truth is ever new and fresh to those who experience it, just as the poetry which records that moment never ceases to delight and move.

4. "Philosophical Implications of Physics," *American Academy of Arts and Sciences Bulletin,* 2, No. 5 (1950).

5   Excess and Mean

A DAUCOCK IS A DAUCOCK IS A DAUCOCK: WHY COME YE NOT TO COURT?

As WE COME TO IT from the sustained brilliance of *Speak, Parrot* and *Colin Clout, Why Come Ye Not to Court?* is a poem that demands an explanation. In the canon, this twelve-hundred-line diatribe is the most ambitious of a group of poems that includes *Against the Scots, Against Garnish,* and *The Douty Duke of Albany,* and there is a temptation to discuss it as a return to a familiar genre (flyting, *sirventes*); but genre classification, while useful, too easily becomes a substitute for genuine criticism; and if my contention that Skelton's poetic history reveals a parallel and progressive complexity of form and matter has any validity, the relative crudity of the poem can be understood only in the context of his entire career.

In the *Bouge of Court,* Skelton reintroduces a sense of urgency into the dream vision by presenting a hero who is unable to make the expected transition from a reliance on false authorities to a recognition of the true; the oppressive sense of alienation and despair which gradually overwhelms both Dread and the reader is unrelieved by any affirmation. In contrast, the hero of *Colin Clout* does turn finally to the true authority, and the affirmation of the closing lines is unmistakable, if limited. These poems mark the boundaries of Skelton's spiritual history; with *Colin Clout,* his attempt to locate the poet in a hierarchy of moral agents is successful. Paradoxically that success takes from him the ordering *dianoia* of what I have termed the mode of definition, and without this control Skelton is once again, as he was in the years before the *Bouge,* the captive of his conventions. *Why Come Ye Not to Court?* is, I think, an involuntary testimony to this.

The reader who approaches Skelton chronologically meets a now familiar historical base ("the countrynge at Cales," 74), an easily recognizable villain ("the mastyve cur," "the bochers dogge"), and lines and phrases which in terms of the Skeltonic universe are "loaded."

Haec vates ille,
De quo loquuntur mille.   [29–30]

There is no man but one.   [110]

They wot not whether to go.   [611]

It were great rewth,
For wrytynge of trewth
Any man shulde be
In perplexyte.   [838–41]

Quia difficile est
Satiram non scribere.   [1213–14]

The boast of prophecy, the dangers of centralization, the need for (moral) "direction," the dilemma of the poet who would be "true," the compulsion to write—they are all here. What is not here, however, is the well-defined conflict which, in other poems, polarizes what is at first a haphazard mass of detail; for in *Why Come Ye Not to Court?* Skelton abandons the "confused" narrator of his most successful poems for the more conventional Juvenalian persona who hurls his moral code at an offending humanity. The results are disastrous. L. J. Lloyd's appraisal of *Against the Scots* is succinct and, for *Why Come Ye Not to Court?,* to the point.

From beginning to end he exhibits not the slightest attempt at selection or balance of judgment. There is no
compression and no subtlety. . . . The monotony of
the general tone is infuriating: the ear wearies of the
ceaseless rattle of gross and often pointless verbiage.
At the end the mind is confused and enervated. One
begins to wonder if, after all, there is not a good deal
to be said for the wretched Scots.[1]

If one does not begin to wonder at the end of *Why Come Ye
Not to Court?* if there is anything to be said for Wolsey, it
is only because eleven hundred lines of unrelieved vituperation have effected a temporary cessation of mental activity.
As Skelton turns from his absorption with the metaphysical
to the personal, from psychological conflict to political and
social criticism, his carefully wrought poetic disappears; the
accumulation of observation is so much dead weight; Wolsey,
who now moves into the foreground of the poem, is grotesque and strangely sympathetic (at least fascinating),
where he was in *Colin Clout* and *Speak, Parrot* an effectively
vague symbol of the forces of chaos. And even more damaging, Skelton's ability to use rhetoric dramatically, to build
subtle characterizations through the manipulation of rhetorical stances, yields to a display of rhetorical (or vituperative)
virtuosity for its own sake; rather than serving, rhetoric
overwhelms.

Why Come Ye Not to Court?, Against Garnish, and *The
Douty Duke of Albany* all fail on the same level,[2] and the
longest of them proclaims its own failure:

1. L. J. Lloyd, *John Skelton: A Sketch of His Life and Writings*
(Oxford, 1938), p. 122.
2. These are essentially less ambitious versions of *Why Come Ye
Not to Court?* The names change, the grievances are not the same, but
the pattern remains. Reasoned criticism inevitably gives way to un-
reasoning attack. The vocabulary of one is the vocabulary of another:
"We set nat a flye / By your Duke of Albany; / We set nat a prane /

> This is the tenor of my byl,
> A daucock ye be, and so shalbe styll.
>
> [1247–48]

That Wolsey is a "daucock" is, unfortunately, the tenor of his "bill," and each of the other poems has its "daucock"— if not Wolsey, then Albany, or a presumptuous scullery boy. The point of course is that no one of these "bills" rises above the statement of the final couplet of *Why Come Ye Not to Court?* Private spite is never left behind; significant trains of thought are allowed to die in the early stages of their development; the larger considerations which may or may not impel the attack are never seen.

These poems more than fail as significant poetry, they are barely literary at all. In *Why Come Ye Not to Court?* words that have occurred again and again direct the reader to a uniformly narrow referent. A daucock is a daucock is a daucock; a losel is a losel is a losel. When Skelton intimates (840 ff.) that he fears reprisals for speaking the truth, the word "truth" implies nothing more than the factual accuracy of his accusations. (It is true that Wolsey eats meat during Lent; it is true that he has a diseased eye.) There is no pattern of imagery, thought, or structure from which single words —daucock, truth, losel, disease—can draw extra-dictionary significance.[3] In the *Bouge of Court,* "They wot not whether

---

By suche a dronken drane; / We set nat a myght / By suche a cowarde knyght" (*Albany,* lines 161–66). "Of the out yles the roughe foted Scottes, / We have well eased them of the bottes / The rude ranke Scottes, lyke dronken dranes" (*Scots,* lines 170–72). "Rankely whan ye swete / Men sey ye wyll wax lowsy, / Drunkyn, drowpy, drowsy" (*Garnish,* III, lines 134–36). Identical charges (low birth, cowardice, avarice, bad breath, presumptuousness) are made with identical techniques (alliteration, assonance, heavy rhymes, accumulation of epithets). More to the point, the total effect of these poems is distressingly similar.

3. "Nature" in Wordsworth's *Tintern Abbey* means much more at the end of the poem than it does in the beginning, and the richness of the word in that poem is quite a different thing from the richness of the

to go" (611) would have borne a multilevel interpretation;
in *Why Come Ye Not to Court?* the line refers to the harried
members of Wolsey's household and to nothing else. The
difference is between language that is symbolic and language
that limits, between poetry and abuse.

Of course, political and social satire is not necessarily
abusive; Skelton enrolls himself in an honorable tradition
when he insists at line 1207 that he is

> Forcebly constrayned
> At Juvenals request,
> To wryght of this glorious gest.

As a model, Juvenal could offer his English disciple more
than one example of an ultimately "public" poem rising
from a well-defined base of personal grievance. In a scene
which may have suggested the title question of *Why Come
Ye Not to Court?,* Juvenal's Umbricius pauses at the gates
of Rome to explain his reasons for quitting the city. "Quid
Romae faciam?"[4] he asks. "What am I to do at Rome?"
The question is pointed and personal, immediately relevant
to the occasion which has prompted it, but as Umbricius replies to his own query, the personal begins to yield to the
general:

> mentiri nescio; librum,
> Si malus est, nequeo laudare et poscere.[5]

---

word in Pope's *Epistle to Burlington.* When Gulliver in the fourth book
of his travels refers to his "own dear countrymen," a host of associations
is operative in the mind of the reader who recalls that the countrymen
in question have been presented as anything but dear, and are not at
this point regarded by Gulliver as his "own."

4. All references are to *Juvenal and Persius,* trans. and ed. G. G.
Ramsay, Loeb Classical Library (London, 1918). The satire under discussion is Juvenal's third.

5. "I do not know how to lie; if a book is bad, I cannot praise it
and be for it."

"I cannot lie" conjures up the host of liars inhabiting the city Umbricius flees. As complaint follows complaint the immediate scene at the gates is replaced in the poem by the sprawling city herself. Umbricius' problems are swallowed up in the larger problems of the society he leaves behind. The specific situation which functions as a structural base is never completely submerged, however, and when the general indictment of a corrupt society has been made, that situation again becomes the focal point, providing a dramatic "frame" for the larger considerations of Juvenal's poem:

> iumenta vocant et sol inclinat, eundum est;
> nam mihi commota iam dudum mulio virga
> adnuit. ergo vale nostri memor.[6]

In Juvenalian (or closed) satire the speaker is less an individual than a spokesman for the code he defends; he is single-toned and only his responsibility (or lack of personality) makes what is almost self-righteousness palatable. This is public poetry and the personal element is but a structural ploy. In Skeltonian (or open) satire at its best, the speaker is anything but responsible (or reliable), and only the terrible reality of a moral dilemma extenuates his rhetorical excesses. This is personal poetry and the public framework is merely a dramatic convenience. In *Why Come Ye Not to Court?* Skelton manages to merge the worst in the two traditions and present a single-toned, irresponsible voice. This is personal spite, a flyting without the saving self-mockery which attends that genre.

The opening *incipit* seems to belie my criticism:

> All noble men, of this take hede,
> And beleve it as your Crede.

6. "But my cattle are calling, the sun is going down, and I must depart; my muledriver has been signalling me for quite a while with his whip. Goodbye and remember me."

This open call to action is followed by a general indictment
which seems to assume a national crisis:

> To hasty of sentence,
> To ferce for none offence,
> To scarce of your expence,
> To large in neglygence,
> To slacke in recompence,
> To haute in excellence,
> To lyght [in] intellegence,
> And to lyght in credence;
> Where these kepe resydence,
> Reson is banysshed thence.   [3–12]

At line 27 the poet repeats his demand for attention and
proclaims himself a *vates,*

> Haec vates ille,
> De quo loquuntur mille.   [29–30]

This is a familiar Skeltonic pose, but in this poem the claims
of prophecy imply a sense of responsibility which is finally
not in evidence.

A second "proem" introduces the personal note that will
lead at line 400 to the title question, "Why come ye not to
Court?":

> For age is a page
> For the courte full unmete,
> For age cannat rage,
> Nor basse her swete swete:
> But whan age seeth that rage
> Dothe aswage and refrayne,
> Than wyll age have a corage
> To come to court agayne.   [31–38]

We are invited to imagine a specific affront, and the situation becomes semidramatic. In the first forty lines, then, a

public appeal is made in a personal context; and the reader who recalls the Juvenalian tradition would expect a structured manipulation of these motifs in which private demands would become society's demands, private grievances, grievances of the realm.

Skelton, however, moves in waves from the general to the particular. He begins traditionally, with a lament for the times, proverbial and nonspecific:

> The tyme dothe fast ensew,
> That bales begynne to brew:
> I drede, by swete Iesu,
> This tale wyll be to trew.   [59–62]

> Our talwod is all brent,
> Our fagottes are all spent,
> We may blowe at the cole:
> Our mare hath cast her fole,
> And Mocke hath lost her sho;
> What may she do therto?   [79–84]

Line 102 reveals the source of disorder:

> For wyll dothe rule all thynge,
> Wyll, wyll, wyll, wyll, wyll;   [102–03]

and the focus on a general submission of reason to will is quickly narrowed to a particular will—Wolsey's:

> There is no man but one
> That hathe the strokes alone;
> Be it blacke or whight,
> All that he dothe is ryght,
> As right as a cammocke croked.   [110–14]

From this heavily ironic comparison of Wolsey's judgment to a crooked stick, Skelton turns to the contemporary scene. In the next 130 lines he touches briefly on the various ills of

the realm, laying them all at Wolsey's door. The wars go
badly:

> Our armye waxeth dull,
> With, tourne all home agayne,
> And never a Scot slayne;   [147–49]

the men are bribed:

> With scutis and crownes of gold
> I drede we are bought and solde;
> It is a wonders warke:
> They shote all at one marke,
> At the Cardynals hat;   [168–72]

the administrative machinery of the realm is inefficient:

> in the Chambre of Starres
> All maters there he marres;
> Clappyng his rod on the borde,
> No man dare speke a worde;   [185–88]

the clergy is lax and corrupt:

> In Lent for a repast
> He eateth capons stewed,
> Fesaunt and partriche mewed,
> Hennes, checkynges, and pygges;
> He foynes and he frygges,
> Spareth neither mayde ne wyfe.   [217–22]

The progression is always inward, moving from the general
statement of a war unfinished or a law unenforced to an
abusive indictment of Wolsey. Skelton seems unable to resist the impulse to attack.

At line 226 he suddenly calls a halt:

> But now upon this story
> I wyll no further ryme
> Tyll another tyme.

The lines which precede this first break (there will be a second and a third at 393 and 834) have moved from a controlled but vigorous invocation to something approaching frenzy. The pattern is repeated throughout—a question, an attempt at a rational reply, an irrational torrent of abuse. The poem seems, as Lloyd remarks, to be written almost in gasps.[7] In *Speak, Parrot* Skelton uses clearly indicated time intervals to unify and dramatize; here the same device marks only a loss of breath and inventiveness. There are only so many ways to express hatred; there are only so many crises to be laid at an enemy's door. Skelton has in these first 230 lines exhausted his supply and he must either transcend his anger or continue to repeat himself endlessly.

At line 230 the first of a series of possible organizational motifs is introduced: "What newes, what newes?" This question marks the beginning of a continual (if one-sided) dialogue. This is a familiar structural device, and its introduction at this point is promising. Question might have been played off against answer to indicate conflicting moral values; dialectic might gradually have raised the level of inquiry, incorporating the personal attack into a larger vision.[8] But the instant rejoinder to this request for news, an

7. *John Skelton*, p. 117. This "narrative pause" and others like it trouble some critics. Edwards seizes upon them to explain the lack of structure he finds in the poem: "the parts of this poetic pamphlet were obviously sent around as they were written, hot from the desk." (*Skelton*, p. 219.) Heiserman feels that they correspond to the tag lines of the traditional political narrative: "Skelton's tags mark off sections of his poem as into the fitts of a narrative work." "When Skelton writes 'And fall to rest a whyle, etc.' he is not really concluding a phase of a story, nor is he completing one of the 'articles' which Edwards says constitutes this 'series' of poems; he is simply pretending to be a minstrel singing a popular lyrical narrative." (*Skelton and Satire*, pp. 264, 255.) Whatever their function in Skelton's plan, these pauses serve to call attention to the poem's wearying length.

8. I am aware that any attempt to rewrite an author's work for him is illegitimate, but the suggestions I throw out here and in the following

allusion to Wolsey's whoring,

> at the naked stewes
> I understande how that
> The sygne of the Cardynall Hat,
> That inne is now shyt up,   [233–36]

only maintains the pre-break level of

> He foynes and he frygges,
> Spareth neither mayde ne wyfe.

As the poem proceeds, it becomes clear that each new section merely recasts or amplifies the original attack. Skelton has returned to the poetic of *amplificatio* as practised by the fifteenth-century rhetoricians he has so often rejected.

The questions hurled at Skelton in lines 230–395— "What here ye of Lancashyre?" (244), "What here ye of the Scottes?" (259), "What here ye of the Lord Dakers?" (269), "Yet what here ye tell / Of our graunde counsel?" (376–77)—elicit an elaboration of the relatively cryptic "Our armye waxeth dull" of the first section. The conduct of several military campaigns is criticized, the criticism predictably returning to the Cardinal, who is by now an almost comically overworked deus ex machina:

> Whyle the red hat doth endure,
> He maketh himselfe cock sure.   [278–79]
>
> For and this curre do gnar,
> They must stand all a far.   [297–98]

---

pages are merely that—suggestions. I point out what Skelton might have done only to point out what he did not do, and to provide a contrast with his technique in other poems. Of course, Skelton is not obliged to write the same poem again, or to imitate or anticipate, respectively, a Juvenal or a Pope; he is obliged, however, to develop a working relationship between the public and personal strains juxtaposed in the first fifty lines of this poem; in this he fails.

> But speke ye no more of that,
> For drede of the red hat.   [379-80]

At the same time, however, Skelton seems to be reaching behind his caricature for a larger perspective. Momentarily, Wolsey's failings are seen as the center of a syndrome that is national. Affairs are in a sorry state not only because one man meddles with all, but because the properly responsible nobles allow this reversal:

> Our barons be so bolde,
> Into a mouse hole they wolde
> Rynne away and crepe,
> Lyke a mayny of shepe.   [289-92]

These lines bathe the opening, "All noble men, of this take hede," in retroactive irony, and recall the irresponsibility theme of *Colin Clout* and *Speak, Parrot*. When a hint of *royal* irresponsibility follows a second break ("Why come ye nat to court? / ... The kynges courte / Shulde have the excellence; / But Hampton Court / Hath the preemynence," 398, 403-06), Skelton seems ready to weave together the strands of his poem. A succession of triphammer couplets ("Strawe for lawe canon / Or for the lawe common, / Or for lawe cyvyll! / It shall be as he wyll," 413-16) echo the earlier cry of "wyll, wyll, wyll, wyll, wyll" and open the way to a comprehensive examination of the entire realm. This is perhaps the high-water mark of the poem and, I fear, its point of no return. Wolsey is here, as he is in *Colin Clout* and *Speak, Parrot,* a conveniently accessible symbol of the dangers of centralization. And the possibilities of Wolsey as king (by default) are infinite. But the concentration of power is less important to Skelton than his distaste for the rival who has somehow won the King's favor despite

> his wretched originall,
> And his base progeny,
> And his gresy genealogy.   [487-89]

Even this characteristic (and traditional) gibe at social climbing might have contributed to the structured documentation of disorder; but Skelton has lost all control; he can only proceed to what he hopes is the verbal destruction of Wolsey. He is ignorant:

> he was parde
> No doctor of devinyte,
> Nor doctor of the law;   [505–07]

he is arrogant:

> His servauntes menyall
> He dothe revyle, and brall,
> Lyke Mahounde in a play;   [592–94]

he is unstable:

> He is so fyers and fell;
> He rayles and he ratis,   [647–48]
>
> He grynnes and he gapis;   [650]

yet, Skelton marvels, he still finds favor with Henry:

> And yet for all that,
> The kynge his clemency
> Despensyth with his demensy.   [677–79]

The King is ironically exonerated when Skelton attributes his blindness to sorcery:

> How he doth hym disceyve,
> I dought, lest by sorsery,
> Or suche other loselry,
> As wychecraft, or charmying.   [659–62]

Witchcraft can be exorcised by Christian ritual, and a mock service celebrating Wolsey's eventual arrival in hell brings to a bitterly personal close a section which seemed to promise an advance from the personal—"Amen, amen, say ye" (834). After 800 lines all pretence that Wolsey's faults are only a symbol of something more important has been abandoned both by Skelton and the weary reader.

Edwards finds a unity in the constant return to the Cardinal: "Loosely strung though it is, however, *Why Come Ye Not To Court?* has a unity, a unity of subject. For everything that has gone wrong . . . Skelton blames one man."[9] For Edwards the subject which unifies is Wolsey, but it is clear even from his own phrasing—"Skelton blames one man"— that the only constant in the entire poem is not Wolsey but Skelton's hatred of Wolsey. Time and again embryonic structural patterns are abandoned for another virtuoso exercise in vituperation. Ideas are tentatively developed—and dropped. Skelton, hinting darkly in lines 791–817 at Wolsey's designs on the papacy, is content to cite them as one more example of his ambition, ignoring, as he does not in *Speak, Parrot,* the *symbolic* threat to his universal order. And when he does (in lines 1043–1162) turn to Wolsey as churchman, it is to report almost salaciously his whoring, gluttony, and simony;[1] larger considerations are buried in a single couplet:

> But yet beware the rod,
> And the stroke of God.   [1134–35]

In *Why Come Ye Not to Court?* length and inclusion or noninclusion of detail are irrelevant considerations. As C. S. Lewis remarks, unjustly I think, of Skelton's poetry in general, "There is no building in his work, no planning, no reason why any piece should stop just where it does . . . and

---

9. *Skelton,* p. 219.

1. "no prechour almost / Dare speke for his lyfe / Of my lordis grace nor his wyfe, / For he hath suche a bull, / He may take whom he wull, / And as many as him lykys; / May ete pigges in Lent for pikys, / After the sectes of heretykis" (1072–79).

no kind of assurance that any of his poems is exactly the
poem he intended to write."[2] It is not enough to blame
Wolsey for England's economic ills,

> He wolde dry up the stremys
> Of ix. kinges realmys,   [954–55]

support the charge with a vague reference to a new tax, and
fall immediately to cursing:

> God save his noble grace,
> And graunt him a place
> Endless to dwell
> With the devyll of hell!   [966–69]

Why is Wolsey drying up the streams of the realm? How is
this connected with other aspects of his behavior aside from
the fact that the same man is involved? Is there a pattern
to his abuses which makes the initial "All noble men, of
this take hede," more than a public airing of private spite?
Skelton himself poses this question at one point—"Perceyve
the cause why?"—and his answer is in a negative way in-
structive because its circularity points to the weakness of the
speaker's position: "He is so ambicyous / So shamles, and
so vicyous, / . . . That he falleth into a *caeciam*, / . . . Or
wylfull blyndnesse / . . . *A caecitate cordis*" (458–59, 463,
466, 472). This idea of a symbolic blindness (God's hardening of the unrepentant heart) fascinates Skelton and he
returns to it at line 530 and again in the closing lines, but in
a way that dissipates its possible effectiveness:

> With a flap afore his eye,
> Men wene that he is pocky,
> Or els his surgions they lye.   [1166–68]

2. *English Literature in the Sixteenth Century*, p. 142.

Balthasor, that helyd Domingos nose
From the puskylde pocky pose,
Now with his gummys of Araby
Hath promised to hele our cardinals eye;
Yet sum surgions put a dout,
Lest he wyll put it clene out
And make him lame of his neder limmes;
God sende him sorowe for his sinnes! [1191-98]

This is the type of detail that Pope or Juvenal might have worked from, not toward. Even in this penultimate position it could have had a unifying effect if Skelton had equated the physical blight with a spiritual blight, and implied that Wolsey's failings (both physical and spiritual) mirror the state of the world; in the same way the famous picture in lines 970-90 of Wolsey torturing the devils in hell[3] might have been the climactic scene in an ordered defense of stability. Here both passages are brilliant but disconnected moments which attest to the intensity of one man's hatred.

As Lewis says, there is no reason at all why *Why Come Ye Not to Court?* should stop when it does. (I suspect the very simple reason to be the poet's inability to think of anything else to say about his enemy.) By allowing his passion to overwhelm him, Skelton succeeds only in stripping his language of subtlety and denying his poem structure. In his desire to destroy Wolsey, he destroys his poem; Wolsey's faults are absorbed by Skelton's, and it is the satiric voice that irritates more than the abuses it condemns. As Juvenal's Umbricius dissects the city he will abandon, repeated

---

3. "graunt him a place / Endlesse to dwell / With the devyll of hell! / For, and he were there, / We nede never feare / Of the fendys blake: / For I undertake / He wolde so brag and crake, / That he wolde than make / The devyls to quake, / To shudder and to shake, / Lyke a fyer drake, / And with a cole rake / Brose them on a brake, / And bynde them to a stake, / And set hell on fyer, / At his owne desyer" (967-83).

references to a retreat in the unspoiled provinces rescue his
criticism from negativity; his ideal is more important than
his injury. Juvenal builds a balanced consideration of his
world on the possibility of a dramatic moment. As his own
protagonist Skelton is consistently negative, abandoning the
verbal heroism of *Colin Clout*. He never rises to a stature
that justifies the boast, "this is the poet of whom thousands
speak." Behind his righteous indignation at Wolsey's supremacy is a plaintive "why not me?" In the end he speaks
not for thousands but only for himself, descending in his
final outburst to a childish taunt:

> Complayne, or do what ye wyll,
> Of your complaynt it shall nat skyll:
> This is the tenor of my byl
> A daucock ye be, and so shalbe styll.
>
> [1245–48]

Why Come Ye Not to Court? is not without its cham-
pions. Heiserman praises the poem as an unusually perfect
sirventes, "not a series of fragments but one of the rare
works which are so 'complete' that they form milestones in
literary history."[4] Heiserman's criterion for completeness,
however, is variety rather than unity; a full complement of
the conventions (authorial apologia, frank and detailed
criticism of political figures, bits of dialogue, composition
in "fits," ironic use of lyric stanzaic patterns, snatches of
song)[5] which characterize the sirventes are to be found in
Why Come Ye Not to Court?; but if the poem succeeds as
a sirventes, it fails as poetry; the evaluations of *Why Come*

---

4. *Skelton and Satire*, p. 266.
5. "We can . . . identify certain characteristics of the *sirventes*. The
poet begins by recording his motives for writing. He addresses directly
those who need chastisement or those who ought to learn of the folly,
cowardice, or viciousness of living rulers. He loosely recounts recent
events, describing some in scenes with snatches of dialogue. All this

Ye Not to Court? as sirventes and as poem are not coexten-
sive, and perhaps, if Heiserman's characterization of the
genre is accurate (loose, disorderly, unsubtle, vicious, crude),
mutually exclusive. Curiously, Heiserman's description of
the poem accords perfectly with my own: "If any order is to
be found in this poem, it is in this narrowing of focus from
an abstract complaint against excess to a jibe at the legate's
eye";[6] we differ only in our conclusions from this evidence.
In a more attractive defense, S. B. Kendle would credit
Skelton with the sophistication we have seen in other poems.
He also recognizes the final absurdity of a critic who out-
herods Herod, but insists that "the rhymes and meter almost
forbid the reader to consider the content of . . . *Why Come
Ye Not to Courte* as literally true";[7] and he sees in the rhetorical excesses and the "mood of irritation for its own sake"
a conscious qualification of a persona whose lack of control is
the poem's subject. Regretfully this sympathetic reading must
be rejected as special pleading, for there is nothing in the
poem to prevent the reader from accepting its pettiness at
face value, no stylistic signposts, no "significant" inconsis-

---

he articulates in great detail within the stanzaic pattern of the love
song. These devices appear and reappear in one shape or another
through the fourteenth and fifteenth centuries. Seldom do they all appear in any one poem, yet most of them can be discovered in *Why
Come Ye Not to Court?*" (p. 249).

6. Ibid., p. 268. Allow me to note here that I am not attempting to
deny the historical existence of conventions. All of Skelton's poems
can be discussed as examples of well-established conventions. *Why
Come Ye Not to Court?* can be seen not only as a sirventes but as a
flyting; *Colin Clout* is in some ways a hybrid descendant of the literature of the "three estates" and the anticlerical Lollard poems; *Philip
Sparrow* is on one level a parody of the mass and therefore a goliardic
poem. My final objection to Heiserman is not that he puts so much
emphasis on conventions, but that he seems to feel that they write
poems.

7. "The Ancestry and Character of the Skeltonic" (dissertation,
University of Wisconsin, 1961), pp. 46–47.

tencies, no observable internal conflict. Perhaps the final
lines could be read as a dramatic qualification of the tour de
force which precedes them. Suddenly Skelton's inoffensive
interlocutor turns tiger and accuses the poet of madness:

> Mayster doctor in your degre
> Yourselfe madly ye overse.   [1220–21]

The reply is an immediate defense of the satirist's art:

> Blame Iuvinall, and blame nat me:
> Maister doctor Diricum,
> *Omne animi vitium,* &c.
> As Iuvinall dothe recorde.   [1222–25]

And a charge of cowardice ("For small is your sadnesse / To
. . . say ill behinde his back") draws only the defiant conclusion: "A daucock . . ." But if this is an attempt at qualification or a belated recognition of disproportion it comes too
late; and at any rate one can easily read this passage straight-
forwardly, with Heiserman's italics: "In this final inter-
change the interlocutor, remaining the cardinal's man even
after the poet's diatribe, calls the *poet* mad."[8] In the end, the
rather peevish old man who demands the attention of his
audience at line 1 does nothing to earn it; he offers only an
intensity which, because it is without an adequate correlative, is sterile. It is not enough.

I believe that Skelton recoils from *Why Come Ye Not to
Court?* (he does not include the poem in his versified bibliography), and that the accommodation with Wolsey which
has so troubled his admirers can be interpreted as a graceful
and courageous retreat from a recognized loss of perspective
rather than a betrayal of his principles. Indeed, it may be
argued that the experience of writing and then reading this
exercise in abuse is a salutary one; for it seems to point out

8. *Skelton and Satire,* p. 265.

to Skelton the necessity of a moral and aesthetic stock-taking. Within a few months he retires to the pastoral sanctuary of Sheriff Hutton, where, in the graceful verse of a simpler age, he looks back on his career.

THE *GARLAND OF LAUREL*

The contrast between *Why Come Ye Not to Court?* and the *Garland of Laurel* is overwhelming and, I think, deliberate. The form is, as it was in 1498, the dream vision, and the narrative movement is familiar. Musing on the apparent omniscience of Mutability, the poet drifts into a dream in which he finds himself at the court of the Queen of Fame. He learns that the court is to pass judgment on his qualifications for entry, and that the Queen is hostile to his candidacy despite the recommendation of Pallas. Skelton is also supported by Chaucer, Gower, and Lydgate; these worthies formally welcome him to the court and introduce him to Occupation, who in turn accompanies him on a tour of the grounds. In the course of their wandering the pair enter a castle to find Skelton's patroness, the Countess of Surrey, weaving a garland for him in anticipation of a favorable verdict. In eleven complimentary lyrics, the poet thanks the Countess and her friends. At that moment he is summoned to the formal hearing where Occupation offers his bibliography as documentation of his right to a place. Skelton is accorded fame by acclamation; the shouts of the crowd awaken him; the dream and poem are over, and an envoy commends the latter to the protection and correction of Cardinal Wolsey, the villain of *Why Come Ye Not to Court?*

But while a summary suggests an action revolving about a single question—shall Skelton be granted admission to Fame's court—Pallas' sponsorship of Skelton assures an affirmative answer, notwithstanding the objections of a minor functionary. In terms of fifteenth-century convention, the

Garland of Laurel presents a form traditionally concerned
with a search for place and the nature of authority, and with
it a hero whose place is secure and whose identification of
the true authority was made long ago; consequently that
hero emerges not as the quester but as the detached observer
of a world which has not yet reached his level of perception.
The poem is thus a comment on Skelton's career; for it im-
poses the control which is the goal of his earlier poems
(and which, as a goal, can no longer serve him) on the frenzy
of *Why Come Ye Not to Court?* The result is a new form,
one that mirrors perfectly the terms of the accommodation
he fashioned so laboriously in 1521. Although the narrative
creaks on toward the trial scene, its seriousness is continually
qualified by the detachment of the central figure; and the
reader, who is surely aware of the poet's stance, is invited to
join him in an effortless romp through the literary world
of the poem.

As Skelton slumbers, he hears Fame protest Pallas' "ryall
commaundement / That in my courte Skelton shulde have
a place" (58–59). Skelton, she complains, has abandoned
the aureate and its conventions:

> For, ne were onely he hath your promocyon,
> Out of my bokis full sone I shulde hym rase;
> But sith he hath tastid of the sugred pocioun
> Of Elyconis well, refresshid with your grace,
> And wyll not endevour hymselfe to purchase
> The favour of ladys with wordis electe,
> It is sittynge that ye must hym correct.   [71–77]

The reader who is familiar with the Skelton canon—and
paradoxically this most personal of poems is his most public,
his apologia—will realize that for him this is praise rather
than criticism. Fame's standards are painfully narrow, and
the restrictedness of her vision is emphasized by the closed
artificiality of the aureate; she is in a most uncomfortable

position, caught between the "rules" of her establishment ("ye know well, I can do no lesse") and the half-serious, half-playful criticisms of a higher authority who pierces through her assumptions and her rhetoric with a Skelton-like thrust: "The sum of your purpose . . . / Is that our servaunt is sum what to dull" (78–79). "Sum what" is perfect; as a qualifier it hints at the need for finer discriminations, and as a relatively colloquial word it emphasizes the pomposity of Fame's presentation. Behind this banter is a serious question, and a familiar one; as Pallas poses it, she echoes the opening lines of *Colin Clout:*

> For if he gloryously pullishe his matter,
> Then men wyll say how he doth but flatter;
>
> And if so hym fortune to wryte true and plaine,
> As sumtyme he must vyces remorde,
> Then sum wyll say he hath but lyttill brayne,
> And how his wordes with reason wyll not accorde.
>   [83–88]

Fame's preference for one diction above another is woefully short of the point; the problem of verbally doing justice to reality is not so easy as Fame would have it, and more often than not we must be careful, lest our inevitable injustices be too unjust and become our epitaphs:

> Beware, for wrytyng remayneth of recorde.   [89]
>
> Who wryteth wysely hath a grete treasure.   [91]

This is of course Skelton's answer as well as Pallas' ("Wherein this answere for hym we have comprisid"), and she concludes her brief lecture with the familiar admission that writing wisely is somewhat of an impossibility, since writing is at best a dangerously imprecise way of communicating:

> How be it, it were harde to construe this lecture;
> Sophisticatid craftely is many a confecture;

Another manes mynde diffuse is to expounde;
Yet harde is to make but sum fawt be founde.

[109–12]

In other words, to return to Fame's original objection to
Skelton's poetry, the advantage of purchasing "the favour
of ladys with wordis electe" (or, as another poet will put it,
of sporting with Amaryllis in the shade) is its possibility;
there are, on the other hand, impossible efforts (*Speak,
Parrot*) which are, even in failure, more important. As a
part of the game he plays with his own poem, Skelton does
return, momentarily, to the amiable precincts of courtly
verse; the lyrics he offers the Countess of Surrey and her
circle are cast in the style which Fame approves, and his
skill in this mode is affirmed by the repeated anthologizing
of lines like these:

It were an hevenly helth,
It were an endles welth,
A lyfe for God hymselfe,
To here this nightingale,
Amonge the byrdes smale,
Warbelynge in the vale.   [994–99]

Mirry Margarete,
As mydsomer flowre,
Ientyll as fawcoun
Or hawke of the towre.   [1019–22]

But Skelton's capitulation to the narrowness of Fame's
aesthetic is only apparent; his performance contains a qualification which allows him to be true to himself. The staple
of courtly compliment is, of course, comparison, and through
the ambiguity of his comparisons Skelton complicates the
simple and conventional machinery of the genre. In a note
to the "ryght noble Countes of Surrey," Eleanor Hammond

remarks that "Queen Tomyris and Agrippina seem extraordinary selections from classical story to compare with English noblewomen."[9] More "extraordinary" is the assertion that the lady Elisabeth Howard is a Cresseid who would stir the appetite of a Pandarus; the acknowledgment of Anne Dakers' fidelity in the line "Paregall in honour unto Penelope" (899) is literally surrounded by the comparisons to Helen and Deianara, which could hardly have made Lord Dakers comfortable; Mistress Margaret Tylney is invited to see herself either as Phaedre or Canace, depending, one might suppose, on the type of incest she prefers. Other ladies find their tributes qualified by a hint of constraint ("What though my penne wax faynt, / And hath smale lust to paint," 954–55)—or by negative assertion ("Though ye wer hard hertyd, / . . . Yet nowe doutles ye geve me cause / To write of you," 1038, 1040–41). In a context like this, the word "doutles" suggests nothing more certainly than a doubt, a doubt that is not diminished by the allusion in the second stanza to Pasiphae's "benygnyte."[1]

Although these are calculated ambiguities, the performance itself is not a calculated insult. Skelton says here in another way what he has said in *Speak, Parrot*. The conventions of fifteenth-century poetry are pleasant but inaccurate, assuming as they do a closed and restricted world of conceit;

---

9. *English Verse between Chaucer and Surrey* (Durham, 1927), p. 518.

1. Edwards notes some of these ambiguities and accounts for them by biographical conjectures. Of course, many poets of this era dipped into standard lists of indiscriminately collected mythological figures when they desired to flatter. I feel that Skelton here follows Chaucer who, when ordered to write some legends of good women, simultaneously obeys and is true to himself. He whitewashes the semi-villainesses of mythology by omitting one half of their legends, undercutting his narrative even as he delivers it. But, of course, the reader who sees Medea presented as a woman betrayed will certainly recall that she slew her children.

what the conventions exclude are the intrusions of the real
world in which the lady on the courtly pedestal may lust
after a stepson or a bull; the use of mythology in the courtly
tradition is restricted by the number of famous ladies who
conform to the ideal (the antifeminist tradition stands this on
its head) and the poet must arbitrarily falsify even myth to
fit it into the artificial mold. Skelton is by no means as didactic as I am forced to be about this; for him this is a not so
private joke, and the joke is on the mode rather than the
Countess for whom he feels an affection that can only be
cheapened by conventional conceit; in the world which will
be there when he awakens, she is the Pallas figure. He is at
home at Sheriff Hutton or as much at home as he can be in
his terrestrial prison, and the ease with which he twits his
friends is a tribute to the intimacy of their society; the
laughter behind these lyrics is of the quality that only friends
enjoy, or provoke.

Indeed, the *Garland of Laurel* is one long peal of laughter
at the expense of the conventions it pretends to follow.
Criticism has traditionally attached a single adjective to the
poem—egotistical: "surely nowhere else in the world has a
poet devoted a work as long as the *Garland,* sixteen hundred
lines of it, to pure self-praise, winding up with the assertion
that he is his country's Catullus, her Adonis, her Homer."[2]

2. Edwards, *Skelton,* pp. 22–23. Edwards exaggerates slightly. Other
poets (not, however, English poets) had not been reluctant to place
themselves in illustrious company. In the fourth canto of the *Inferno*
Dante is introduced by Virgil to Homer, Horace, Ovid, and Lucan:
"Thus I saw assembled the fair school of that Lord of the loftiest Song
who soars above the others like an eagle. . . . And far more of honor
yet they did me, for they made me of their band, so that I was the sixth
amid so much wisdom" (trans. Charles Eliot Norton, Cambridge, Mass.,
1920, p. 26). E. Schulte (*La Poesia di John Skelton,* Napoli, 1963,
pp. 170–205) attempts to connect Skelton to the Italian humanists
through these boasts. The parallels she cites are less convincing than
the exact parallels in Skelton's classical sources, Horace, *Odes* 3.1,4,
and Ovid, *Amores* 3.15.

But to a reader familiar with innumerable protestations of authorial inadequacy, Skelton's assertions are a recognizable spoof of the modesty topos. In the same way, the invocation to Dame Rhetoric which often attends the admission of ignorance and the search for "facoundius termes," is here replaced by a tipsy procession "of a thousande poetes assembled togeder" (286). They are led by Apollo, who anticipates the triumphal scene by recalling plaintively ("O thoughtfull herte, was evermore his songe!") the metamorphosis of Daphne from nymph to laurel. Rather than celebrate the codifications of Quintilian or de Vinsauf, the literary great march to the harp of Orpheus and the stimulus of Bacchus:

> But blessyd Bachus most reverent and holy,
> Of clusters engrosid with his ruddy flotis
> Theis orators and poetis refreshed there throtis.
>
> [369–71]

It is from this procession that Chaucer, Gower, and Lydgate emerge to set the scene for a dramatization of the inevitable tribute and obeisance; and again Skelton mocks his genre even as he complies with its rules. Characteristically aloof, he stands aside as his predecessors move forward to welcome him. Properly impressed, but hardly cowed (as he admires their apparel, he notes "Thei wantid nothynge but the laurell"), he accepts their praise as his ceremonial due and replies in kind:

> How all that I do is under refformation,
> For only the substance of that I entend,
> Is glad to please, and loth to offend.   [411–13]

When Lydgate in turn complains rhetorically that his fellows have "preventid" (anticipated) his salutation, Skelton, amused at the idea of the prolific monk with nothing to say, serenely assures him that his words are as usual more than adequate:

> So have ye me far passynge my meretis extollyd,
> Mayster Lidgate, of your accustomable
> Bownte. [435–37]

The entire scene is as Skelton notes a "devyse," and when his sponsors importune him to advance, the poet draws back, but only "under the forme," for the sake of ceremony:

> So finally, when they had shewyd there devyse,
> Under the forme as I sayd tofore,
> I made it straunge, and drew bak ones or twyse,
> And ever they presed on me more and more. [443–46]

This is not disrespect or arrogance; the smile these lines provoke is directed not at the English triumvirate whose reputations are secure against even a real attack, but at the mechanical eulogies which stereotype them and immobilize their successors. Like the Countess of Surrey, Gower, Chaucer, and Lydgate are Skelton's friends, and he shares his laughter with them.

Of course the lightness of tone which characterizes the *Garland of Laurel* is possible only because the consideration of real, as distinct from literary, problems is suspended;[3] and in the poem Skelton takes care to remind us that this suspension is temporary and artificial. As Pallas toys with Fame in the opening scene, she contrasts her servant (Skelton) and the crowds who have won admission to Fame's court previously:

3. If we were to classify the dream according to Macrobius' categories, we might say that it is an *insomnium* in potential since the nightmare figures are neutralized and cannot approach the dreamer, and an *oraculum* in actuality since Pallas controls the proceedings.

But whome that ye favoure, I se well, hath a name,
Be he never so lytell of substaunce,   [176–77]

Some have a name for thefte and brybery;
Some be called crafty, that can pyke a purse;
Some men be made of for their mokery;
Some carefull cokwoldes, some have theyr wyves curs.
                                                [183–86]

It is in this way that we are introduced to the threatening
rout that hangs on the fringes of the *Garland's* world
throughout, reappearing at lines 246, 492, 602, and 740. The
forces of disorder are always at the gate, and from the first
Skelton puts before us all the familiar problems which, although they will not be allowed to enter Sheriff Hutton,
are still with him. Once again the specter of uncertainty
("How oftyn fortune varyeth in an howre, / Now clere
wether, forthwith a stormy showre; / All thynge compassyd,
no perpetuyte," 11–13) "encraumps" his mind. But the
specter is no longer as formidable as it once was. In the
Bouge of Court, Dread can neither find a ballast within himself nor turn from the arbitrariness of Fortune to a greater
deity. In the *Garland of Laurel,* Skelton provides symbolic
assurance that his resources are equal to the challenge of a
difficult world. As the poet meditates himself into a slumber,
he leans for support on

    a stumpe
Of an oke, that somtyme grew full streyghte,
A myghty tre and of a noble heyght,
Whose bewte blastyd was with the boystors wynde.
                                                [17–20]

In Christian symbolism, the oak is "a symbol of Christ or
the Virgin Mary," which "because of its solidity and endurance . . . is also a symbol of the strength and faith of

virtue, and of the endurance of the Christian against adversity."[4] Both meanings are operative here, providing a contrast to the *Bouge of Court:* the tree in its bareness and height is the obvious counterpart, in the natural world, of the aging and enduring poet himself; and its religious signification completes the formula of Christian heroism, faith not void of deeds. The affirmation of faith is more explicit at line 829 as Skelton pauses before presenting his lyrics to send up this prayer:

> As a mariner that amasid is in a stormy rage,
> Hardly bestad and driven is to hope
> Of that the tempestuows wynde wyll aswage,
> In trust wherof comforte his hart doth grope,
> From the anker he kuttyth the gabyll rope,
> Committyth all to God, and lettyth his shyp ryde;
> So I beseke Ihesu now to be my gyde.   [829–35]

This might seem incongruous in context were not the dual framework of the poem so well established and so flexible. Skelton's humor and detachment, the easy condescension he turns on the world of his own production—these are the manifestations of a faith which lifts him beyond concern. The question of worldly fame has long since ceased to trouble him. Committed to a vision and a certainty which transcend this world, he is able to solace himself with the promise of things hoped for, and in the *Garland* he allows himself a momentary glimpse of his final reward. Strolling with his guide, Occupation (or poetry), through the "grounds" of the poem, the poet notices "innumerable people" pressing at every gate. They are, as Occupation identifies them, Fame's true subjects, the worshipers of

4. George Ferguson, *Signs and Symbols in Christian Art* (New York, 1961), p. 35.

worldly values who lie in wait for the Colin Clouts and the
Skeltons:

> Forsothe, quod she, theys be haskardis and rebawdis,
> Dysers, carders, tumblars with gambawdis.   [607–08]

> Fals flaterers that fawne the, and kurris of kynde
> That speke fayre before the and shrewdly behynde;
> Hither they come crowdyng to get them a name,
> But hailid they be homwarde with sorow and shame.
>   [619–22]

Suddenly the onrushing rout is struck by a cannon blast, and
the resulting mist plunges Skelton into darkness and fear
("that aventuris . . . made me sore agast"); but when the
"clowdis . . . clere" and the "myst" is "rarifid," the intruders
are gone and the poet finds himself in an arbor where

> birdis on the brere sange on every syde;
> With alys ensandid about in compas,
> The bankis enturfid with singular solas,
> Enrailid with rosers, and vinis engrapid;
> It was a new comfort of sorowis escapid.   [653–57]

This is, of course, the *locus amoenus* of classical tradition,
the Elysium-like landscape where one can look back serenely
on "sorowis escapid." Appropriately, this Elysium is popu-
lated by poets and landscaped with "poetic" foliage, "a goodly laurell tre, / Enverdurid with levis contynually grene."
Even here the poem continues to comment on its antecedents; the lady of many another garden is replaced by a tree
(one thinks of Marvell's "not as a nymph, but for a reed").
In the top of the tree, firing an olive branch, is the phoenix,
who, like poets, seems to die but repeatedly revives; and
surrounded by the Dryads and Muses, Apollo harps while

Iopas sings forever as he does in the *Aeneid* (1.740) of the
universe's mysteries:

> Of wandryng of the mone, the course of the sun,
> Of men and of bestis, and whereof they begone.
>
> [691–92]

> of the winter days that hy them so fast,
> And of the wynter nyghtes that tary so longe,
> And of the somer days so longe that doth last,
> And of their shorte nyghtes.   [700–03]

Not until Spenser's Colin Clout pipes while the Graces
dance before him is there a more compelling statement of
the divinity of poetry. In a line that anticipates Wyatt, Occupation leans forward to ask, "Is this after your appetite?"
and Skelton's response is immediate:

> Jupiter hymselfe this lyfe myght endure;
> This joy excedith all worldly sport and play,
> Paradyce this place is of syngular pleasure.
>
> [715–17]

The comparison is actually a tautology; this *is* Paradise, the
"place of pleasure perdurable" whose loss his own Parrot
laments, and behind the wish that he might dwell there
forever is the certainty that he will. The presence of Envyous
Rancor in a "pyle" just beyond the arbor (740) accentuates
again the distance between the true poet and his earthbound
detractors. The *Garland* is less a tribute to Skelton than to
poetry, and to Skelton's peculiar identification of poetic inspiration and grace. When Occupation greets Skelton in
Fame's Palace, she reminds him of "tymes past / . . . when
at the port salu / Ye firste aryved; whan broken was your
mast / Of worldly trust, then did I you rescu; / Your storme
dryven shyppe I repared new" (540–44). The allusion is
surely to the "ship" imagery of the *Bouge of Court* and *Colin*

Clout. Although Dread is betrayed by the weakness of the mast of worldly trust, Colin Clout fashions a new mast (his pen) with the aid of Occupation and literally writes himself past the paradoxes of worldly trust into the "port salu." Skelton can smile at the blindness of others, at the ceremony of a court whose ritual formalizes arbitrariness, only because his prophetic gift allows him to see what others cannot see, and commits him to the authority of a court that is not arbitrary. His prophetic and poetic insights are, however, gifts, and his willingness to acknowledge this (as he does in the prayer at line 829) more than balances the presumption of a self-laureation; the images of the oak, ship, and arbor are redeeming and brilliant reminders that the source of his confidence is his humility.

In the climactic (now anticlimactic) hearing scene, the principals come together once again to play out their ceremonial roles. Disconcerted by Skelton's premature acceptance of the garland, the Queen of Fame wraps herself in the authority of the aureate and the royal we:

> And for as moche as, by the hy pretence
> That ye have now thorow preemynence
> Of laureat triumphe, your place is here reservyd,
> We wyll understande how ye have it deservyd.
>
> [1124–27]

And Skelton, with mocking obsequity, assures her that she is famed for proceeding according to reason except when "hastyve credence by mayntenance of myght / Fortune to stande betwene you and the lyght" (1133–34), or to paraphrase, except where there is a possibility of proceeding otherwise. Fame has the hearing Pallas promised her, receiving exactly what she asks for, and deserves. For some 350 lines she must listen to Skelton's apparently endless bibliography (only the applause of the court interrupts the recital); unfortunately, the joke is partly on us, for we must suffer through it too; but if we do, we are rewarded with the amusing spectacle of Skelton as critic deliberately misinterpreting his own poems: *Colin Clout* is a trifle of honest mirth (1234), *Speak, Parrot* a poem in commendation of ladies (1188); the only defense is the defense of *Philip Sparrow* against the charge of dishonoring a maid (1254); *Why Come Ye Not to Court?* is not noted. Of course, as the critical history of the *Garland* proves, these distortions and omissions succeed only in calling attention to themselves and to the censored poems. In an envoy, Skelton emphasizes again the inoffensiveness of his poem and, by implication, of all his poetry. The *Garland,* he declares, is written "to deffend, / Under the banner / Of all good manner, / Under proteccyon / Of sad correccyon, / With toleracyon / And supportacyon / Of reformacyon" (1571–78), and a petition *Ad serenissimam Majestatem Regiam, pariter cum Domino Cardinali* identifies the source of this "correccyon." Those who are disturbed at this apparent turnabout should read more closely. Poetry, to repeat an earlier observation, is not logic; Pallas remarks "wryting remayneth of record," Occupation echoes "wordes be swordes," and Skelton himself says pointedly *"Quod scripsi, scripsi,"* what I have written, I have written (1456), an allusion to Pilate's refusal to strike the phrase "King of the Jews" from the inscription on the cross (*John,* 19:22). *Colin Clout, Speak, Parrot,* and *Why Come Ye Not to Court?* survive beyond the *Garland* and despite Skelton's bibliographical retraction. Just as he writes for himself behind a mock deference to the courtly lyric, his poetic "surrender" to Wolsey is made on his own terms, in a way which makes their joint efforts in 1527 on behalf of the Church possible.

With a winning grace, Skelton, in the final lines, turns his humor on himself. The last of his works cited by Occupation is the translation of Diodorus Siculus, "Out of fresshe Latine into Owre Englysshe playne, / . . . Sex volumis"

(1499, 1502). Edwards' comment on its "plainness" is sufficient: "the *Diodorus* survives, in its one incomplete manuscript, as the *reductio ad absurdum* of the theory that a thing
should be said not as accurately, but in as many different
ways as possible."[5] The poet himself remarks on its length
in a marvel of understatement: "Who redyth it ones, wolde
rede it againe" (1501). When the garland of laurel itself is
mentioned, the bibliography is mercifully interrupted by the
acclaim of the crowd (which Skelton scorns) and the dreamer
awakes to see Janus

> With his double chere,
> Makynge his almanak for the new yere;
> He turnyd his tirikkis, his volvell ran fast:
> Good luk this new yere! the olde yere is past.
>   [1515–18]

The last line is, I think, the crowning irony. "Luck" as a
determinant does not operate in Skelton's universe; in all
its guises—Fortune, Fame, Mutability—it has been exorcised
in the course of the poem. For the poet the new year offers
no uncertainty *sub specie aeternitate;* it simultaneously
brings him closer to the promise of Paradise and confers on
him for an intermediate period the responsibilities (earthly)
of the seer. The still point that is the *Garland of Laurel* has
been welcome; the poem allows him to recover the perspective lost in the irresponsibility of *Why Come Ye Not to
Court?* and to reaffirm the vision which supports that perspective; but the withdrawal it affords is but preparation for
a reinvolvement in the real world, where poets are few and
rare and heresy never dies.

5. *Skelton,* pp. 25–26.

6   Observations and Qualifications

OBSERVATIONS

WHEN CENTURIES OF readers and scholars have more or
less agreed on the nature of a poet's achievement, the burden
of proof rests with the critic who insists on a reassessment.
The Skelton who emerges from these pages is neither Pope's
"beastly" Skelton nor Lewis' "playful" Skelton. He is, to be
sure, occasionally beastly and often playful, but he is also
much more. In *Philip Sparrow, Bouge of Court, Colin Clout,
Speak, Parrot,* and a number of lyrics he asks all the important questions, and his answers inform a poetry that is at
once complex and ordered. He refuses to simplify: an awareness of the limitations of art as well as of mortality pervades
his every line. Why have so many given Skelton what would
seem to be less than his due?

There are, I think, several answers to this question. Anything that is new in my reading is the result of a single
assumption—that at the center of a Skelton poem is the
psychological (spiritual) history of its protagonist. This does
not imply any crude equation of poet and persona; neither
does it allow us to banish the historical Skelton from his
own poem; but it does provide a framework that absolves
Skelton from a score of criticisms, and transforms what seem
at first to be random observations into ordered structures.
As comment on the Calais conference, *Speak, Parrot* is unsatisfactory, discursive, and very possibly inaccurate, but as
an examination of the burdens of prophecy, it is profound

and, one might add, thoroughly traditional. As biography, *Philip Sparrow* is questionable (Jane Scrope was perhaps twenty-one years of age when it was written), but as a reconsideration of the distance between innocence and experience and of the relationship between literary artifice and sincerity, it is masterful. As a sustained attack on a corrupt Church in the manner of either *Jack Upland* or *The Reply of Friar Daw Topias, Colin Clout* is inconsistent and confusing, but as a statement of one believer's reaction to the corruption of *his* Church, it is satisfying, coherent, and again traditional.

The objections to this way of reading Skelton might be historical; it could be said that in these pages he is illegitimately made to leap three centuries to adopt the first-person stance and the poetic method of a sensibility not yet born, of an age when the certainties of his fixed universes will give way to the uncomfortable freedom of the individual soul and the search for stability. But it is on historical grounds, I would maintain, that this "new" Skelton is most defensible. The furniture of his mind, the stuff of his literary experience is surely medieval, and in medieval literature, he would have found several traditions which might have brought him to the technique of the doubt-torn or questing narrator:

(1) The *Psychomachia* or *Romance of the Rose* tradition, where for different reasons the "faculties" of man are fragmented and allegorized in a "drama" which moves from a psychic imbalance to a restoration of equilibrium. In contemporary literature the battle for Man-soul would have been familiar to Skelton in the morality play, while the ritual of courtship had fallen into the mechanizing hands of Lydgate (*Temple of Glass*), not to be revitalized until the tenth Canto, Book IV of the *Faerie Queene*.

(2) The wanderer-guide tradition in which the aspiring but confused (and sometimes miserable) narrator is brought

to understanding or acceptance by an interlocutor who is either the agent of divinity or someone who has successfully passed through a similar state of spiritual confusion. Boethius' *Consolation of Philosophy,* the Middle English *Pearl,* and *The Divine Comedy* come to mind at once. Skelton undoubtedly knew Boethius and possibly the *Pearl.* His acquaintance with Dante is less certain, but he would have caught the Dantesque flavor and seen a small-scale model of his method in the *House of Fame,* a poem that demonstrably influenced him, and a poem whose first-person voice is concerned in part with the place and efficacy of poetry in an apparently chaotic world.

(3) The *Piers Plowman* tradition in which the good man as truth-seeker observes (usually in a dream) the moral anarchy of the world and attempts to come to terms with it. In the fifteenth century the Piers figure loses its complexity, its capacity for carrying the vision of a capacious mind, and becomes instead the innocent-turned-cynic of "London Lickpenny" or the conveniently anonymous and single-toned critic of *Jack Upland.*

As distinct as they are, these traditions share a pattern: the first-person narrator loses his way and indulges momentarily in the kind of questioning or complaint which characterizes what Irving Babbitt called the romantic flight from center,[1] and which I see as the formal signature of Skelton's poetry; and always that narrator is returned to the security of an order whose relevance has been reasserted rather than weakened in the process of exploration and redefinition, returned in the poem by a guide or by his own reasoning, ultimately by the poet who allows rather than shares his protagonist's doubts. Thus the soul in the *Psychomachia* moves from that state when "exoritur quotiens turbatis sensibus intus / seditio atque animam morborum rixa

1. See *Rousseau and Romanticism* (Meridian Edition, 1955), pp. 189–201.

fatigat"[2] to the calm of a "holy alliance" "Christi sub
amore";[3] Boethius from the classic complaint of the first
verse paragraph to the admonition of Philosophy (" 'Sed
medicinae,' inquit 'tempus est quam querelae' ")[4] to understanding (" 'Animadverto,' inquam 'idque, uti tu dicis, ita
esse consentio' ");[5] the dreamer of the *Pearl* from the tor-
ment ("bale") of a heart that "bolne and bele"[6] to the acceptance of God's will, "Lorde, mad hit arn that agayn the
stryven / Other proferen the oght agayn thy paye";[7] Dante
from the loss of "la diritta via" to the assured statement of
his faith in Canto 24 of the *Paradisio,* "Fede e sustanza di
cose sperate / ed argomento delle non parventi";[8] and
Chaucer (who restores his equilibrium despite, not because
of, his eagle guide) from the despair of "Fro fantome and
illusion / Me save" to the dignity of "I wot myself best how
y stonde."[9] In each poem what we see is a mind in the act
of composing itself; and in each the technique allows the
poet to insist on, and the reader to make, discriminations
which would be impossible in a more straightforward
presentation. Gordon's description of the *Pearl* will serve
them all: "Dramatically the debate represents a long process
of thought and mental struggle."[1] What must be kept in

2. Lines 7–8, in *Prudentius,* trans. H. J. Thomson, Loeb Classical Library (London, 1949), p. 278: "when there is disorder among our
thoughts and rebellion arises within us."
3. Line 735.
4. *De consolatione,* trans. H. F. Stewart and E. K. Rand, Loeb
Classical Library (London, 1918), p. 134. " 'But it is rather time,'
saith she, 'to apply remedies, than to make complaints.' "
5. Ibid., p. 371. " 'I observe it,' quoth I, 'and I acknowledge it to
be as thou sayest' " (Book V, Prose II).
6. Ed. E. V. Gordon (Oxford, 1953), i, line 18.
7. Lines 1199–1200.
8. Trans. John D. Sinclair (New York, 1961), p. 346, lines 64–65.
9. Lines 493–94, 1778.
1. *Pearl,* p. xix. The kind of structure I am trying to describe is
similar, I think, to what Stephen Gilman calls vertical debate, "a
dialogue between a narrator and an allegorical personage who comes

mind is that the struggle is (at least in the poem) the protagonist's and not the poet's. We may, without danger to
our perspective, entertain the possibility (and, in Skelton's
case, the probability) that the poem is a recreation of the
poet's own spiritual history, but it is a history recollected in
tranquility. And we must not forget that for the medieval
mind, the romantic stance of rebellion and doubt was to be
used in the continual reaffirmation of the necessity of obedi-
ence and faith, not accepted as a legitimate end.

In short, what I am trying to say is that there is nothing
remarkable in Skelton's repeated presentation of a doubting
narrator, and some evidence (his enthusiasm for the *House
of Fame*) suggests a certain inevitability in his choice. Why,
then, to return to my question, has no one offered this theory
previously? The answer is complex: (1) There is a specificity
and topicality in Skelton's adaptation of the technique that
is alien to the majority of the traditions which may have
influenced him. (2) The disproportion of interest in the
"Skeltonic" has prevented critics from asking some very
basic questions. (3) There is a general refusal—and (1) and

---

to him on the basis of admitted infallibility" (*The Art of 'La Celestina,'*
[Madison, 1956], pp. 159–60). Morton Bloomfield uses Gilman's term
in his *Piers Plowman as a Fourteenth-Century Apocalypse* (New
Brunswick, 1961), pp. 20–21. Bloomfield's account of the characteristics
of such poems fits Skelton's "satires" nicely: "Langland seems to be
struggling to find an authoritative answer to the question of salvation
and perfection, and by the multitude of his instructors, Langland in a
sense admits his failure. . . . The weakness of this genre from the point
of view of aesthetic considerations—a weakness Langland does not
altogether rise above—is a tendency to bog down in endless talk. Langland, too, tends to use this genre in somewhat confused fashion,
changing his instructors." Of course, in Skelton's poems, and perhaps
in *Piers Plowman,* the infallible instructor of Gilman's definition is not
present, and the narrator is forced to conduct the vertical debate by himself. This, then, becomes the problem of the poem—to find an authority
that is infallible—and the rejection or debunking of pseudo-authorities
becomes the poem's action.

(2) are part of this—to consider Skelton as a man faced with problems which determined his poetic as well as his political actions.

Heiserman would have us believe that Skelton, operating in an atmosphere where genre distinctions provided a generally accepted way of thinking about literature, manipulated and interchanged topoi of various traditions in order to find new (fresh) ways to make old observations. If one examines the evidence (the canon itself) with these distinctions in mind, Heiserman's description of it seems reasonable; but as always, when a grillwork of assumptions is brought to bear on an artifact, the assumptions themselves are illuminated, not the artifact; and Heiserman finally tells us a great deal about the possibilities available to a Skelton who is a kind of literary "chemist" and very little about the Skelton who lived and thought from 1460 to 1529. The evidence indicates the union of a technique associated with moral allegory, and therefore with generality, with the specificity of popular invective, and while Heiserman attempts to explain this by referring to the history of convention, I would extend the area of inquiry to include the less clearly defined but undeniably relevant considerations of biography and milieu. I make no extravagant claims for the "historical" analysis which follows; indeed I shall do no more than describe the components of the situation and leave the reader to draw the lines of cause and effect; but it does seem possible that there is something in the conjunction of the facts I am about to put forward which explains Skelton and his poetry.

(1) In the fifteenth century the traditions of medieval court poetry were atrophied while the reigning aesthetic produced a literature of disassociation and artificiality. As always in such periods, techniques which had been used because they provided vehicles for a complex exploration of reality became ends in themselves. The forms are there but

the questions which invested them with a transcendence beyond the mechanical are no longer asked with the same intensity. It is not the familiarity of a literary mode that breeds contempt but the insincerity and facileness of those who adopt it; Dr. Johnson's strictures on the easy and vulgar pastoral might well have been addressed to those who struck the pastoral stance (which is still viable today) too easily and without a genuine involvement in the problems the form could accommodate. The machinery of the psychology of love is still visible in Lydgate's *Temple of Glass,* but the insight into psychological process is absent, and as mere ritual the poem becomes tedious; in the *Siege of Thebes,* the same poet joins the famous pilgrimage to Canterbury and momentarily adopts a first-person naïveté which is promising; but his tale owes nothing to the pose and it is clear that for him the technique is only a formal tribute to his master; in the *Assembly of Gods* the education of the befuddled dreamer does receive more than passing emphasis; but between the conventional opening and the final pray-for-me are great stretches in which he is silent save for a feeble "Methink I saw"; and the relationship between the psychomachia of stanzas 88 through 210 and his own doubts, a relationship which should dictate the direction of every line, must be mechanically explained by Doctrine at the close of the poem. Toward the end of the century some literary men realize that the old forms are museum pieces in an age that needs more than nostalgia from its literature; but their only response to the problem is to lay a series of inadequate forms side by side, effecting a kind of consecutive qualification. Thus in the *Court of Sapience* a psychomachia is undercut by an encyclopedia which is in turn dismissed by a recital of the Creed; and in the *Pastime of Pleasure* Hawes presents, with no qualification at all, a five-thousand-line journey through the familiar intricacies of a chivalric education only to suggest in a three-hundred-line retraction that his hero erred when he began the journey at line 112. Both poets lose their readers by failing to structure qualification into the narrative as it proceeds. This is Skelton's accomplishment, one which prepares the way for Spenser and the *Faerie Queene.*

(2) At the same time the horror of the Wars of the Roses engendered a less polished and more topical poetry. This verse is not always simple in the sense of being plain; the devices, as Heiserman and Kinsman have shown,[2] are heavily allusive and even obscure; but the obscurity is protective rather than doctrinal, and when deciphered the allusive pattern is seen to draw fairly predictable parallels between the contemporary situation and biblical or "historical" times. The emotional impulse behind the poem is elemental, even crude, and correspondingly the perspective is narrow (one thinks, for example, of Skelton's political flytings, *Against the Scots, Against Garnish,* and *Why Come Ye Not to Court?*); above all, the sense of contact with specific situations and identifiable people is in direct contrast with the "gentilesse" (somewhat artificial in the fifteenth century) and detachment of the aureate tradition. Charles Muscatine, remarking on the coexistence in the fifteenth century of these attitudes and their respective styles, speaks of an "exaggerated dualism." "The age self-consciously perpetuates chivalry in social rituals, with processions and tournaments, the creation of knightly orders and cults of love. . . . On the other hand it is also an age of realism."[3] Helmut Hatzfeld suggests that the "naturalistic view and the sym-

2. See Heiserman, *Skelton and Satire,* pp. 177–86, 251–62, and Kinsman's 1949 Yale dissertation, "John Skelton, Satirist: The Tradition of Fifteenth-Century Political Verse Satire."
3. *Chaucer and the French Tradition* (Berkeley and Los Angeles, 1957), p. 245.

bolic tradition" become "coordinates of style,"[4] and we have seen how Skelton reverses the process and makes of the stylistic antithesis a moral and philosophical problem.

(3) And in England the nexus of the Skeltonic problem is provided by the intrusion into the symbolic perspective of the Middle Ages of two "facts" from the "real" world, the administrative revolution of Wolsey and Henry VIII in which the power structure of a modern state replaces the federalism of a feudal state, and the religious revolution of Wycliffe, only temporarily checked by the more immediate demands of a civil war. We know now, of course, that neither revolution was a sudden one, that their dramatic and visible phases marked the culmination of a lengthy process; but from the perspective of the moment, the emergence of the star chamber and the proliferation of heresies and heretics must have seemed providential or diabolic.

(4) Into this matrix of historical, philosophical, and literary patterns steps John Skelton, born 1460—fifteenth-century rhetorician, sometime courtier, priest and tutor, political pamphleteer, moralist, prophet—died 1529. For nearly forty years only a stylistic crispness distinguishes him from the poets who form the fifteenth-century aureate tradition —Lydgate, Hoccleve, and his contemporary, Hawes. He does the accepted things and does them well. He translates Diodorus and Cicero into fashionably ornate English, writes graceful elegies, pious meditations, elaborate compliments, cynical love lyrics. If there is an intensity to his melancholy which suggests that it may be more than rhetorical, if there is an edge to his cynicism that is close to bitterness, we murmur something appreciative about "realism" and pass on to Wyatt. But in 1498 the *Bouge of Court* is written and the accomplished rhetorician who would have fitted so nicely into

4. "Geist und Stil der flamboyanten Literatur in Frankreich," *Estudis Universitaris Catalans,* 22 (1936), 185. Quoted and translated in Muscatine, *Chaucer and the French Tradition,* p. 246.

the final paragraph of a lengthy essay on the fifteenth century is replaced by the unique figure who defies categorization. Again the facts only add dimension to, rather than explain, the mystery. The horror of the *Bouge* is followed by an eight-year exile which may or may not be self-imposed; the return to London sees a return to the narrowness of the old perspective, for the nationalism of *Against the Scots* and the didacticism of *Magnificence* are a disappointment after *Philip Sparrow*. But suddenly, in 1521, an old man begins a third career, and in two years produces nearly five thousand lines of poetry so individual that literary history hardly recognizes the existence of Henry VII's laureate, who now becomes the first poet of the English Renaissance.

But of course he is not anything of the kind, and the fact that he looks as if he ought to be explains in part the difficulty of placing him. What Skelton does is infuse the old forms, which symbolize for him a desirable and hopefully still viable way of life, with the intrusive mass of a specific historical moment. What he does not do is reject the abstract formulae which this specificity replaces; they are temporarily inadequate; and he comes more and more to realize that their inadequacy is both personal and a condition of the human situation, that any new formulae are likely to be equally and more dangerously inadequate. Skelton's poetry gives us neither the old made new nor the new made old, but a statement of the potentiality for disturbance of the unassimilated. It is a poetry which could only have been written between 1498 and 1530, when the intrusive could no longer be ignored as Lydgate had ignored it and before it had become part of a new and different stability as it would after 1536. This, perhaps, explains why Skelton seems neither to fit a pattern nor establish one; the conditions which produce him, to which he responds, do not exist before or after him. The explanation of his uniqueness is not in his manipulation of conventions (which may be the effect, not the cause) but in his verbal response to a moral and philosophical problem. Ernst Curtius points out that an aesthetic is or should be a justification that is more than literary. "The ultimate basis of the problem and of all its manifestations is a metaphysical one: the incessant question of what the poet is to do in the world."[5] If this study has any central thesis, it is that for one man in the early sixteenth century the problem of what to do in the world and the problem of style are one.

It is a mistake, however, to consider under style only the Skeltonic. Whatever its origin, this short-line verse form has less to do with the excellences of Skelton's poetry than has traditionally been supposed. In *Speak, Parrot* and the *Bouge of Court*—two of his more impressive poems—the Skeltonic does not appear at all, while *Against the Scots, The Douty Duke,* and *Why Come Ye Not to Court?*—his "beastly" poems—are largely in Skeltonics. The Skelton I describe in these pages realizes that although metrical and stanzaic patterns can reinforce meaning within the arbitrary limits of an artifact by supporting (*Colin Clout*) or undercutting (*Philip Sparrow*) assumed rhetorical stances, in isolation they are morally and philosophically neutral. In other words, alone, meter and stanza mean nothing. Maurice Pollet reads the *Replication* and decides that the Skeltonic is "le résultat d'une soumission quasi mystique aux dictées de l'inspiration, une sorte de sténographie de la poésie inspirée."[6] Perhaps so in that poem; but in *Speak, Parrot,* where there is no Skeltonic, the signature of inspiration is not the meter, but the virtuosity with which the title figure pushes a satirical device—the juxtaposition of old and new times—to an obscurity suggesting clairvoyance. This is done, of course, "in context"; for the relationships between formal components and their capacity for conveying meaning do

5. *European Literature and the Latin Middle Ages,* p. 469.
6. *John Skelton,* p. 192.

not antedate the artifact, but are established in the process
of composition. Consequently, a poet who wishes to make
fine discriminations will make use of several formal patterns
to which he can, in the course of the poem, "attach" meanings; and a poem which relies on a single pattern (the Skeltonic) to carry its meaning is likely to sacrifice complexity
for intensity.

Eleanor Rumming is a case in point. Every commentator,
be he hostile or sympathetic, describes it in similar terms.
For Alan Swallow, Eleanor Rumming is a "complete portrait
being achieved through the accumulation of many . . . images."[7] Auden states that its effect "is like looking at the
human skin through a magnifying glass."[8] "We get a vivid
impression of riotous bustle, chatter and crazy disorder,"[9]
remarks Lewis. "Portrait," "looking," "impression"—the
emphasis is always on the poem's visual impact, almost as
if it were a gigantic mural. Tillemans, for the opposition,
makes essentially the same point when he declares that "the
poem resembles strikingly a dramatic piece without dramatic
action";[1] and Richard Hughes articulates the constant which
is to be found in each of these statements.

> It is the processional manipulation of vivid impressions,
> the orchestration, the *mental* rhythm which strikes me.
> So far from calling it a realistic poem, I would call it
> one of the few really abstract poems in the language.
> Its aesthetic effect is that of a *good* cubist picture.[2]

Exactly. The *Tunning of Eleanor Rumming* is a picture,
a verbal painting—and designedly nothing more. Tillemans'

7. "John Skelton: The Structure of the Poem," *Philological Quarterly, 32* (1953), 36.
8. "John Skelton," in *The Great Tudors,* ed. Katherine Garvin
(London, 1935), p. 66.
9. *English Literature in the Sixteenth Century,* p. 138.
1. "John Skelton, A Conservative," *English Studies, 28* (1946), 146.
2. Introduction to *Poems by John Skelton* (London, 1924), p. xiv.

objection to the lack of action (or to be more precise, of interaction) misses the point. As a painting all its conflicts are only potential, and it is morally neutral. Indeed, when one of Eleanor's customers threatens to mar the unity of tone (in effect a consistent tonelessness) Skelton enters to rebuke her:

> among all
> That sat in that hall,
> There was a pryckemedenty [an affected one],
> Sat lyke a seynty,
> And began to paynty,
> As thoughe she would faynty.   [580–85]

Affectation has no place in either Eleanor Rumming's make-shift tavern or Skelton's poem. As the "pryckemedenty" rises from her seat, the poet steps forward to make the one value judgment in the poem,

> She was not halfe so wyse,
> As she was pevysshe nyse,   [588–89]

and dispatches the offender with a couplet:

> We supposed, I wys,
> That she rose to pys.   [594–95]

By including himself in the scene ("We"), he serves notice to his characters and his readers that no moral or philosophical considerations will be allowed to disturb the surface (there is after all nothing else) of his tableau. .

The Skeltonic is the ideal vehicle to carry the mental rhythm (progressive accretion) of a verbal painting. Since the rhyme can be prolonged, as Lewis says, "as long as the resources of the language hold out,"[3] and since the aural logic of the rhyme leash calls attention to the tag ends which in *Eleanor Rumming* are visually descriptive, to read the

3. *English Literature in the Sixteenth Century*, p. 136.

poem is to see a canvas prepared before (or through) your
very eyes.

Skelton begins by drawing his central figure, who is

> Droupy and drowsy,
> Scurvy and lowsy,   [15–16]

> Comely crynklyd,
> Wondersly wrynkled.   [18–19]

An extended description of Eleanor is followed by an account
of her brewery,

> And somtyme she blennes
> The donge of her bennes
> And the ale together.   [201–03]

Her customers are first clothed:

> Wyth theyr heles dagged,
> Theyr kyrtelles all to-jagged,
> Theyr smockes all to-ragged,
> With tytters and tatters   [123–26]

and then positioned:

> Instede of coyne and monny,
> Some brynge her a conny,
> And some a pot with honny,
> Some a salt, and some a spone,
> Some theyr hose, some theyr shone.   [244–48]

Three hundred and eight lines of this (exactly half the poem)
complete the background of the scene and in lines 309–616
the poet turns to the foreground, adding detail to what has
been only an outline:

> And than come haltyng Jone,
> And brought a gambone.   [326–27]

> Than Margery Mylkeducke
> Her kyrtell she did uptucke.   [418–19]
>
> There came an old rybyde,
> She halted of a kybe,   [492–93]
>
> And fell so wyde open
> That one myght se her token,
> The devyll thereon be wroken!
> What nede all this be spoken?   [496–99]

"What nede all this be spoken?" Indeed; the accumulation of
detail is approaching the point of diminishing returns, and
at line 617 the poet concludes abruptly:

> God gyve it yll hayle!
> For my fyngers ytche;
> I have wrytten to mytche
> Of this mad mummynge
> Of Elynour Rummynge.
> Thus endeth the gest
> Of this worthy fest.   [617–23]

No space on his canvas remains unfilled. The poem does not
end; it stops, but it stops not because Skelton's imagination
has given out (I think he might have gone on in this vein
forever), but because additions would add nothing to the
effect of what is essentially a mood piece. Skelton has done
nothing more nor less than portray in words the chaos and
confusion of a sixteenth-century "still." In this poem Skelton is once again the sophistic rhetorician who responds to
the traditional challenge, descant on a theme; indeed the
sophist Hermogenes might be describing *Eleanor Rumming*
when he writes

> An ecphrasis is an account in detail, visible as they
> say, bringing before one's eyes what is to be shown.
> Ecphrases are of persons, actions, times, places, seasons,

and many other things. . . . The virtues of the ecphrasis are clearness and visibility; for the style must . . . operate to bring about seeing.[4]

Skelton's training in the old rhetoric, rather than any enthusiasm for the new humanism, is responsible for the visual "realism" so many critics have noted.

As "one of the few really abstract poems in the language," *Eleanor Rumming* pleases (if it pleases at all) because of its virtuosity. One doesn't think about the poem, one only takes it in. The danger, of course, is that the reader will tire of the "mad mummynge" before Skelton does, and it is primarily because he is carried forward by the Skeltonic with its tumbling kinetic movement that he reads on until the picture is complete. It is in this kind of poem, one which demands from its reader a single sustained response, that the Skeltonic shows to best advantage. Without it *Eleanor Rumming* would hardly be bearable, for as Lewis reminds us, this is not significant art: "The technique is . . . crudely related to the matter; disorder in life rendered by disorder in art . . . the thing is legitimate, it works, but we cannot forget that the art has much better cards in its hand."[5] One of those "better cards" is *Colin Clout,* also a poem of detail, but detail informed by carefully worked out patterns of thought. Again the Skeltonic (irregular and cascading) reinforces the sense of confusion which is to be opposed to the still point of the final image, but in no sense does it carry the poem. Similarly in *Philip Sparrow* the continual flow of the Skeltonic supports the bubble-like inconsequentiality of Jane's monologue, but the same meter, now associated in the reader's mind with the girl, will be part of a more complex set of effects when it is parodied by the

4. Quoted by C. S. Baldwin in *Medieval Rhetoric and Poetic* (New York, 1928), pp. 35–36.
5. *English Literature in the Sixteenth Century,* p. 139.

sophisticated rhetorician of lines 834 to 1260. Of course,
when the Skeltonic is neither a component in a series of
structural movements nor the sole support of a reasonably
attractive mood, but is married instead to something cheap
(scorn) or vicious (hate), the result is an intensity that becomes unbearable. In *Against the Scots, The Douty Duke,*
and *Why Come Ye Not to Court?* wave after wave of hate
and scorn overwhelm the reader, who goes on only because
he is literally hypnotized by the rhythm of the rhyme leashes,
a rhythm which finally does not accentuate, but anesthetizes.

The Skeltonic, I think, meant less to Skelton than it has
to his admirers.[6] For a stylistic way of talking about problems which were both eternal and contemporary, he turns
not to the Skeltonic but to the ready-made antithesis of the
aureate and plain; but even here the antithesis is used, not
platonized (accepted as an absolute statement). What Skelton says is that the plain style is the best style, not the perfect
style; as he comes to terms with his projected mission, he
learns to make a distinction between the certainty of inspiration and the uncertainty of communication. It is the medium, not the style, which is the difficulty; no vehicle can
adequately carry the inspiration. Poet-prophets are few and
rare not only because they know the truth, but because they
know how difficult it is to promulgate it. The "bestness" of
the plain style is an admission of inadequacy ("the limitation
which makes affirmation possible"); the "bestness" of the
plain style is a personal, historical thing which becomes real

6. S. B. Kendle ("The Ancestry and Character of the Skeltonic")
obliquely supports this assertion when he concludes, after exhaustive
investigation, that the Skeltonic may not have been as unique as we
have tended to think: "The significant point is that within the body
of medieval English poetry, with its fusion of native and foreign traditions, there existed not only a great deal of verse embodying the same
general rhythmical principles that governed the Skeltonic, but also a
specific literary form almost directly analogous to the Skeltonic"
(p. 139).

only against the background of the aureate; the bestness of the plain style is illusory; in another age, when *it* becomes the affectation, the aureate will return; the bestness of the plain style is only one part of the meaning of a Skelton poem, for the aureate even as it is rejected says something, stands for something, which remains in the Skeltonic universe even as it is deplored. In short, the attitudes and values which are attached to the two styles are not their own, but Skelton's. In this perspective the Skeltonic and rhyme royal become fluid (unattached to definite attitudes or stances), formal patterns which are used to frame more central formal patterns (of diction) which are themselves only artificially fixed. Through the nineteenth century Skelton was known only for *Eleanor Rumming,* but if my statement of his concerns and methods is at all accurate, with no poem are we further from the "true Skelton"; for it is only when he indulges either his rage or his sense of the grotesque, when he writes for immediacy rather than illumination and clarification, when, in sum, he sacrifices all the complex considerations which move and plague him to his emotions that the Skeltonic becomes all. It may fairly be said, I think, that Puttenham, Pope, Graves, and Lewis saw Skelton as "rude," "beastly," "homely," and "playful," respectively, because they were willing to; this should not prevent us from being willing to see more.

QUALIFICATIONS

One last question remains: how much more? What, after all this, can we say about Skelton and his place in English literature? Paradoxically our reassessment of his achievement reaffirms (in different terms) the assessment of centuries; an awareness of Skelton's sophistication and formal complexity involves a recognition of the limitations which have justly relegated him to the rank of minor poets. I have

argued that the strength of his poetry lies in the way questions are framed in the context of a specific historical moment through the filter of an acute and involved mind; but
in this strength, there is weakness; for that context and that
mind are so unique as to be too specialized to interest. The
moment which was Skelton's could not have existed before
1485, and when the intrusions which alarmed him were
assimilated into the structure of a Protestant England, it became unlikely that it would ever exist again. There have,
of course, been periods when fact strained against assumption, but nothing comparable to the shock of the Reformation, except perhaps for the First World War, which was
followed in the 1920s and 1930s by a Skelton revival.

Of course, Skelton's limitations can hardly be explained
away by a reference to opportunity. One hundred years after
Skelton's death, another poet-prophet used the difficulty of
fulfilling a mission in a special circumstance (the Common-
wealth) as the basis of his poetry. Milton, of course, lived to
see the Restoration and the failure of his mission and also
to write his greatest verse. The comparison can only be suggestive; there is in Skelton a lack of warmth and compassion,
an inability to understand (as Milton and Chaucer surely do)
the attractiveness of the human values which draw men
from the worship of God and the maintenance of His order.
Skelton's robustness, his vaunted "love of life," is an illusion.
In *Eleanor Rumming* the vigor is clinical; in the political
poems, it is vicious; in the first part of *Philip Sparrow* the
sensitivity is the half-admiring, half-condescending mimicry
with which we usually meet attitudes we cannot understand.
It is in the cynicism of the poet in *Philip Sparrow,* in Dread's
distrust, in Parrot's indignation, in Colin Clout's determination, that we find the real Skelton, and what comes through
is a will and a faith that rise above, but do not qualify, a
great world-weariness. In the end, the terms in which he sees
his problem and the vision which allows him to bypass

rather than solve it are such that only poet-prophets can
fully share them. He remains for most of us a fascinating,
but restricted, instance of the Western mind at work.

There are also faults of composition. J. M. Berdan wrote
in 1920 that when "his mind is started upon one line of
thought, he is unable to select; he goes on and on. . . .
Skelton had not learned the value of emphasis."[7] I would
modify this judgment, since Skelton's "lines of thought,"
it seems to me, are somewhat different than Berdan conceived them; but as a statement of a tendency, Berdan's
criticism is not inaccurate. In the opening pages of this study,
I suggested that Skelton's muse needs the control afforded
by the decision to write a poetry of definition in which "the
fiction to be maintained . . . is that of a mind in the actual
processes of thought, emotion, and speech."[8] Subsequently,
I extended the point to a discussion of satire, attempting
to define definitional satire; and in this chapter I have discussed the difference between Skelton and his fifteenth-
century predecessors and contemporaries as the difference
between a mind which mistakes rhetorical stances for reality
and involvement, and a mind which manipulates rhetorical
stances to approximate the complexity of reality. It is when
he abandons his intellectual and literary integrity that Skelton returns to the fifteenth-century dependence on form and
paradoxically to a poetry that is formless, a series of rhetorical ecphrases which are elaborated for their own sake and
which exist in no relationship whatsoever to any emotional
or intellectual gestalt. As we have seen, rhetorical formulae,
like the more familiar "natural" symbolism of the nineteenth
century, can be used to carry, even create, meaning. But just
as the daffodils, daisies, and rivers of Wordsworth's verse
degenerate to ornament in the hands of less committed dis-

7. *Early Tudor Poetry* (New York, 1920), p. 217.
8. Maynard Mack, in *Major British Writers,* ed. G. B. Harrison et al.
(New York, 1959), *1,* 756.

ciples (imitators) who make of Wordsworth's symbolism (rhetoric) their reality, so the more "artificial" symbolism of the Middle Ages can become, in the absence of a genuine involvement, an art-for-art's-sake in spite of itself. Skelton's less admirable poems are little more than ecphrases or digressions which might serve as illustrations in a rhetorical manual of "how to's" under the heading "how to hate."

Even when the urgency of the problems I have described does grip him and determines the form of his poem, Skelton cannot escape the heritage of the fifteenth century which emphasizes the part because there is no idea of the whole. His practice of adding to a finished poem without truly incorporating the addition is an instance of this. (I do not include *Speak, Parrot* in this observation because the pattern of accretion is a part of the meaning.) In *Ware the Hawk* it is impossible to tell whether the ninety lines of invective mark the last stage in the narrator's progressive loss of control, or indicate the poet's abandonment of his comic perspective for a real anger. Does Skelton become the persona he mocks? In *Philip Sparrow* a lengthy diatribe against envy, which would not be out of place were it considerably shorter, threatens to obscure the all-important distinction between the first and second parts of the poem, and the third section is an annoying footnote. Skelton makes it all too easy for a reader or critic to mistake a minor theme for a major one, and Berdan's charge, unfortunately, can be substantiated in part by some of his finest work.

What finally demands our attention and respect, I believe, is the honesty of the man, the willingness to make fine, often difficult, discriminations, to recognize his own limitations and perhaps sins, to reject the security and fame which a more limiting poetic milieu had granted him as a young man. Behind the questions I have asked in this study is the assumption that poetry is significant insomuch as it deals responsibly with the complexities of existence. In his essay "The Pathetic

Fallacy," Ruskin describes the poet of the first order as "having a great centre of reflection and knowledge in which he stands serene," whereas a lesser poet "views all the universe in a new light through his tears."[9] Although Skelton is certainly not a poet of the first order, he seems finally to have Ruskin's "great centre of reflection"; his heroes, and he is one and all of them, do not view the universe through either tears or laughter, but learn to confront it, if not serenely, at least unflinchingly. If his poetry is unpolished, even unfinished, it rings true and deserves from us the consideration due any genuine attempt to make sense of things. Skelton himself claims no more:

> though my ryme be ragged,
> Tattered and jagged,
> Rudely rayne beaten,
> Rusty and moughte eaten,
> If ye take well therwith,
> It hath in it some pyth.

Lewis said it best: "He stands out of the streamy historical process, an unmistakable individual, a man we have met."[1] I would like his friends who read this to feel that they have met him again.

9. *Selections and Essays,* ed. F. W. Roe (New York, 1918), p. 121.
1. *English Literature in the Sixteenth Century,* p. 143.

Index